The Literature of Terror

The Literature of Terror

A HISTORY OF GOTHIC FICTIONS from 1765 to the present day

David Punter

VOLUME 2

THE MODERN GOTHIC

An imprint of **Pearson Education**

Harlow, England · London · New York · Reading, Massachusetts · San Francisco
Toronto · Don Mills, Ontario · Sydney · Tokyo · Singapore · Hong Kong · Seoul
Taipei · Cape Town · Madrid · Mexico City · Amsterdam · Munich · Paris · Milan

Pearson Education Limited
Edinburgh Gate
Harlow
Essex CM20 2JE
England

and Associated Companies throughout the world

Visit us on the World Wide Web at:
http://www.pearsoneduc.com

First published in 1996

ISBN 0 582 290554 PPR

British Library Cataloguing-in-Publication Data

A catalogue record for this book is available from the British Library

Library of Congress Cataloging-in-Publication Data
Punter, David.
    The literature of terror : a history of gothic fictions 1765
to the present day / David Punter.
        p.   cm.
    Previous ed. published in 1 v.
    Includes bibliographical references (p.   ) and index.
    Contents: v. 1. The gothic tradition
    ISBN 0–582–23714–9 (v. 1)
        1. English literature—History and criticism.   2. Gothic revival
(Literature) 3. Horror tales, English—History and criticism.
    4. Horror tales, American—History and criticism.   5. American
literature—History and criticism.   I. Title.
    PS408.G68P8   1966
    823'.0872909—dc20   95–30686
                                                                CIP

Transferred to digital print on demand, 2003

Typeset by 20 in 10/12pt Baskerville
Printed and bound by Antony Rowe Ltd, Eastbourne

Contents

Preface to the First Edition

This book has grown out of a combination of interests. First and most important is my fascination with much of the literature, which has been considerably increased by experiences of teaching it to students, at Cambridge, but with far more interesting results over the last five years at the University of East Anglia. Associated with this has been a growing dissatisfaction with the adequacy of available approaches to Gothic, a point to which I address myself several times in the course of the text. Behind this, however, there lurks a more general dissatisfaction, which can be summed up like this: it has seemed to me that the most valuable general approaches to literary criticism, which I take to be grounded in Marxist and sociological ways of thinking, have acquired the habit of falsely restricting themselves (with one or two honourable exceptions) to examining literary material which we can broadly term 'realist'. I hope this book can be seen as a contribution to a dialogue about this persistent tendency.

I want to use this brief Preface to make a few methodological points, some large and some small. First, I assume that the consequence of my remark above is that the best literary criticism is written from a standpoint which is at least implicitly interdisciplinary. However, I have found the task of fulfilling this demand while attending to an enormous range of material difficult. It seems to me that the main orientation of the book has therefore remained 'critical'; on the other hand, I hope that it suggests lines of argument which could be borne out by the proper processes of cultural research, even where considerations of space and time have prevented me from filling out the relevant connections.

Second, I have planned this book as an introduction to Gothic fictions for the student and for the interested general reader, and have adopted one or two devices in furtherance of this end. In terms of quotations and references, I have varied procedure. With fiction which is currently available, I have cited the most readily obtainable version, even where this might be a paperback reprint. With fiction which is unavailable outside central libraries, I have reverted to the usual scholarly procedure, citing the original text. With poetry, where textual variation is of greater consequence, I have relied on standard editions of complete works where possible. There are various points in the text where I have had to take a choice as to whether to support my argument with esoteric quotations, or with those which are more frequently referred to in the critical literature. I have consistently tended towards the latter, as conducive to furthering a continuing and focused *debate* about the nature of Gothic.

Third, I am aware that some of these comments may make the reader suppose that he or she will find much reference in the text to Marx and to Marxists. This is not the case. On the other hand, there is a good deal of specific reference to Freud. It would be ponderous to attempt an explanation of this here; I hope the reasons emerge in the course of reading. It is, however, perhaps worth pointing out the obvious, that Marx had little to say about literature in general, and nothing whatever about Gothic fictions, whereas Freud's theory both contains an implicit aesthetic dimension and centres upon an analysis of fear; the uses to which I have put this configuration seem to me at no point incompatible with an underlying historical materialism.

I began to write this book in 1976. Since then there has been a sizeable increase in the quantity of criticism of Gothic. I have rarely included explicit reference to this very recent critical material in the text (although I am aware that some arguments, about, for instance, the relations of women to and in Gothic and about the formal nature of Gothic, have crept in anyway). This is because this material is as yet largely unavailable to the student or general reader. There are, however, relevant references in the Bibliography.

Finally, I should point out that the chapter divisions are not based on a simple historical sequence. My principle of organisation has been based on historical progression, but has also taken into account other considerations. Each chapter is centred on what I take to be, in one way or another, a coherent body of literary work; and most of the chapters also specialise in one of a series of linked critical approaches to the material.

D.G.P.
University of East Anglia
December 1978

Preface to the Second Edition

In producing a second, revised edition of *The Literature of Terror*, I initially found myself confronting a well-nigh impossible task. The original version was begun in 1976, completed in 1978, and published in 1980. Since those years, a flood of critical material on the Gothic has appeared; furthermore, whole sets of assumptions about critical thinking have been modified or overturned, and my own conception of the nature of criticism and interpretation has inevitably altered in explicit and implicit ways. Perhaps even more important, there is a whole history of writing over these last fifteen or so years which has not merely added to but *changed* the notion of what Gothic might be seen to be about, what it might be conceived to be; if there was a 'canon' in the late 1970s, then that canon, or more correctly those coordinates of canon-formation, can now only be radically different.

While trying to think about these difficulties, I found myself reading the Preface to the second, revised edition of an entirely different book, *Imagined Communities* by Benedict Anderson, and what he says there seems so sensible that I would like to quote it here as part of a signature to my own efforts: to adapt his book, he says, 'to the demands of these vast changes in the world and in the text is a task beyond my present means. It seemed better, therefore, to leave it largely as an 'unrestored' period piece, with its own characteristic style, silhouette, and mood'.

Some restorations, however, I have attempted. In both volumes, I have updated the Bibliography. In the first volume I have also added a brief 'Appendix on Criticism', which attempts to offer some guidance about recent criticism of the 'classic' Gothic canon. And in the second volume, in the most significant additions, I have added a further chapter on the contemporary Gothic and have also substantially revised the chapter originally entitled 'Towards a theory of the Gothic'. I am not at all sure I have managed these changes seamlessly; but I hope that at least they provide, along with the separation of the book into two volumes, some further starting-points for considering the Gothic not only in its historical formation but also as a contemporary phenomenon, and one with considerable implications for the wider cultural and social sphere.

D.G.P.
University of Stirling
January 1995

Acknowledgements

We are grateful to the following for permission to reproduce copyright material:

Little Brown and Company for an extract of poetry taken from *Interview with the Vampire* by Anne Rice published in 1976; *The Prelude* by William Wordsworth, edited by Stephen Gill, published in 1970 by permission of Oxford University Press; Routledge Publishers for an extract taken from *Essays on Man 1732–4, The Poems of Alexander Pope*, edited by John Butt.

CHAPTER 1

Gothic and decadence

Robert Louis Stevenson, Oscar Wilde, H. G. Wells, Bram Stoker,
Arthur Machen

What is remarkable about the 'decadent Gothic' of the 1890s is that
out of a cross-genre with only doubtfully auspicious antecedents
should have proceeded, in the space of eleven years, four of the
most potent of modern literary myths, those articulated in Robert
Louis Stevenson's *Dr Jekyll and Mr Hyde* (1886), Oscar Wilde's *Picture
of Dorian Gray* (1891), H. G. Wells's *Island of Dr Moreau* (1896) and
Bram Stoker's *Dracula* (1897). Here again we have a burst of symbolic energy as powerful as that of the original Gothic: alongside
Frankenstein's monster, the Wandering Jew and the Byronic vampire
we can set the *Doppelganger,* the mask of innocence, the maker of
human beings and the new, improved vampire of *Dracula.* As we
look at these books, we shall see certain interconnections – at any
rate in terms of theme, even where authorial stances may be quite
different – but one thing can be said at the outset which underlines
the meaning of decadence in connection with these texts, and that
is that they are all concerned in one way or another with the
problem of degeneration, and thus of the essence of the human.
They each pose, from very different angles, the same question,
which can readily be seen as a question appropriate to an age of
imperial decline: how much, they ask, can one lose – individually,
socially, nationally – and still remain a 'man'? One could put the
question much more brutally: to what extent can one be 'infected'
and still remain British?

The text in which these questions are least on the surface is also
the earliest of them, *Dr Jekyll and Mr Hyde*, which needs no introduc-

tion as the best-known *Doppelganger* story of them all. It follows on
from an easily identifiable Gothic tradition, including James Hogg's
Confessions of a Justified Sinner (1824) and Edgar Allan Poe's 'William
Wilson' (1839), both of which influenced Stevenson, yet it has captured the popular imagination more strongly than any of the others,
feasibly partly because of its 'contemporary', metropolitan setting
and detective-story trappings, but feasibly also because of a stranger
phenomenon, its obvious connection with *actual* late Victorian fears
about similarly untraceable murders, centred on the archetype of
Jack the Ripper. It is interesting in passing to note that, while *Jekyll
and Hyde* itself is not in any overt way concerned with the Gothic
problem of the aristocracy, popular imagination nevertheless has
had its way by tying the text in with this body of semi-legendary
history which unmistakably *is* aristocracy-oriented: the one thing
nobody ever seems to have thought about Jack the Ripper was that,
when unmasked, he might be someone working class or unknown.

Jekyll and Hyde is, from one aspect, the record of a split personality,
and the nature of the split is in its general outline one now familiar
to a post-Freudian age, although one which Stevenson outlines with
particular sensitivity: 'the worst of my faults', says Jekyll, describing
his youth,

> was a certain impatient gaiety of disposition, such as has made the
> happiness of many, but such as I found it hard to reconcile with my
> imperious desire to carry my head high, and wear a more than
> commonly grave countenance before the public. Hence it came about
> that I concealed my pleasures; and that when I reached years of
> reflection, and began to look round me, and take stock of my progress
> and position in the world, I stood already committed to a profound
> duplicity of life. Many a man would have even blazoned such
> irregularities as I was guilty of; but from the high views that I had set
> before me, I regarded and hid them with an almost morbid sense of
> shame. It was thus rather the exacting nature of my aspirations, than
> any particular degradation in my faults, that made me what I was, and,
> with even a deeper trench than in the majority of men, severed in me
> those provinces of good and ill which divide and compound man's
> dual nature.[1]

This is a very rich passage. One must, of course, be careful not to
interpret it as the narrative voice, since it is part of Jekyll's own
statement, and Jekyll is certainly remarkably pompous and possibly
a self-deceiver. However, Jekyll's view seems to be that the split in
his being has derived much less from the presence within his psyche
of an uncontrollable, passionate self than from the force with which
that self has been repressed according to the dictates of social

convention. The original tendency of Jekyll's *alter ego*, so he claims, was by no means towards the vicious, but rather towards the 'loose', a neutral desire for certain kinds of personal freedom which has been repressed by the 'imperious' need not only to conform to, but also to stand as a public example of, strict virtue. Jekyll's problem, surely, is largely put as a social one, and one can interpret it in two connected ways: literally, as the problem of a member of a 'respectable', professional upper middle class, who is supposed to 'body forth' social virtue in his person and to eschew any behaviour, however harmless, which might tend to degrade that stance, and also metaphorically as the problem of a member of a 'master-race'. Jekyll's difficulties are those of the benevolent imperialist: they are not at all to do with the political problem of sanctioning brute force, but with the maintenance of dignity under adverse circumstances. It is strongly suggested that Hyde's behaviour is an urban version of 'going native'. The particular difficulties encountered by English imperialism in its decline were conditioned by the nature of the supremacy which had been asserted: not a simple racial supremacy, but one constantly seen as founded on moral superiority. If an empire based on a morality declines, what are the implications for the particular morality concerned? It is precisely Jekyll's 'high views' which produce morbidity in his relations with his own desires. Thus, of course, the name of his *alter ego*: it is the degree to which the doctor takes seriously his public responsibilities which determines the 'hidden-ness' of his desire for pleasure. Since the public man must be seen to be blameless, he must 'hide' his private nature, even to the extent of denying it be any part of himself. And although this is in one sense a problem locatable within a particular historical development, we can also sense in it echoes of older Gothic problems: it is, Jekyll claims, his 'aspirations' which render him particularly liable to psychic fragmentation, just as the younger Wringhim's aspirations towards total purity caused his breakdown.

But Jekyll's aspirations are of two kinds: they are moral and social aspirations, but they are also scientific aspirations, as in the case of Frankenstein. The great strength of *Jekyll and Hyde* lies in its attempt to connect the two more clearly even than Mary Shelley had done, and to show that Jekyll's familiar desire to 'make another man' stems from problems in the organisation of his own personality. Like *Frankenstein* (1818) and *The Island of Dr Moreau*, *Jekyll and Hyde* relies upon and even exploits public anxieties about scientific progress and about the direction of this progress if undertaken in the absence of moral guidance, but this aspect seems to be largely

metaphorical. The scientific emphasis is very perfunctory; Jekyll himself slides over it, suggesting that details would only bore. What he does not slide over is his series of attempts to comprehend the precise nature of the relation between himself and Hyde, which Stevenson carefully avoids describing merely as a relation of opposites. Hyde is not Jekyll's opposite, but something within him: the fact that he is smaller than the doctor, a 'dwarf', demonstrates that he is only a part whereas Jekyll is a complex whole, and this is underlined in one of Stevenson's more startling insights: 'Jekyll had more than a father's interest; Hyde had more than a son's indifference' (*Works*, IV, 75). This, of course, was precisely the aspect of relationship which Mary Shelley suppressed in connection with Frankenstein and his monster, probably because such 'unnatural' creativity seemed too close to a parody of the divine. Stevenson admits to Hyde's status as a parodic 'son of God', but only at the expense of certain other authorial repressions, principally sexual.
· Not only does the relation between Jekyll and Hyde exclude women, the whole tale moves – like *Dorian Gray* and *Dr Moreau* – in a world substantially composed of leisured bachelors, and even when Stevenson ostensibly tries to portray Hyde's tendency towards sexual excess and deviance, which could hardly not be at the root of Jekyll's fastidious disgust, he can get almost nothing on paper.

Most of Hyde's nastiness is withheld: Stevenson deals with it merely in generalities, and whether this is because of Jekyll's revulsion or of a poverty in Stevenson's ability to imagine the sexually criminal remains obscure: 'into the details of the infamy at which I thus connived (for even now I can scarce grant that I committed it)', Jekyll says, 'I have no design of entering; I mean but to point out the warnings and the successive steps with which my chastisement approached' (*Works*, IV, 72). He does then proceed, however, to allude to one incident, which we have already been told about, when Hyde has been seen to meet a child at a street corner, and to have 'trampled calmly over the child's body and left her screaming on the ground'. 'It sounds nothing to hear', says Enfield, who is telling Utterson the story, 'but it was hellish to see' (*Works*, IV, 6). He is right: it does sound nothing to hear, and it is not even very easy to imagine. It lingers in the memory, but only because of its strangeness, which may have been Stevenson's purpose. It is, of course, symbolic: it is designed to show the inhumanity of Hyde where a more purposive crime would not. Hyde is described here as a kind of Juggernaut, and it is his 'thing-ness' which finally appals Jekyll: 'this was the shocking thing; that the slime of the pit seemed to utter cries and voices; that the amorphous dust gesticulated and sinned; that what was dead, and had no shape, should usurp the offices of life' (*Works*, IV, 83).

Again, there is a problem here, a further reticulation of the *Doppelganger* structure, about the relation between Stevenson and Jekyll. It is reasonable that Jekyll should not want, or be able, to acknowledge Hyde as in any way human, and indeed that onlookers like Enfield should hold whatever opinion they please, but Stevenson himself appears to stop short of certain realisations. If it is indeed repression which has produced the Hyde personality, further denial of Hyde's claims can only result in an ascending scale of violence. And this, of course, is exactly what happens, but Stevenson shows no clear signs of knowing why. Jekyll's later attempts at repression compound Hyde's fury: 'my devil had been long caged, he came out roaring' (*Works*, IV, 76). There is an underlying pessimism in the book which results from Stevenson's difficulty in seeing any alternative structure for the psyche: once the beast is loose, it can resolve itself only in death. Jekyll rather feebly suggests at one point that, if he had been in a different frame of mind when he first took the drug, the second self thus released might have been very different: the prospect of an alternative Hyde, constructed of sweetness and light, is attractive but perhaps somewhat unrealistic.

Julia Briggs's work suggests that the issue of the relations between the human and the bestial which occurs in Stevenson, Wells, Stoker and later in such writers as Forster and Lawrence springs largely from the attempt to deal with Darwinian revelations about the nature of evolution.[2] Thus Jekyll's transformation is a change of state of the most extreme kind: when he takes the drug, 'the most racking pangs succeeded: a grinding in the bones, deadly nausea, and a horror of the spirit that cannot be exceeded at the hour of birth or death' (*Works*, IV, 68). This is the reversion of the species, the ever-present threat that, if evolution is a ladder, it may be possible to start moving *down* it. Not surprisingly, this threat cannot be named in the text: Jekyll says that he has brought on himself 'a punishment and a danger that I cannot name' (*Works*, IV, 37), and Hyde is constantly spoken of as possessing unexpressed deformities. As in much Gothic, there is a dialectical interplay here between the unspeakable and the methods of verification evidenced in the complexity of narrative structure, but post-Darwinian fears have given a new twist to the concept of degeneration. Early in the story, Utterson suggests that something unspoken from the past may be coming to claim Jekyll:

> He was wild when he was young; a long while ago, to be sure; but in
> the law of God, there is no statute of limitations. Ah, it must be that;
> the ghost of some old sin, the cancer of some concealed disgrace;
> punishment coming, *pede claudo*, years after memory has forgotten
> and self-love condoned the fault. (*Works*, IV, 19)

But in the context of the tale, Utterson is, despite the encouraging
pun in his name, an old-fashioned moralist, and his attempt to
impose a conventional 'sins of the fathers' explanation fails. If Hyde
represents a 'ghost' and a 'cancer', it is a general one: the absence
of just limitations goes farther than Utterson cares to think. The
human being may be the product of a primal miscegenation, a
fundamentally unstable blending, which scientific or psychological
accident may be able to part.

And this problem of the double self is, of course, also central to
The Picture of Dorian Gray, the record, as Wilde puts it in Radcliffean
terms, of the 'terrible pleasure' of 'a double life'. The gilded Dorian

> used to wonder at the shallow psychology of those who conceive the
> Ego in man as a thing simple, permanent, reliable, and of one
> essence. To him, man was a being with myriad lives and myriad
> sensations, a complex multiform creature that bore within itself strange
> legacies of thought and passion, and whose very flesh was tainted with
> the monstrous maladies of the dead.[3]

A casual wish on Dorian's part severs the links, and he becomes
free to live a life of vice and self-indulgence without losing his looks
or his youth, while his portrait records his depravity in terms of
physical decay.

The problem of distinguishing narrator from character is very
great in Wilde, particularly because of his aphoristic habits: it is not
easy to know what to make of the multiple resonances of Dorian's
opinion that

> It was the passions about whose origin we deceived ourselves that
> tyrannised most strongly over us. Our weakest motives were those of
> whose nature we were conscious. It often happened that when we
> thought we were experimenting on others we were really
> experimenting on ourselves. (*Dorian*, p. 59)

Here, as elsewhere, *Dorian Gray* incorporates the problems of the
1890s in a jewelled nutshell. We have a burgeoning awareness of
the existence of the unconscious, of that fountain from which spring
desires and needs a thousand times stronger than those to which
we can admit; a sense of the dire situations which result from
the liberation of those passions; and the complicated metaphor of
experimentation, which runs through all four of these texts. In

Dorian Gray, it is perfectly clear that one cannot restrict the concept of experimentation to science: Dr Jekyll and Dr Moreau experiment on malleable flesh, Sir Henry Wotton and Dorian – in different ways, but there are *Doppelganger* complexities here too – artificially mould the mind.

Artifice is perhaps the key term: how much, if at all, do scientific and psychological discoveries help us to mould ourselves, and are the possible shapes into which they can project human life necessarily at all desirable. It is characteristic of Wilde's late romanticism that the means of moulding should be not science but the art of painting, but the tenor of the metaphor is the same: is there anything we can *do* with this knowledge, on the one hand of our myriad-mindedness and on the other of our proximity to the beasts, which will be other than harmful?

The answer of the 1890s was unanimous: No. This is more surprising in Wilde than in the other writers, because it places limits of a severe kind on his apparent decadence: *Dorian Gray* encourages no faith in artifice, either artifice on others or the self-artifice which is supposed to be the crux of decadence. Wilde's fear of decay is even more vividly expressed than those of Stevenson or Wells: Dorian throws a pall over his picture,

> to hide something that had a corruption of its own, worse than the corruption of death itself – something that would breed horrors and yet would never die. What the worm was to the corpse, his sins would be to the painted image on the canvas. They would mar its beauty, and eat away its grace. They would defile it, and make it shameful. And yet the thing would still live on. It would be always alive.
>
> (*Dorian*, p. 119)

Wilde has no doubt that Dorian's repressed desires are as horrible as Jekyll's, not only morally horrible but also inelegant; the much-vaunted divorce between moral and aesthetic categories is simply not there in *Dorian Gray*, which is structurally a simple morality tale, more so even than *Jekyll and Hyde*, and certainly more so than *Dracula*. Like Stevenson, Wilde is locked in the realisation that repression gets you both ways: Sir Henry advocates liberation, claiming that if we repress our desires 'we degenerate into hideous puppets, haunted by the memory of the passions of which we were too much afraid, and the exquisite temptations that we had not the courage to yield to' (*Dorian*, p. 23). Dorian does his slightly insipid best to avoid this fate, but ends up in exactly the same state. Sir Henry's anthropological speculations have a lot to be said for them:

> The mutilation of the savage has its tragic survival in the self-denial
> that mars our lives. We are punished for our refusals. Every impulse
> that we strive to strangle broods in the mind, and poisons us. . . . The
> only way to get rid of a temptation is to yield to it. Resist it, and your
> soul grows sick with longing for the things it has forbidden to itself,
> with desire for what its monstrous laws have made monstrous and
> unlawful. (*Dorian*, p. 18)

So far so good: 'sooner', perhaps, 'murder an infant in its cradle
than nurse unacted desires'.[4] But Dorian cannot escape doom that
way, and possibly Wilde's reasoning is similar to Stevenson's: both
Dorian and Hyde 'go native', they both renounce the repressive
morality of the dominant culture, but all they achieve is an assimi-
lation to the apparently even worse 'morality' of the lower classes.
Wilde's version of the London environment is again Stevenson's,
and again lifted out of Dickens but shorn of even the severely
truncated sympathy we find in *Oliver Twist* (1838): Dorian
remembers

> wandering through dimly-lit streets, past gaunt black-shadowed
> archways and evil-looking houses. Women with hoarse voices and
> harsh laughter had called after him. Drunkards had reeled by cursing,
> and chattering to themselves like monstrous apes. He had seen grotesque
> children huddled upon doorsteps, and heard shrieks and oaths from
> gloomy courts. (*Dorian*, p. 88)

There are two possible but contradictory conclusions one might
draw from this nexus of urban visions: on the one hand, that
Dickens, Stevenson, Wilde were themselves too deeply imbued with
middle-class morality to grant any validity to alternative kinds of life,
on the other that they had seen too clearly the depredations which
that morality had wrought upon its underdogs to grant any credence
to the survival of lower-class integrity. It has been said that decadence is fundamentally a middle-class attitude, and this is borne out
by *Dorian Gray*. There is, says Basil Hallward, the artist, 'a fatality
about all physical and intellectual distinction, the sort of fatality that
seems to dog through history the faltering steps of kings' (*Dorian*,
p. 3). But, elegant though this thought may be, it does not support
the conclusions of the story: Schedoni, in Ann Radcliffe's *The Italian*
(1797), could indeed claim kudos from such a fatality, as could any
Byronic hero, but Dorian is not of the same stature at all. His crimes
and his feelings are alike petty and dilettante, and his doom evokes
neither compassion nor the more elevated sympathies of tragedy.
Again, Wilde tries to fuse psychological speculation with character-

istics taken from the older Gothic, but does not convince us of the grandeur of necessity:

> There are moments, psychologists tell us, when the passion for sin, or
> for what the world calls sin, so dominates a nature, that every fibre
> of the body, as every cell of the brain, seems to be instinct with fearful
> impulses. Men and women at such moments lose the freedom of
> their will. They move to their terrible end as automatons move.
>
> (*Dorian*, p. 190)

This reminds us less of the fate of the tragic hero than of the indulgent self-assessment of Count Fosco in Wilkie Collins's *The Woman in White* (1860), but Fosco has a saving irony absent from *Dorian Gray*: he is also considerably more effective, in almost any terms, than any of Wilde's characters.

As the core Gothic theme of *Jekyll and Hyde* is the *Doppelganger*, the core theme of *Dorian Gray* is the quest for immortality, accompanied with appropriate speculations on the relations between art and life and between beauty and vice. A significant twist in Wilde's dealings with these themes, however, is that his protagonist is hardly a hero but rather a hero-worshipper, whose *own* hero, Sir Henry, is really rather unconnected with the doom which afflicts Dorian. The vitality, the fire, the primitive barbaric energy of the Gothic hero are absent. Wilde himself talks about the continuing power of Gothic images to affect the psyche:

> There are few of us who have not sometimes wakened before dawn,
> either after one of those dreamless nights that make us almost
> enamoured of death, or one of those nights of horror and misshapen
> joy, when through the chambers of the brain sweep phantoms more
> terrible than reality itself, and instinct with that vivid life that lurks in
> all grotesques, and that lends to Gothic art its enduring vitality, this art
> being, one might fancy, especially the art of those whose minds have
> been troubled with the malady of reverie.   (*Dorian*, p. 131)

But his attempts to reinvoke this condition are tired, perhaps with the natural fatigue of accomplished paradox, perhaps because of the lack of bite in the social fears on which he plays. Dorian chooses to ape an aristocratic life-style, but he is not an aristocrat, at least not in any of the more worrying senses. It is, finally, unclear how much seriousness Wilde invests in this matter of style. When Lytton Strachey says of Horace Walpole that 'he liked Gothic architecture, not because he thought it beautiful, but because he found it queer',[5] the sensibility sounds very much like Wilde's, and the embarrassment one feels at *Castle of Otranto* (1764) is similar to that in *Dorian Gray*. Who is being made fun of in a passage like this:

From the corner of the divan of Persian saddlebags on which he was
lying, smoking, as was his custom, innumerable cigarettes, Lord Henry
Wotton could just catch the gleam of the honey-sweet and honey-
coloured blossoms of a laburnum, whose tremulous branches seemed
hardly able to bear the burden of a beauty so flame-like as theirs; and
now and then the fantastic shadows of birds in flight flitted across the
long tussore-silk curtains that were stretched in front of the huge
window, producing a kind of momentary Japanese effect, and making
him think of those pallid jade-faced painters of Tokio who, through
the medium of an art that is necessarily immobile, seek to convey the
sense of swiftness and motion. (*Dorian*, p. 1)

Most probably the target is the reader: in any case, the primary
effect of *Dorian Gray* is surely, unlike that of *Jekyll and Hyde*, cathartic.
Where *Jekyll and Hyde* raises issues and does not resolve them, thus
remaining to haunt the mind, *Dorian Gray* wraps up issues in a way
that purges them of real importance. Dorian is not at root a figure
whose fate affects the rest of us.

In terms of this schema, Wells's *The Island of Dr Moreau* is definitely
more closely related to *Jekyll and Hyde*, and of course even more so
to *Frankenstein*, another text which owes a large part of its continuing
popularity precisely to its failure to establish a coherent pattern out
of its intellectual elements. Since it is perhaps rather less well known
than *Jekyll and Hyde* or *Dorian Gray*, it may be as well to give a brief
account of the plot. It is the first-person narrative of Edward Prendick, introduced by his nephew, who confirms the minimal points
that his uncle has been shipwrecked and rescued, with an interval
of almost a year between, but states that his uncle's version of the
intervening time has never been accepted. Prendick's own account,
thus introduced, tells how he was rescued from a ship's boat by a
strange craft equipped with a drunken captain, a collection of animals, and a man named Montgomery, an outcast ex-medical student
who appears to be in charge. Due to an altercation with the captain,
Prendick is put off with the others at their island destination, and
there encounters Moreau himself. He is surprised by many features
of the island, which, he is assured, is a kind of biological research
station, but particularly by its other inhabitants, some of whom
appear to be men, although of no race he has ever encountered,
others to be somehow between men and animals. He is also disturbed by screams of pain heard during the nights, and eventually
forms the conclusion that Moreau, whose name he has now remembered as that of an exiled vivisectionist, is reducing men to an
animal state by surgery, for dire purposes of his own. An explanation
follows, in which Prendick is humiliated to find that Moreau is

doing exactly the reverse and trying to form a man from the beasts, with varying success. The mixed crop of failures which inevitably accrues lives in a village of hovels on the island, restrained from violence by laws which Moreau has implanted in them, but these start to become ineffective and the beast-men return to the beast, killing Moreau and Montgomery on the way. Prendick manages to survive amid the wreckage of the island society, and is eventually rescued.

On the surface, this is another fable about the dangers of scientific progress unrestrained by moral compunction: we are clearly meant to be appalled both by the pain caused to the animals and by the condition to which many of them are reduced.

> Had Moreau had any intelligible object I could have sympathised at least a little with him. I am not so squeamish about pain as that. I could have forgiven him a little even had his motive been hate. But he was so irresponsible, so utterly careless.[6]

But Prendick's attitude is by no means consistent, which renders many of the scientific points ambiguous. Writing, we must remember, *after* his return to civilisation, he comments on the moment when he remembers where he had previously heard Moreau's name, and adds that when his experiments became known

> the doctor was simply howled out of the country. It may be he deserved to be, but I still [*sic*] think the tepid support of his fellow investigators, and his desertion by the great body of scientific workers, was a shameful thing.   (*Moreau*, p. 38)

The principal problem, however, concerns the status of pain in the story. At one level, Moreau appears to be practising an extreme form of surgery with variable results, but at another he seems to be performing a less clearly scientific kind of operation, in which the important feature of the 'humanising' process is the actual experience of pain for its own sake. 'Each time I dip a living creature into a bath of burning pain', says Moreau, 'I say, This time I will burn out all the animal, this time I will make a rational creature of my own' (*Moreau*, p. 84). Human rationality, for Moreau, seems to be largely dependent on transcending pain: 'the store men and women set on pleasure and pain . . . is the mark of the beast upon them, the mark of the beast from which they came. Pain! Pain and pleasure – they are for us, only so long as we wriggle in the dust . . .' (*Moreau*, p. 81). Yet it is by the threat of further pain that Moreau keeps control over the beast-men: presumably this is supposed to be a mark of their inadequacy, yet Moreau implants fear of pain in them as a substitute for a moral law.

The purely scientific point is thus confused with a set of moral arguments about the difference between man and beast, as it is in *Frankenstein*; and similarly Prendick's objections to Moreau's procedures are considerably vitiated by his admiration for Moreau himself, grudging as it is. In the discussion where Moreau reveals his true aims, Prendick says that he found himself 'hot with shame at our mutual positions' (*Moreau*, p. 76). Like previous hero/villains, Moreau exercises an enormous power over his fellow men. When Prendick first ventures on a journey to discover the island's secrets, Moreau catches him: 'he lifted me as though I was a little child' (*Moreau*, p. 56), says Prendick, and when Moreau dies, Montgomery collapses completely and returns to drink: 'he had been strangely under the influence of Moreau's personality. I do not think it had ever occurred to him that Moreau could die' (*Moreau*, p. 115). Moreau is described, oddly, as having an exceptional, perhaps godlike, serenity, evidenced precisely in the absence of motive by which Prendick is fascinated: 'you cannot imagine', says Moreau to Prendick, rightly, 'the strange colourless delight of these intellectual desires' (*Moreau*, p. 81).

Thus far, the ambiguity of the text is a common Gothic ambiguity, in which the seeker after forbidden knowledge is condemned while being simultaneously surrounded by a halo of admiration. With very pleasing irony Wells portrays Montgomery after Moreau's death venting his spite and fear on the puritanical Prendick: 'You logic-chopping, chalky-faced saint of an atheist, drink', he shouts, 'you're the beast. He takes his liquor like a Christian' (*Moreau*, p. 116). Certainly we are left feeling that there is a genuine vision at the root of Moreau's behaviour, even if through rejection it has turned obsessional, and it is also very difficult to answer the questions which the text raises about the happiness of the beast-men in the way Wells appears to want them answered: how does one determine whether a half-man is more or less happy or pained than the beast from which he came?

But Moreau is not only a Faustian seeker: he is also a more contemporary symbol. At one point Moreau, Montgomery and Prendick go forth to reassert their control over the beast-men, who come out of the jungle towards them:

> As soon as they had approached within a distance of perhaps thirty yards they halted, and bowing on knees and elbows, began flinging the white dust upon their heads. Imagine the scene if you can. We

three blue-clad men, with our misshapen black-faced attendant, standing in a wide expanse of sunlit yellow dust under the blazing blue sky, and surrounded by this circle of crouching and gesticulating monstrosities, some almost human, save in their subtle expression and gestures, some like cripples, some so strangely distorted as to resemble nothing but the denizens of our wildest dreams. (*Moreau*, p. 98)

This is the Gothic vision of empire on which the book is founded. The 'black-faced' attendant is, of course, literally black-faced because he is himself a beast-man, but the play on black and white is nonetheless sustained throughout. Moreau himself is both white-haired and white-faced; Prendick, as we have seen, is 'chalky'; it is 'white dust' with which the dark-skinned beast-men cover themselves as a sign of submission. Moreau, whose island is, significantly, marked on maps as 'Noble's Isle', is the white 'aristocrat' who presides over a colonial society in which the fears of reversion which we have already seen in *Jekyll and Hyde* and in *Dorian Gray* are ever-present, both in the beast-men and in the 'white trash' Montgomery. His attempts to prevent this reversion are unsuccessful but ultimately heroic, for he dies, surely, in the attempt to purify the race.

None of this, of course, is to think of Wells as a racist: far from it. The point is that *The Island of Dr Moreau* represents a confluence of, first, old Gothic themes of aspiration and dominance; second, the fears about human status and dignity generated by Darwin; and third, as a natural metaphorical accompaniment, images of white imperialism in its decline. But just as in *Dorian Gray*, the strands do not hold together: like Sir Henry Wotton, Moreau has considerable insight into the operations of repressive ideology, but his advocacy of alternatives is condemned by the text. 'Very much', says Moreau, 'of what we call moral education is . . . an artificial modification and perversion of instinct; pugnacity is trained into courageous self-sacrifice, and suppressed sexuality into religious emotion' (*Moreau*, p. 79). But Wells fails to keep this suggestion, with its Freudian and Darwinian connotations, firmly in mind, and describes Moreau's process of humanisation in two rather different ways. The first beast-man Moreau makes is said to have begun his new life 'with a clean sheet, mentally; had no memories left in his mind of what he had been' (*Moreau*, p. 82). Yet Moreau is also said not to be experimenting with freedom from conditioning, but rather to be forming beast-men who will be obedient to his own moral and social ideas:

they had certain Fixed Ideas implanted by Moreau in their minds, which absolutely bounded their imaginations. They were really hypnotised, had been told certain things were impossible, and certain things were not to be done, and these prohibitions were woven into the texture of their minds beyond any possibility of disobedience or dispute.

(*Moreau*, pp. 87–8)

As Frankensteinian creator, Moreau wants to form a free being, free from the natural constraints of pain and pleasure; as imperialist, he wants to form a slave, and the best kind of slave, of course, does not know that he or she is one.

The arguments are partly difficult to sort out because Moreau is not himself particularly concerned with the little society of rejects which he is producing; as far as he is concerned they are merely signs of failure. It is Montgomery who takes an interest in them. The society which thus accidentally emerges is one which repeats many features of ordinary human societies: an interesting and resonant one is that 'the females were less numerous than the males, and liable to much furtive persecution in spite of the monogamy which the Law enjoined' (*Moreau*, p. 89). More important, their 'human-ness' does not stick: they retain 'the unmistakable mark of the beast'; 'the stubborn beast flesh grows, day by day, back again' (*Moreau*, pp. 46, 83). At a very basic level, the message is a simple and conservative one: do not interfere in the natural order. What is left doubtful, however, is whether such interference is wrong on *moral* grounds, or merely impossible to achieve fully, and also to what extent the experience of pain is an essential part of Moreau's process. Answers to the two hypothetical questions which one would like to ask – what Prendick or Wells would think if Moreau were successful, and what the situation would be given the benefits of anaesthesia – cannot be extrapolated from the text.

If this makes for a somewhat confused work, it also makes for a rich one. The story has strong elements in it of Defoe and more particularly Swift. The language used by and to the beast-men is oddly biblical, which reinforces the image of a perverted island paradise, and the ending, with Prendick returning to civilisation only to find that he keeps regarding his fellow men as themselves bearing the mark of the beast, is identical to the ending of *Gulliver's Travels*. *The Island of Dr Moreau* brings the reader face to face with a problem which had accompanied Gothic visions since the time of William Godwin and Mary Shelley, but which had been given an extra twist by Darwin: where do we locate the blame for terrors which are the effect of social conditioning? It could simply be said that Moreau's ends do not justify his means, but Prendick at least seems to feel rather doubtful about this, and there are strong hints that the kinds of pressure under which the beast-men live are not really all that different from ordinary social pressures. Moreau's island is partly a microcosm, partly a polemical distortion: its terrifying effect derives partly from Wells's handling of conventional adventure-story techniques, but more from the sense of vertigo with which we apprehend the relation between the beast-men and ourselves.

Fundamentally, all three of these works are concerned with the problem of the liberation of repressed desires. The discoveries of Darwin combined with psychological developments to produce, first, a revelation that the personality contains depths which do not appear on the surface of everyday intercourse, and second, a fear that the Other thus postulated may relate to the bestial level which evidences human continuity with the animal world. In the light of this double supposition, experiments of the kind made deliberately by Jekyll and Moreau and accidentally by Dorian Gray become fraught with more terror than a similar experiment implied in *Frankenstein,* because experimentation is coming to be seen as tinkering with the self. Thus the 'double self' which had been hypothesised by Hogg and others received a basis in scientific speculation, and the whole question of man's relations to the beasts came to be examined – and mythologised – anew. But a myth supposes two moments in time: the moment of origin, creation, differentiation which needs explanation, and the contemporary moment in terms of which communicable myth must be cast. Thus Stevenson, Wilde and Wells found themselves necessarily assimilating the intellectual problems of their age to the actual social structures within and about which they wrote. In the case of Stevenson, the problem of the beast within becomes cast in terms of the difficulties of professional, public, respectable life: the doctor, of course, is the symbol of the union between scientific exploration and respectability. In the case of Wilde, the whole issue is cast archaically in the old Gothic categories of aristocratic life-style and its relation to primal cruelty. In *The Island of Dr Moreau,* as befits the work of a writer more politically concerned than Stevenson or Wilde, the question of reversion is linked to a series of agonising speculations on the inner significance of empire, with its attendant insistence on the preservation of both class and racial integrity.

The whole complex of problems received by far its most significant treatment, however, in Bram Stoker's greatly underrated *Drac-*

ula, which is not only a well-written and formally inventive sensation novel but also one of the most important expressions of the social and psychological dilemmas of the late nineteenth century. For obvious reasons, the intellectual content of *Dracula* has not been taken seriously; yet it deserves to be, less because of any distinction in Stoker's own attitudes and perceptions than as a powerful record of social pressures and anxieties. It has always been a difficult book to place, largely because if one accepts the conventional view of the expiry of Gothic before the middle of the nineteenth century *Dracula* becomes a kind of sport; but in fact it belongs securely with *Jekyll and Hyde, Dorian Gray* and *The Island of Dr Moreau*, while transcending all of them in its development of a symbolic structure in which to carry and deal with contradictions. The use of the term 'myth' to describe a work of written literature is open to abuse, but if there is any modern work which fits the term adequately, it is *Dracula*, if on the grounds of reception alone.

At the heart of *Dracula* (if the pun may be forgiven) is blood. The vampire thrives on the blood of others, and the whole effort of Van Helsing and his colleagues is to fight this one-way flow of blood, by transfusion and any other possible means. 'The vampire live on', says Van Helsing in his broken English, 'and cannot die by mere passing of the time; he can flourish when that he can fatten on the blood of the living. Even more, we have seen amongst us that he can even grow younger; that his vital faculties grow strenuous, and seem as though they refresh themselves when his special pabulum is plenty. But he cannot flourish without this diet; he eat not as others.'[7] Here, as elsewhere in *Dracula*, is a religious inversion, brought out the more strongly by the biblical tone of Van Helsing's discourse: the blood is the life. Stoker is well aware of the rich possibilities for ambiguity and bitter humour in this central motif. When Van Helsing recounts the ship's captain's response to his vampire passenger, there is a vertiginous interplay of conventional swear-words and deeper ironic significance: Dracula

> give much talk to captain as to how and where his box is to be place; but the captain like it not and swear at him in many tongues, and tell him that if he like he can come and see where it shall be. But he say 'no'; that he come not yet, for that he have much to do. Whereupon the captain tell him that he had better be quick [*sic*] – with blood – for that his ship will leave the place – of blood – before the turn of the tide – with blood.
>
> (*Dracula*, pp. 322–3)

But the blood which gives Dracula his life is, as usual in vampire legendry, not merely literal. Dracula the individual needs blood, but Dracula is not merely an individual; he is, as he tells Harker, a dynasty, a 'house', the proud descendant and bearer of a long aristocratic tradition. He recites to Harker a catalogue of the gallant feats of his ancestors, ending thus:

> when, after the battle of Mohács, we threw off the Hungarian yoke, we of the Dracula blood were amongst their leaders, for our spirit would not brook that we were not free. Ah, young sir, the Szekelys – and the Dracula as their heart's blood, their brains, and their swords – can boast a record that mushroom growths like the Hapsburgs and the Romanoffs can never reach. The warlike days are over. Blood is too precious a thing in these days of dishonourable peace; and the glories of the great races are as a tale that is told. (*Dracula*, pp. 38–9)

The long historical progression of the bourgeoisie's attempts to understand the significance of noble 'blood' reaches a point of apotheosis in *Dracula*, for Dracula is the final aristocrat; he has rarefied his needs, and the needs of his house and line, to the point where he has no longer any need of any exchange-system or life-support except blood. All other material connections with the 'dishonourable' bourgeois world have been severed: the aristocrat has paid the tragic price of social supersession, yet his doom perforce involves others. Cheated of his right of actual dominion, his power is exerted in mere survival: his relationship to the world is the culmination of tyranny, yet it is justified in that it is not his own survival that he seeks but the survival of the house, and thus, of course, the survival of the dead. Stoker brings out the ambiguity in the legends very well when Dracula tells Harker his history:

> In his speaking of things and people, and especially of battles, he spoke as if he had been present at them all. This he afterwards explained by saying that to a 'boyar' the pride of his house and name is his own pride, that their glory is his glory, that their fate is his fate. Whenever he spoke of his house he always said, 'we', and spoke almost in the plural, like a king speaking. (*Dracula*, p. 37)

It is impossible to tell whether what is at stake is Dracula's personal longevity or his total identification with his line.

And if one looks again at the old legends themselves, what emerges as very obvious is that they were partly invented to explain the problem of the connection between aristocracy and immortality. To the peasantry of central Europe, it may well have seemed that the feudal lord *was* immortal: the actual inhabitant of the castle upon the mountain might change, but that might not even be known. What would have been known was that there was always a

17

lord; that by some possibly miraculous means life and title persisted, at the expense, of course, of peasant blood, in the literal sense of blood shed in battle and in cruelty. Dracula can no longer survive on blood of this kind; he needs alternative sources of nourishment to suit his socially attenuated existence. The dominion of the sword is replaced by the more naked yet more subtle dominion of the tooth; as the nobleman's real powers disappear, he becomes invested with semi-supernatural abilities, exercised by night rather than in the broad day of legendary feudal conflict.

But thus far *Dracula* is merely another variant on the vampire legendry which we have already seen in John Polidori's 'The Vampyre' (1819), another modification of pre-bourgeois fears of tyrannical violence imaged in terms of the primal fear of blood-sucking. What makes *Dracula* distinctive is Stoker's location of this set of symbols within late Victorian society. Over against the 'house' which Dracula represents Stoker places the bourgeois family, seen around the moment of maximum bonding, on the eve of marriage. *Dracula* is a dramatised conflict of social forces and attitudes: opposite the strength of the vampire we are shown the strength of bourgeois marital relations and sentimental love, as in Mina's letter to Lucy after her marriage to Harker.

> Well, my dear, what could I say? I could only tell him that I was the happiest woman in all the wide world, and that I had nothing to give him except myself, my life, and my trust, and that with these went my love and duty for all the days of my life. And, my dear, when he kissed me, and drew me to him with his poor weak hands, it was like a very solemn pledge between us . . .
> Lucy dear, do you know why I tell you all this? It is not only because it is all sweet to me, but because you have been, and are, very dear to me. It was my privilege to be your friend and guide when you came from the schoolroom to prepare for the world of life. I want you to see now, and with the eyes of a very happy wife, whither duty has led me; so that in your own married life you too may be all happy as I am.
> (*Dracula*, p. 115)

The list of structural oppositions is long. Dracula stands for lineage, the principal group of characters for family; Dracula for the wildness of night, they for the security of day; Dracula for unintelligible and bitter passion, they for the sweet and reasonable emotions; Dracula for the physical and erotic, they for repressed and etherealised love. And at the kernel of this structure is embedded the further opposition between Dracula and his arch-enemy Van Helsing, who is imported to put a stiffening of science and reason into the 'team':

He is seemingly arbitrary man, but this because he knows what he is talking about better than any one else. He is a philosopher and a metaphysician, and one of the most advanced scientists of his day; and he has, I believe, an absolutely open mind. This, with an iron nerve, a temper of the ice-brook, an indomitable resolution, self-command, and toleration exalted from virtues to blessings, and the kindliest and truest heart that beats – these form his equipment for the noble work that he is doing for mankind – work both in theory and practice, for his views are as wide as his all-embracing sympathy.

(*Dracula*, p. 121)

Van Helsing is a superman, and therefore combines in himself a number of contradictory qualities, but the emphasis in his character is on order, neatness, reserve, in Freudian terms on those aspects of the ego which serve the purpose of quashing the tendency towards chaos and libidinal fulfilment which would otherwise disrupt social and psychological organisation. Dracula's is the passion which never dies, the endless desire of the unconscious for gratification, which has to be repressed – particularly on the eve of marriage, of course – in order to maintain stable ideology. He is 'undead' because desire never dies; gratification merely moves desire on to further objects. There is, for Dracula as for the unconscious, no final satisfaction, for his very nature is desire.

Towards these structures the text manifests a socially revealing ambivalence. One of the aspects of decadence was the supremacy of the moment of attraction in the continual dialectic of attraction and repulsion which characterised the relation between the dominant middle class and its 'un-dead' predecessor. From the bourgeois point of view, Dracula is, like Schedoni, Frankenstein and Dorian Gray, a manic individualist; from his own point of view, which is not absent in the text, he is the bearer of the promise of true union, union which transcends death. From the bourgeois point of view, Dracula stands for sexual perversion and sadism; but we also know that what his victims experience at the moment of consummation is joy, unhealthy perhaps but of a power unknown in conventional relationships. Dracula exists and exerts power through right immemorial; Van Helsing and his associates defeat him in the appropriate fashion, through hard work and diligent application, the weapons of a class which derives its existence from labour. Lest some of this seem fanciful, we can cite some of Stoker's dream symbolism:

I didn't quite dream; but it all seemed to be real. I only wanted to be here in this spot – I don't know why, for I was afraid of something – I don't know what. I remember, though I suppose I was asleep, passing through the streets and over the bridge. A fish leaped as I went by,

and I leaned over to look at it, and I heard a lot of dogs howling –
the whole town seemed as if it must be full of dogs all howling at
once – as I went up the steps. Then I had a vague memory of something
long and dark with red eyes, just as we saw in the sunset, and
something very sweet and very bitter all around me at once; and then
I seemed sinking into deep green water, and there was a singing in
my ears, as I have heard there is to drowning men; and then everything
seemed passing away from me; my soul seemed to go out from my
body and float about the air. I seem to remember that once the West
Lighthouse was right under me, and then there was a sort of agonising
feeling, as if I were in an earthquake, and I came back and found you
shaking my body. I saw you do it before I felt you.

(*Dracula*, p. 108)

This reads almost like a case study in emotional ambivalence. Beginning by establishing that there is a difficulty in assessing Dracula's
reality *vis-à–vis* the world's, Lucy then goes on to demonstrate that
Dracula represents the 'un-known', that which is not available to
consciousness, and to illustrate this with a succession of images of
the unconscious: the leaping fish, emerging from psychic depths
like Coleridge's fountain, the howling dogs, symbol of yearning and
wordless need, and the 'something long and dark with red eyes',
which is Dracula but also prefigures the phallic connotations of the
lighthouse. She sinks into the primal fluid of the unconscious,
assailed by sensations which she can only describe as contradictory,
'sweet' and 'bitter', and her soul and body separate as she abandons
responsibility for her situation. Dracula, the unconscious, takes the
sins of the world on his shoulders because his existence, and
the acquiescence of his victims, demonstrate the limitations of the
moral will. Lucy, of course, can only experience the consummation
of the lighthouse and the earthquake while in this trance-like state,
and then translates her experience back into 'safe' terms, 'you
shaking my body'. She sees Mina before she feels her because she
is sinking into the liberation which her conventional self denies:
every time Dracula strikes it becomes harder for his victim to return
to normality.

The myth in *Dracula*, more clearly even than in other versions of
the vampire legends, is an inversion of Christianity, and particularly
of Pauline Christianity, in that Dracula promises – and gives – the
real resurrection of the body, but disunited from soul. Stoker's
attitude to this is of course shocked, but then Stoker appears from
the text to be almost traumatised by a specific sexual fear, a fear
of the so-called 'New Woman' and the reversal of sexual roles which
her emergence implies. Mina is afraid that 'some of the "New

Women" writers will some day start an idea that men and women should be allowed to see each other asleep before proposing or accepting. But I suppose the New Woman won't condescend in future to accept; she will do the proposing herself. And a nice job she will make of it, too! There's some consolation in that' (*Dracula*, p. 100). Behind the smugness lies disturbance; it is ironic, but with an irony familiar in the Gothic from Radcliffe on, that precisely the authorial conservatism of *Dracula* makes its rendition of the threats to comfortable Victorian sexual and familial life pointed and perceptive. A crucial scene occurs when Arthur visits Lucy, who is failing fast. When he first sees her, she 'looked her best, with all the soft lines matching the angelic beauty of her eyes'. But as she sinks into sleep, this model of femininity and passivity begins to change:

> Her breathing grew stertorous, the mouth opened, and the pale gums, drawn back, made the teeth look longer and sharper than ever. In a sort of sleep-waking, vague, unconscious way she opened her eyes, which were now dull and hard at once, and said in a soft, voluptuous voice, such as I had never heard from her lips:-
> 'Arthur! Oh, my love, I am so glad you have come! Kiss me!'
> (*Dracula* pp. 167–8)

Upon which Van Helsing, whose role is to protect against this kind of overt passion and reversal of roles, comes between them. And this scene is prefigured by the 'key-note' scene where Harker is menaced in Dracula's castle by the three female vampires:

> All three had brilliant white teeth that shone like pearls against the ruby of their voluptuous lips. There was something about them that made me uneasy, some longing and at the same time some deadly fear. I felt in my heart a wicked, burning desire that they would kiss me with those red lips. It is not good to note this down; lest some day it should meet Mina's eyes and cause her pain; but it is the truth.
> (*Dracula*, p. 46)

It is hard to summarise *Dracula*, for it is such a wide-ranging book, but in general it is fair to say that its power derives from its dealings with taboo. Where taboo sets up certain bounding lines and divisions which enable society to function without disruption, Dracula blurs those lines. He blurs the line between man and beast, thus echoing the fears of degeneracy in Stevenson, Wilde and Wells; he blurs the line between man and God by daring to partake of immortal life and by practising a corrupt but superhuman form of love; and he blurs the line between man and woman by demonstrating the existence of female passion. In his figure are delineated so many primitive fears: he is a shape-changer, a merger of species, the harbinger of ethnic collapse. His 'disciple' Renfield regards him as a god; and his satanic aspects are all the more interesting if we remember that his real-life ancestor gained his reputation for cruelty because of his assiduity in defending the Christian faith against the marauding Turk.

Where Moreau constitutes an ambiguous and accidental threat to empire from without, destroying genetic and racial barriers which are essential to smooth government, Dracula threatens it from within, attacking the whole concept of morality by preying upon and liberating aspects of the personality which are not under moral control, and colonising on his own behalf by infection in a savage and quite unintentional parody of imperialism. The ironic refrain of Wilde's *Ballad of Reading Gaol* (1898), the perception that you always kill the thing you love, that only love allows the proximity which can lead to real damage, is given a savage new twist by Stoker, in whose text one can see the traces of the illimitable desire which turns love into possession and demands incorporation of the love-object. Dracula is the logical culmination of the Victorian and Gothic hero, the hero in whom power and attraction are bent to the service of Thanatos, and for whom the price of immortality is the death of the soul.

Before turning from the problematic of decadence to other forms of Gothic which continued to exist in late nineteenth-century and early twentieth-century fiction, there is one other writer whose work, beginning in the 1890s and continuing through to the 1920s, merits some comment: Arthur Machen. Machen's books have never received much attention, a fact about which he grew increasingly bitter, yet they are the best in the rather sickly field of genre work which took up Darwinian anxieties as a basis for terror. In 1894, Machen published a novella called *The Great God Pan*, in which yet another doctor performs on a young girl an operation which is designed to open her 'inner eye' to the continuing diabolical existence of the Great God; the operation drives her mad, after which her child, born of her union with Pan, proceeds to confront a series of other people with visions of the horror which underlies the quiet surface of life. It is, as Machen says, 'an old story, an old mystery played in our day, and in dim London streets instead of amidst the vineyards and the olive gardens'.[8] The old story is the story of Moreau and Dracula, the story of the breaking of taboo boundaries and the dreadful consequences which result: Pan is a 'presence, that was neither man nor beast, neither the living nor the dead, but all things mingled, the form of all things but devoid of all form'

(*Pan*, p. 20), and when the hell-child finally dies she goes through the stages of the reversion of the species to the 'primal slime':

> I saw the form waver from sex to sex, dividing itself from itself, and then again reunited. Then I saw the body descend to the beasts whence it ascended, and that which was on the heights go down to the depths, even to the abyss of all being.   (*Pan*, p. 109)

The paradox of *The Great God Pan* is that the visitation which liberates the human being from the repression of false assumptions also destroys the barriers which retain human individuation: the liberation of desire returns man to a primal association with the beast and destroys the soul:

> I knew I had looked into the eyes of a lost soul . . . the man's outward form remained, but all hell was within it. Furious lust, and hate that was like fire, and the loss of all hope, and horror that seemed to shriek aloud in the night, though his teeth were shut; and the utter blackness of despair.   (*Pan*, p. 91)

This is a lurid version of the process which converted Jekyll into Hyde; and it happens, as one might expect, almost exclusively to aristocrats.

The Three Impostors (1895) is a rather more complex book and an interesting example of a text composed of a series of interlocking stories, all of which are lies. It is indebted to Stevenson's *New Arabian Nights* (1882), and moves through a range of settings which bear comparison with Conan Doyle's. The stories vary in terms of the order of interpretation which they advance, but the most significant of them are committed, like *The Great God Pan*, to asserting a pseudo-'natural' explanation for apparently supernatural events. Professor Gregg, another unfortunate seeker after forbidden knowledge, is convinced that the horror stories of folk legendry mask facts which are amenable to scientific discovery: he rejects 'the supernatural hypothesis of the Middle Ages', saying that 'invention, no doubt, and the Gothic fancy of old days, had done much in the way of exaggeration and distortion', and advances a different hypothesis: 'what if the obscure and horrible race of the hills still survived, still remained haunting wild places and barren hills, and now and then repeating the evil of Gothic legend, unchanged and unchangeable as the Turanian Shelta, or the Basques of Spain?'[9] Here Machen's Celtic sensibility verges on a theory of history according to racial conspiracy; it is perhaps not surprising that he felt attracted towards Fascism.[10]

In one sense at least, *The Three Impostors* might be described as a truly decadent book, in that its content turns back upon itself and is used as the excuse for a series of ironic arguments about the nature of fiction. Its protagonists are involved in pondering the strangeness of the real, while continually being subjected to unsolicited stories which do nothing whatever to help the problem, since their tellers cannot be trusted. Machen's continual theme is 'the awful transmutation of the hills' (*Impostors*, p. 119): the possibility that the merest sideslip of vision might offer us a world which is wholly other, and show us the real and awful faces of the demons who manipulate evolution to serve their own ends.

This transmutation is also the theme of Machen's most impressive work, *The Hill of Dreams* (1907), which has been described as the most decadent book in the English language. Its decadence is not formal but thematic, the closest connection being to Swinburne. The hero, Lucian Taylor, finds the world resistant both to his desires and to his attempts to write a novel, and enters into a dark bath of pain and sacrifice in which he revolves an endless obsession with the single moment of dubious love which he has experienced; but what is distinctive is that Machen manages to describe algolagnic indulgence without losing his sense of the irony which results from Lucian's conflict with the real world:

> Never did he fail to wake at the appointed hour, a strong effort of will broke through all the heaviness of sleep, and he would rise up, joyful though weeping, and reverently set his thorny bed upon the floor, offering his pain with his praise. When he had whispered the last word, and had risen from the ground, his body would be all freckled with drops of blood; he used to view the marks with pride. Here and there a spine would be left deep in the flesh, and he would pull these out roughly, tearing through the skin, On some nights when he had pressed with more fervour on the thorns his thighs would stream with blood, red beads standing out on the flesh, and trickling down to his feet. He had some difficulty in washing away the bloodstains so as not to leave any traces to attract the attention of the servant; and after a time he returned no more to his bed when his duty had been accomplished. For a coverlet he had a dark rug, a good deal worn, and in this he would wrap his naked bleeding body, and lie down on the hard floor, well content to add an aching rest to the account of his pleasures. He was covered with scars, and those that healed during the day were torn open afresh at night; the pale olive skin was red with the angry marks of blood, and the graceful form of the young man appeared like the body of a tortured martyr. He grew thinner and thinner every day, for he ate but little; the skin was stretched on the bones of his face, and the black eyes burnt in dark purple hollows. His relations noticed that he was not looking well.[11]

The Hill of Dreams is an over-lush book, and the baroque quality of Machen's prose sometimes becomes absurd, yet it has a power which is partly derived from his refusal to sever Lucian completely from reality: where a Keatsian hero might be able to retreat to a world of beauty, or a Swinburnian one to a permanent semi-mystical indulgence in pain, Lucian remains in contact with his environment, albeit transmuted by his special vision. His apocalyptic view of London is comparable with Baudelaire's urban nightmares in intensity if not in execution:

> Voices, raucous, clamant, abominable, were belched out of the blazing public-houses as the doors swung to and fro, and above these doors were hideous brassy lamps, very slowly swinging in a violent blast of air, so that they might have been infernal thuribles, censing the people. Some man was calling his wares in one long continuous shriek that never stopped or paused, and, as a respond, a deeper, louder voice roared to him from across the road. An Italian whirled the handle of his piano-organ in a fury, and a ring of imps danced mad figures around him, danced and flung up their legs till the rags dropped from some of them, and they still danced on. A flare of naphtha, burning with a rushing noise, threw a light on one point of the circle, and Lucian watched a lank girl of fifteen as she came round and round to the flash. She was quite drunk, and had kicked her petticoats away, and the crowd howled laughter and applause at her. Her black hair poured down and leapt on her scarlet bodice; she sprang and leapt round the ring, laughing in Bacchic frenzy, and led the orgy to triumph.
>
> (*Hill of Dreams*, pp. 203–4)

Machen takes to an extreme point tendencies already existing within decadent Gothic: like Dracula's, Lucian's is the desire which tends towards death, but unlike Dracula Lucian does not have the supernatural privilege of attaining gratification, except in his final dream:

> And presently the woman fled away from him, and he pursued her. She fled away before him through midnight country, and he followed after her, chasing her from thicket to thicket, from valley to valley. And at last he captured her and won her with horrible caresses, and they went up to celebrate and make the marriage of the Sabbath. They were within the matted thicket, and they writhed in flames, insatiable, forever. They were tortured, and tortured one another, in the sight of thousands who gathered thick about them; and their desire rose up like a black smoke.
>
> (*Hill of Dreams*, p. 266)

Machen provides an epilogue to English decadence, in which beauty and death are represented as inextricably fused at the root of the moment of passion.

Notes and references

1. **Robert Louis Stevenson**, *Works*, ed. L. Osbourne and Mrs R. L. Stevenson (30 vols, London, 1924–6), **IV**, 65.
2. See **Julia Briggs**, *Night Visitors: The Rise and Fall of the English Ghost Story* (London, 1977), pp. 20–1, 79–81.
3. **Oscar Wilde**, *The Picture of Dorian Gray*, ed. Isobel Murray (London, 1974), p. 143.
4. **William Blake**, *The Marriage of Heaven and Hell* (1790–3), in *The Poetry and Prose of William Blake*, ed. David V. Erdman (New York, 1965), p. 37.
5. **Lytton Strachey**, *Characters and Commentaries* (London, 1933), p. 40.
6. **H. G. Wells**, *The Island of Doctor Moreau* (London, 1973), p. 104.
7. **Bram Stoker**, *Dracula* (New York, 1965), p. 245.
8. **Arthur Machen**, *The Great God Pan and The Inmost Light* (London, 1913), p. 101.
9. **Machen**, *The Three Impostors*, introd. Julian Symons (London, 1964), pp. 110–12.
10. This is, of course, only one of many examples in the Gothic – as in literature in general – of an oblique relation between a writer's political tendency and the political content of his writings; a simple point, but one so far largely ignored in criticism of the genre.
11. **Machen**, *The Hill of Dreams* (New York, 1923), pp. 101–2.

CHAPTER 2
Later American Gothic

Ambrose Bierce, Robert W. Chambers, H. P. Lovecraft

In America, the early 1890s saw the appearance of two volumes of short stories by the West Coast journalist and literary pundit Ambrose Bierce: *Tales of Soldiers and Civilians* (1891) and *Can Such Things Be?* (1893). The first book, as the title suggests, was divided between stories based on Bierce's experiences in the Civil War and other tales; what is most immediately striking about both groups in the book is the intensity of their preoccupation with death, which is no less strong in the second volume. It has been pointed out that of the sixty-eight short stories Bierce wrote, only two are not to do with death; and the kinds of death which form focal points of action run the gamut of violence and terror. On the strength of these stories he was hailed, somewhat prematurely, as the new Poe, but although Poe was clearly a pronounced influence, there are vital differences of emphasis and tone. Chiefly, what Bierce has in common with Poe is an economy. In his role as literary critic he consistently sneered at the novel, claiming it to be a temporary eccentricity of literary history, incapable of the intensity and compression which were the virtues of the short story, and as a writer his greatest skill lies in paring his story down to the bare and grisly bones, an 'un-fleshing' to reveal the skull beneath the skin. Yet even there, where economy and brevity in Poe are generally supplemented by a momentary but intense involvement with the psychological state of the protagonist, Bierce gives his reader almost nothing to compensate for the absence of developed character. As a writer his stance is brutal: this, he implicitly says, is what occurred, in all its nastiness. It carries no particular significance, and even if

27

it had, the realisation would have come too late for the protagonist. Although one can find a few moments of tenderness in the Civil War reminiscences, the rest of the stories are, like his journalism, informed by a bitter cynicism, so complete that it cannot even emerge as anger. When the 1891 volume was published in England its title was changed to *In the Midst of Life*, that death which in Bierce's stories is in the midst of life comes almost to fill the entire screen, sapping energies and souls and rendering feelings and emotions redundant even before they have been formed.

As a writer of the 1890s, Bierce's connection with the problems of decadence is more tenuous than in the case of his British contemporaries, but it is nonetheless there. He spent time in Britain, and was able to observe the way in which culture there was being influenced by French writers who in turn drew their inspiration from his master, Poe. As a journalist, his main concern was with the exposure of political and moral corruption, although he sometimes attempted this in a rather haphazard manner: his reputation was for savage honesty, to which a Calvinist upbringing, although he nominally rejected it and apparently entertained nothing but contempt for his childhood days and for his family, can hardly have failed to contribute. Bierce, like other American writers of the time, saw himself as maintaining a set of standards which were coming under constant threat from the depredations of big business and political manipulation. The actual political stance which this produced was a complex and sometimes contradictory one: Bierce prided himself on his anglophilia and his conservatism, yet this conservatism, since it professed allegiance to the democratic principles of the American constitution, often resulted in very radical opinions as to the changes necessary in order to preserve. If, thought Bierce, the fundamental rights of man could be guaranteed in the present time only by the abolition of private property and by enforced economic equality, then this was the price which a conservative might have to pay to avoid the injustices of an emergent corporate state. But this was the enthusiastic, crusading side of Bierce; the stories present a different aspect, a Bierce who, perceiving the omnipresence of death and the defeat of hope, stood back from the degeneracy of real life and composed warning fables about futility while the world burned. The stiff upper lip was a protection against decay and the collapse of ideological values.

A good example of the interlocking of horror and generalised social commentary in Bierce is the grimly humorous 'The Famous Gilson Bequest'[1] which begins with the summary small-town trial and hanging of Milton Gilson for horse-stealing and other crimes. Gilson's will bequeathes his all to his main enemy, Brentshaw, with one condition: that if anyone can come forward and *prove* Gilson's criminality, the estate shall pass to him. When it turns out that Gilson did indeed have considerable property in the East, Brentshaw promptly becomes his most earnest defender; he wastes his life, and all of the money, in defending his posthumous reputation. In the final scene he goes, prematurely aged and broken, to visit Gilson's grave. It has been opened by a flood, and he sees a vision of the dead man's ghost, engaged in stealing the ashes of the other occupants of the graveyard, a vision which causes his own death. Until this very last scene, Bierce manages not to commit himself about Gilson's guilt, but at that point we realise that Brentshaw's life has been spent in the service of lies and deceit, that the bequest has indeed spread corruption through the whole town and has compounded the dishonesty of Gilson's own life. The flooding of the graveyard is an image of the contamination of guilt.

The habit of reserving the point of his story for the final line or paragraph is a mannerism for which Bierce has been attacked, but in certain cases it works extremely well. The outstanding example, and Bierce's best-known story, is 'An Occurrence at Owl Creek Bridge', which opens with Peyton Farquhar about to be hanged from the bridge for treachery during the war. As he falls, however, the rope breaks and he finds himself in the river. His would-be executioners shoot at him, but he avoids their bullets and reaches the bank. After a lengthy and difficult journey, he manages to find a road which leads back to his home, and struggles along it, 'fatigued, footsore, famishing'. Then,

> He stands at the gate of his own home. All is as he left it, and all bright and beautiful in the morning sunshine. He must have travelled the entire night. As he pushes open the gate and passes up the wide white walk, he sees a flutter of female garments; his wife, looking fresh and cool and sweet, steps down from the veranda to meet him. At the bottom of the steps she stands waiting, with a smile of ineffable joy, an attitude of matchless grace and dignity. Ah, how beautiful she is! He springs forward with extended arms. As he is about to clasp her he feels a stunning blow upon the back of the neck; a blinding white light blazes all about him with a sound like the shock of a cannon – then all is darkness and silence!
>
> Peyton Farquhar was dead; his body, with a broken neck, swung gently from side to side beneath the timbers of the Owl Creek Bridge.

It is a trick, but it is also more than a trick; it is an economical portrayal of the moment of awakening from hope. He draws us far enough into the dream for us not to want to come back, and ends by promising us that, whatever else death may be, it will be more unjust and terrible than we had suspected, it will come upon us precisely in the moment of freedom and will laugh at our delusion. The very fact of Bierce's refusal of 'character' intensifies the tragic moment by universalising the experience. It seems, in fact, to be the case that Bierce's style produces a situation in which, since so many of the accustomed markers of realism are missing anyway, there is no difference in texture between dream and reality; since life is itself spread so thinly, only the moment of death can give us confrontation with the significant.

Jay Martin uses the word 'surreal' in connection with this aspect of Bierce's technique,[2] and for certain of the stories this is highly appropriate, insofar as the symbolism attains to an unhealthy life of its own to which we have to attempt to attach our own meanings. 'The Death of Halpin Frayser' works in this mode, and is also one of the most Poe-esque of the stories. It opens, like 'Ligeia', with a quotation about the 'real' and complex nature of death:

> For by death is wrought greater change than hath been shown. Whereas in general the spirit that removed cometh back on occasion, and is sometimes seen of those in flesh (appearing in the form of the body it bore) yet it hath happened that the veritable body without the spirit hath walked. And it is attested of those encountering who have lived to speak thereon that a lich so raised up hath no natural affection, nor remembrance thereof, but only hate. Also, it is known that some spirits which in life were benign become by death evil altogether.

The difference from Poe is marked in the attribution, to 'Hali', a mythical authority who was later to become part of the mythology of H. P. Lovecraft, and more importantly in the directness of Bierce's statement about the 'hate' of the zombie. The story itself then opens with characteristic abruptness:

> One dark night in midsummer a man waking from a dreamless sleep in a forest lifted his head from the earth, and staring a few moments into the blackness, said: 'Catherine Larue'. He said nothing more; no reason was known to him why he should have said so much.

A dark tale unfolds of murder and guilt, during which occurs the celebrated description of the forest of blood:

> It was now long after nightfall, yet the interminable forest through which he journeyed was lit with a wan glimmer having no point of diffusion, for in its mysterious lumination nothing cast a shadow. A shallow pool in the guttered depression of an old wheel rut, as from a recent rain, met his eye with a crimson gleam. He stooped and

plunged his hand into it. It stained his fingers; it was blood! Blood, he then observed, was about him everywhere. The weeds growing rankly by the roadside showed it in blots and splashes on their big, broad leaves. Patches of dry dust between the wheelways were pitted and shattered as with a red rain. Defiling the trunks of the trees were broad maculations of crimson, and blood dripped like dew from their foliage.

The plot itself is confused and confusing; what is impressive is the sense of fatality which Bierce imparts to Frayser's doomed journey. Like most of Bierce's other characters, he has neither free will nor any comprehension of the forces around him – or, indeed, within him: Mary Grenander's book on Bierce contains a detailed and convincing Freudian explication of the story,[3] and the whole 'journey' metaphor which recurs throughout the corpus has clear Freudian undertones. Frayser moves in dreams and half-light, while around him gather the monstrous shapes of familial persecution which propel him towards an undeserved and horrible end.

This kind of self-sufficing symbolism has been historically associated with the prose poem, and so it is in Bierce. 'An Inhabitant of Carcosa' presents a man who finds himself isolated amid unrecognised ruins; his discovery of his own grave reveals to him that these are the ruins of the great city in which he once lived. It draws on the feelings of graveyard poetry and on the tradition of the 'ruins of empire' which goes back to Count Volney and to Shelley's 'Ozymandias'[4]: 'scattered here and there, more massive blocks showed where some pompous tomb or ambitious monument had once flung its feeble defiance at oblivion'. Yet in Bierce this tendency towards the fragmentary, reminiscent of the attempts by Nathan Drake and other early Gothic writers to encapsulate the feeling of terror in a single literary episode or scene, is sometimes accompanied by a sophisticated and even scornful understanding and use of narrative perspectives. 'The Moonlit Road' is a particularly interesting example, in which the story of a fatal night is told in succession by one Joel Hetman, whose life has been ruined by the death of his mother and the later disappearance of his father; by the father, whose memory and sense of identity has gone, but who suspects from his recurrent nightmares that it was he who killed his wife, in a fit of jealousy; and then by the shade of the wife, from whose account we discover that the object of this jealousy, a mysterious and unseen visitor, is as inexplicable to her as to her husband. When all the stories have been told, we are left with a yawning gap. Bierce mocks expectations of solution by showing that the passage into the world of ghosts is accompanied by not a whit of greater understanding on the part of the deceased wife:

> No, I have no knowledge of what it was. The sum of what we knew at
> death is the measure of what we know afterward of all that went
> before. Of this existence we know many things, but no new light falls
> upon any page of that; in memory is written all of it that we can read.
> Here are no heights of truth overlooking the confused landscape of
> that dubitable domain. We still dwell in the Valley of the Shadow,
> lurk in its desolate places, peering from brambles and thickets at its
> mad, malign inhabitants. How should we have new knowledge of that
> fading past?

To complete the picture of despair, it turns out that it was the apparition of the dead wife, undertaken by her to comfort the husband, whom she does not know to have been her murderer, which caused his flight, his loss of memory and his reduction to the extremes of poverty and decay. As Grenander rightly if rather confusingly puts it, Bierce concentrates on making 'the intellectual awareness on which the whole psychology of his protagonist's terror rests a wrong one; hence all the emotional and sensory reactions which follow are erroneous, and the reader's perception of this gruesome inappropriateness to the real situation is what gives their peculiar distillation of horror to these tales' (Grenander, p. 94). Almost all of the action of the stories is based on mistakes, mistakes of perception and of self-conception, which result, inevitably, in death.

In a style of military precision Bierce metes out to his readers Old Testament prophecies and warnings of doom, a doom which is nonetheless unavoidable because it is laid down in advance. It is partly this tone of peremptory and irritable warning which causes the 'familiar fascistic ring' of which Edmund Wilson speaks,[5] and it is also partly Bierce's assumption of an aristocratic role in relation to his audience. His literary and cultural tastes looked back to the English eighteenth century, which he saw as a time of order and stability which nevertheless permitted a controlled benevolence based on an awareness of social and intellectual distinction; he saw this as the best that could be achieved to palliate the terror of mortality. His combination of Puritan and military morality is responsible for the form of his more complex stories, in which deliberate difficulties are set in the path of understanding: 'The Suitable Surroundings' is virtually narrated backwards; 'The Night-Doings at "Deadman's" ' announces its mockery of the reader in its subtitle, 'A Story That is Untrue'. Life for Bierce was a 'sickness unto death', but this perception permitted of no defiant grandeur, merely a stoical mixture of acceptance and resentment, a knowledge that the shock of realising truth would kill, but that this does not matter, because such realisation can in any case only come at the very point of predestined death.

In the same year as Bierce's *Can Such Things Be?*, another volume of horror stories was published in America, *The King in Yellow* by Robert W. Chambers. Chambers went on to become a successful writer of magazine potboilers, alternating between historical romance and 'tales of fashionable life' set in and around New York; he never followed in the direction in which *The King in Yellow* pointed. What is perhaps chiefly remarkable about the book is that it actually demonstrated the possibility of an American writing horror fiction which was *not* obviously derivative from Poe, and this was all the stranger in that Chambers had spent several of his youthful years in Europe studying art, and was even more aware than Bierce of the decadent interest in Poe. Those stories which were most clearly influenced by this aspect of his experience are couched in a lush, incantatory prose which is directly connected with the Bierce of 'An Inhabitant of Carcosa', though not at all with the morbid and cynical Bierce of 'Halpin Frayser' or the Civil War stories; connected both mythologically and stylistically, as one can see from the very brief 'In the Court of the Dragon'.[6] Here the narrator is inexplicably pursued by a figure of doom. His endeavours to escape are hampered by dreamlike immobility but eventually take him to a church, where he again perceives the same figure; the story concludes with the hero's perception of the real world being overwhelmed by the alternative diabolic vision offered by the pursuer.

> I crept to the door; the organ broke out overhead with a blare. A dazzling light filled the church, blotting the altar from my eyes. The people faded away, the arches, the vaulted roof vanished. I raised my seared eyes to the fathomless glare, and I saw the black stars hanging in the heavens: and the wet winds from the Lake of Hali chilled my face.
>
> And now, far away, over leagues of tossing cloud-waves, I saw the moon dripping with spray; and beyond, the towers of Carcosa rose behind the moon.
>
> Death and the awful abode of lost souls, whither my weakness long ago had sent him, and had changed him for every other eye but mine. And now I heard *his voice*, rising, swelling, thundering through the flaring light, and as I fell, the radiance increasing, increasing, poured over me in waves in flame. Then I sank into the depths, and I heard the King in Yellow whispering to my soul: 'It is a fearful thing to fall into the hands of the living God!'

The vices and virtues of Chambers's style are difficult to separate:

the ornateness, and the attempt at poetic rhythm, are only partly achieved, and Chambers's seemingly adolescent pride in 'literariness' can be hard to take, yet behind this lies a singular attempt to recreate a type of horror which flows not directly from psychological obsession in the manner of Poe or Bierce but from blasphemy. Chambers, it is true, is very concerned with the workings of the mind at the point of breakdown, but his best effects come from connecting observation of mental operations with a sub-Baudelairean diabolism.

A good example, and one of the best of the stories, is 'The Repairer of Reputations'. This is an internal study of megalomaniac insanity, but its interest lies less in the process of mental disintegration which it depicts than in its creation of a decadent mythology, with a devil-figure to match, whose name, not accidentally chosen, is Wilde. It is set thirty years into the future (1920), in an America curiously transformed into a place of security and beauty: 'everywhere good architecture was replacing bad and even in New York, a sudden craving for decency had swept away a great portion of the existing horrors'; this brave new world has also repealed 'the laws prohibiting suicide', and Government Lethal Chambers provide a conveniently unembarrassing point of exit for those for whom American world domination and consequent national self-confidence are too much to take. The first-person narrator, Castaigne, who has ominously suffered from a serious accident which, he informs us, has 'fortunately left no evil results' – except an increased ambitiousness – comes across the book *The King in Yellow*, which is both a symbolic work of blasphemy and also, clearly, an apotheosis of 'yellow-bookery', and is so affected by it as to believe in the predictions about his own glorious future made to him by Wilde. Wilde himself is, in a certain sense, laughable; the terror comes through in Castaigne's cheerful acceptance of him as a prophet and semi-divinity:

> When he had double-locked the door and pushed a heavy chest against it, he came and sat down beside me, peering up into my face with his little light-coloured eyes. Half a dozen new scratches covered his nose and cheeks, and the silver wires which supported his artificial ears had become displaced. I thought I had never seen him so hideously fascinating. He had no ears. The artificial ones, which now stood out at an angle from the fine wire, were his one weakness. They were made of wax and painted a shell pink, but the rest of his face was yellow. He might better have revelled in the luxury of some artificial fingers for his left hand, which was absolutely fingerless, but it seemed to cause him no inconvenience, and he was satisfied with his wax ears. He was

very small, scarcely higher than a child of ten, but his arms were magnificently developed, and his thighs as thick as any athlete's. Still, the most remarkable thing about Mr Wilde was that a man of his marvellous intelligence and knowledge should have such a head. It was flat and pointed, like the heads of many of those unfortunates whom people imprison in asylums for the weak-minded. Many called him insane but I knew him to be as sane as I was.

Chambers's little joke in the last sentence is one of the many points at which he alerts the reader to the discrepancy between the narrator's view of the world and those of the other people with whom he comes into contact; the scratches on Wilde's face are caused by his persistent habit of fighting murderous duels with his cat, but Castaigne puts this down to harmless eccentricity. He is convinced that Wilde has at his command a secret army of adherents who are going to reinstate him (Castaigne) to his rightful position at the head of 'the Imperial Dynasty of America', and has as token of his eventual success a collection of crown jewels. The adherents, however, are no less psychologically suspect than Wilde, and the 'jewels' are 'theatrical tinsel'; Castaigne's eventual attempt to appear in all his promised glory is thwarted by the efforts of his relatives, and by the simultaneous and bloody defeat of Wilde by this remarkable cat.

> Mr Wilde lay on the floor with his throat torn open. At first I thought he was dead, but as I looked, a green sparkle came into his sunken eyes, his mutilated hand trembled, and then a spasm stretched his mouth from ear to ear. For a moment my terror and despair gave place to hope, but as I bent over him his eyeballs rolled clean around in his head, and he died. Then while I stood, transfixed with rage and despair, seeing my crown, my empire, every hope and every ambition, my very life, lying prostrate there with the dead master, *they* came, seized me from behind, and bound me until my veins stood out like cords, and my voice failed with the paroxysms of my frenzied screams. But I still raged, bleeding and infuriated among them, and more than one policeman felt my sharp teeth. Then when I could no longer move they came nearer . . .

The reactionary revolution which Wilde and Castaigne have intended comes to nothing; it is revealed as a thing of dream and madness by those forces (policemen, soldiers, an 'armourer') devoted to the perpetuation and protection of a grotesquely caricatured welfare state. Chambers's displaced aristocrats lack the self-destructive grandeur of Poe's, or of Dracula, who would not have sullied his teeth with the blood of policemen.

In 'The Demoiselle d'Ys', the American hero, travelling in a bleak part of Finistère, loses himself, tries to sleep and awakens to find that 'a great bird hung quivering in the air above my face'. He encounters a lady who talks mainly of falconry, in terms long outmoded, and accompanies her hunting. He is taken to her chateau, falls in love with her, and is invited to 'win her'. At the climactic moment,

> as she lay trembling on my breast, something struck my foot in the grass below, but I did not heed it. Then again something struck my ankle, and a sharp pain shot through me. I looked into the sweet face of Jeanne d'Ys and kissed her, and with all my strength lifted her in my arms and flung her from me. Then bending, I tore the viper from my ankle and set my heel upon its head. I remember feeling weak and numb, – I remember falling to the ground.

When he awakes a second time, the crushed viper is still there, but apart from that there is only a heap of mouldering ruins. He gets up, dragging his 'numbed foot', and falls 'before a crumbling shrine carved in stone for our Mother of Sorrows'. It is a memorial to Jeanne d'Ys, who died in 1573; upon it lies 'a woman's glove still warm and fragrant'.

To mention just one further story, 'The Mask' begins with a successful experiment to perpetuate living beauty:

> Although I knew nothing of chemistry, I listened fascinated. He picked up an Easter lily which Geneviève had brought that morning from Notre Dame and dropped it into the basin. Instantly the liquid lost its crystalline clearness. For a second the lily was enveloped in a milk-white foam, which disappeared, leaving the fluid opalescent. Changing tints of orange and crimson played over the surface, and then what seemed to be a ray of pure sunlight struck through from the bottom where the lily was resting. At the same instant he plunged his hand into the basin and drew out the flower. 'There is no danger', he explained, 'if you choose the right moment. That golden ray is the signal.'
>
> He held the lily toward me and I took it in my hand. It had turned to stone, to the purest marble.

The story turns on the relationships between the sculptor, Boris, his wife Geneviève and Alec the narrator. Geneviève reveals under the influence of fever that she really loves Alec, upon which he, with the weakness endemic in decadent heroes, goes into a decline. He pulls out of it to discover that Geneviève, stricken to the soul by her revelation, her removal of the mask, has plunged herself into a pool of the magic fluid, upon which Boris has shot himself. The marble Geneviève is placed in an unfinished sculptural group of Boris's, along with a figure of the Madonna. Alec does the decent thing and boards the 'Orient express for Constantinople', but after two years he is drawn back to the sculptor's abandoned house, to find that strange things are happening: two goldfish and a rabbit which Boris had petrified come back to life. Alec sees the Easter lily, and goes to pick it up:

> But the flower I lifted from the table was fresh and fragile and filled the air with perfume.
> Then suddenly I comprehended and sprang through the hall-way to the marble room. The doors flew open, the sunlight streamed into my face and through it, in a heavenly glory, the Madonna smiled, as Geneviève lifted her flushed face from the marble couch, and opened her sleepy eyes.

The implication of the smile on the face of the *Madonna* is an example of Chambers's technique at its most economical.

His French and American exquisites have a touch of life – and of humour – quite foreign to the Poe tradition; terror comes to them not in the blackness of underground passages and dungeons but in the blindness of too much streaming sunlight, the 'scalloped tatters of the King in Yellow'. Where Poe looked back to Coleridge and to the romantic versions of the 'long night of the soul', Chambers found his inspiration in the fatal ambivalence of beauty which preoccupied Keats and Shelley. Yet what Chambers does have in common with Poe is a particular relation to 'modernism': to put it simply, his stories do not feel like complete wholes but like assembled fragments, in the course of which questions are deliberately left open. Vague pieces of mythology are introduced and fade out of sight; at the end of 'The Yellow Sign', a figure appears 'and the bolts rotted at his touch', but the doctor who is called to explain 'a horrible decomposed heap on the floor' has 'no theory, no explanation'. The stories are themselves 'tatters', one of Chambers's favourite words, fragmentary manifestations of evil which are not *produced* by dislocation of sensibility, although that dislocation tears gaps in the world through which evil may come – and through which may also come, simultaneously, a beauty which it is death or madness to behold.

Chambers's stories also mark a curious point in the transmutation of horror fiction into 'pulp'; Lewis Pattee refers to his 'fineness', 'finesse', 'deftness and lightness of touch', and H. L. Mencken assents to 'a fundamental earnestness and a high degree of skill', but Mencken also, and in the same breath, talks of 'the shoddiness in Chambers, the leaning towards "profitable pot-boiling" '.[7] One way of looking at these contradictory judgements is by saying that Chambers had in his horror stories very little to express but a high awareness of the elliptical techniques which terror fiction invites, techniques which he was to go on to waste on the weary dialogue of upper-class New York alcoholics. His literary devices are polished but unrooted; at least, however, he, like the earlier writers of terror-fiction, regarded the genre, if only briefly, as worthy of effort and poise, as a fit field in which to practise that evasion of crudity and naturalism which was a linchpin of the decadent aesthetic. His stories are not obviously concerned with any of the great themes of decadence except that of the Medusa, but their style is at times more truly decadent than anything to be found in Wilde; where Wilde tries to use paradox to overturn a rationalist framework, Chambers works obliquely, always suggesting a wider dominance of evil and decay without being drawn into portraying the dimensions of that dominance.

From Hawthorne and Poe, Bierce and Chambers, the blood-stream of American Gothic flows a little anaemically into the work of H. P. Lovecraft. Lovecraft is a literary sore point: ever since his death in 1937, his life and work have been submerged in a cultism which transcends anything lavished on Mervyn Peake or J. R. R. Tolkien, yet the few critics who have bothered to spend any time reading him have been massively dissatisfied; perhaps the main exception is the bizarre Colin Wilson who unequivocally finds Love-craft to be 'a very bad writer', but grants at least that he was 'not an isolated crank', that he was 'working in a recognisable romantic tradition; but everything is overdone, exaggerated to a point at which it ceases to be acceptable as art'.[8] Various points in this general assessment might be criticised; but what might be salvaged is that this 'romantic tradition' is, in most of its significant features, the Gothic tradition, although Lovecraft, like Chambers, did not take his Gothic direct from Poe.

Ironically, this has caused critical problems. When Edmund Wilson comments that he has 'never yet found in Lovecraft a single sentence that Poe could have written, though there are some – not at all the same thing – that have evidently been influenced by Poe',[9] this is hardly surprising, because Lovecraft saw terror in a very different way from Poe. Where Poe refers fear back to the 'life within', Lovecraft is utterly devoid of psychological interest; his terrors are entirely those of the unintelligible outside, of the indi-vidual cramped by alien encroachment. Julia Briggs is closer to the truth when she refers to Lovecraft as a 'disciple' of Machen, and compares the so-called 'Cthulhu Mythos' – the organising structure behind much of Lovecraft's best-known work – to elements in Machen's *The Three Impostors* and *The Children of the Pool* (1936) (Briggs, p. 73). As Lovecraft himself wrote,

> All my stories, unconnected as they may be, are based on the funda-
> mental lore or legend that this world was inhabited at one time by
> another race who, in practising black magic, lost their foothold and
> were expelled, yet live on outside, ever ready to take possession of this
> earth again.[10]

The structure is common to Machen, Lovecraft and Algernon Blackwood, and in at least two important respects it is the structure of
the original Gothic: in that it hinges on an unassimilable fear of the
past, and in that primal crime is symbolised in terms of unholy
aspiration after forbidden knowledge, a forbidden knowledge
imaged by Lovecraft in a whole range of invented books. These
books, of which the best known is the imaginary *Necronomicon,* are
both *grimoires* and, like Chambers's *King in Yellow,* works which
madden by their blasphemous potential.

The fundamental structure of terror in most of Lovecraft's work
is a simple one. In a New England setting, reminiscent scenically and
in its claustrophobic intensity of Hawthorne's, he recounts fables of
degeneration. In this respect, his work unites the fears of the *histori-*
cal past which preoccupied the writers of the early nineteenth
century with anxiety about the *species*-past, as in the post-Darwinian
British writers, and it is this important conjunction which is responsible for such strength as his writing has. His backcloth brings
together a number of thinly disguised East Coast towns, chosen for
their historical 'depth of field', with those other depths, of the sea
and of outer space, breeding-grounds for the primitive but powerful
exiled beings who await their chance to return and topple the flimsy
dominion of humanity. Horror often comes at the point where sea-
beings become amphibious and begin to crawl out of their domain.
A typical explicatory passage occurs in *The Lurker at the Threshold,*
partly written by Lovecraft and completed after his death by his
indistinguishable disciple August Derleth, which takes as its 'evidence' the survival of strange cults in the South Seas:

> Such cult-survivals are common enough, and don't often come to
> public notice, but this one was published because of certain adjunctive
> discoveries – the queer mutations present on the bodies of certain of
> the natives killed in a shipwreck just off the coast – the presence of primal
> gills, for instance, of vestigial tentacles arising from the torso, and in
> one case, of scaly eyes in an area of squamous skin near the navel of
> one of the victims, all of whom were known to have belonged to the
> Sea-God cult.

Lovecraft goes on to mention 'dark hints . . . that there has been carnal traffic between certain sea-dwellers and some of the natives of the Carolines', and it is from this act of miscegenation that the action of the book derives. That the resulting beings are akin to the amphibia of prehistory is further evidenced in the sympathy felt towards them by actual amphibia: the author of the *Necronomicon*, according to Lovecraft, has 'intimated . . . that the terrestrial amphibia were both unusually active and unusually vocal in the presence of their primal relatives, "be they visible or invisible, to them it maketh no difference, for they feel them, & give voice" '.[11]

The appalling feature of this aspect of Lovecraft's writing is that, reading through not only his fiction but also his letters, one realises that the terms which he applies to his invading non-human monstrosities are precisely the same as those in which he describes members of all American ethnic groups with the exception of the caste of East Coast 'Old Americans' to which he belonged. It is unnecessary to document the point here; the biography of Lovecraft by L. Sprague de Camp contains page after page of outpourings about the dangers of racial pollution, focusing on Jews, Mexicans, blacks and every variety of European.[12] Lovecraft regarded himself as unable to survive in New York because of the effects of this pollution, which he claimed, produced in him feelings of uncontrollable revulsion, which are identical to the feelings which his heroes experience when confronted with the 'unnatural'. It is difficult to say which in Lovecraft is the greater, his fear of the past, principally in the shape of a fear of decadent European and primitive civilisations corroding the upright values of New England (and especially Providence, Rhode Island), or his fear of the future, manifested as a detestation of machines, commercialism and anything which might vitiate the illusory social stability to which he obsessively clung. Philosophically, this combination of anxieties reduced Lovecraft to total stasis: the oddly appropriate – in its very distastefulness – term which de Camp uses is 'futilitarianism', by which he means to denote Lovecraft's self-defensive insistence on the meaninglessness of the cosmos, a frequent emphasis in his fiction. Paradoxically, though, Lovecraft does not bemoan the coming of mechanisation in the terms one might expect, as an erosion of feeling in the name of rationality and order, but from an opposite perspective: mechanisation was to him a concomitant of irrationality, insofar as it marked a fall from the kind of orderly natural virtue which he, rather oddly, regarded as the hallmark of his 'golden age', the British eighteenth century.

Certainly, however, his fear of the past is tempered with a tra-
ditionally Gothic emphasis on the past's attractiveness; his heroes
behave towards haunted surroundings with the mixture of terror
and self-sacrifice which has since become a convention of pulp
fiction and of many horror films:

> Gilman believed strange things about Keziah, and had felt a queer
> thrill on learning that her dwelling was still standing after more than
> two hundred and thirty-five years. When he heard the hushed Arkham
> whispers about Keziah's persistent presence in the old house and the
> narrow streets, about the irregular human tooth-marks left on certain
> sleepers in that and other houses, about the childish cries heard near
> May-Eve, and Hallowmass, about the stench often noted in the old
> house's attic just after those dreaded seasons, and about the small,
> furry, sharp-toothed thing which haunted the moldering structure and
> the town and nuzzled people curiously in the black hours before
> dawn, he resolved to live in the place at any cost.[13]

The stance of false naïvety is far from Poe; in Lovecraft there is an
open collusion with the reader which seems designed to prevent
him from interesting himself in the protagonist's mind or feelings,
and focuses his attention directly on the action and on the terror-
figures themselves. When, as he so often does, he employs the
familiar Gothic theme of the 'sins of the fathers', we are left in little
doubt about what those sins were; the only question is whether
Lovecraft can muster a re-visitation dread enough to represent
adequately that past which will not lie still.

The curious thing which has happened to Lovecraft, and which
has also happened to Tolkien, the development of a connected cult
which continues and in some ways supersedes the biographical and
literary facts, should probably itself be seen as to do with Gothic.
Lovecraft developed to a high point the insistence on verification
which characterised so many of the early Gothic writers – Mary
Shelley, Charles Maturin, Hogg and others. Not only did he continually emphasise the reliability of his fictional 'root' manuscripts, he
even invented a town and a university in which his actions are
consistently located. Those who laboured to publish his work after
his death did so by establishing a press which bore the name of his
imaginary town, Arkham, the result, paradoxically, being to cast
doubt upon the relative reality of Lovecraft himself, a doubt pleasantly reinforced by the facts that, first, a great deal of 'his' fiction
was either completed or in fact written by other people, and second
much of his *actual* work was in the form of 'ghost-writing' [sic] for
others.

To return, however, to the work itself and to the ways in which Lovecraft can be seen as an inheritor of Gothic traditions, one is initially struck by the deliberate archaism of much of his language. He was possessed of a concept of the 'literary' which was in full accord with his general taste for things eighteenth-century: much of his very early work consisted of poor imitations of Augustan poetry and provides clear evidence, if such were needed, of his longing for the qualities of reason, order, stability which he found so lamentably missing from the modern world. Lovecraft's greatest fear was of disorder, chaos, the situation which would result if the walls of convention which surrounded both human perception and the cosmos were to be breached. This is one of many passages in which he describes, as the culmination of a story, the final vision of meaninglessness which lies beyond these walls, to which we might all be brought by tampering with the natural – and, by implication, the social – order:

> Screamingly sentient, dumbly delirious, only the gods that were can tell. A sickened, sensitive shadow writhing in hands that are not hands, and whirled blindly past ghastly midnights of rotting creation, corpses of dead worlds with sores that were cities, charnel winds that brush the pallid stars and make them flicker low. Beyond the worlds vague ghosts of monstrous things; half-seen columns of unsanctified temples that rest on nameless rocks beneath space and reach up to dizzy vacua above the spheres of light and darkness. And through this revolting graveyard of the universe the muffled, maddening beating of drums, and thin, monotonous whine of blasphemous flutes from inconceivable, unlighted chambers beyond Time; the detestable pounding and piping whereunto dance slowly, awkwardly, and absurdly, the gigantic, tenebrous ultimate gods – the blind, voiceless, mindless gargoyles whose soul is Nyarlathotep.[14]

At other times, Lovecraft talks of Azathoth, the blind, idiot god who dwells at the centre of the universe, and is a principle of chaos; and in all these passages, repetitive as they are, there is a curious consistency of form and content, partly because individual words – here, for instance, 'tenebrous' – are used almost without regard for meaning, but merely as elements in an incantation. The very fact of the repetitiveness is also part of Lovecraft's point: no matter how various the supernatural adventures, or how diverse the minor manifestations of evil, the final vision is single and unchanging: beneath the solid surface of the world lurks the threat of the random. To reach it is self-defeating, for it resists interpretation; it defeats the mind for it is itself 'mindless'. Therefore human life must be bounded by convention and by rigid schemes of social classification, a view which Lovecraft bore out in his person; only conventions and classes protect us from the mindless and destructive pleasure of the instincts – which are, surely, the blind 'gargoyles' of which he speaks.

The Dream-Quest of Unknown Kadath, a long piece written in the early 1920s, relies on a crucial opposition between the 'mild gods of earth' and the 'other gods'[15]; those anthropomorphised qualities through whose passive benevolence we continue to live and those 'others' whose purposeless lust for dominion threatens the normal boundaries of that life. The opposition is again clear in Freudian terms, but with a significant difference: in Lovecraft's cosmology the forces of psychological compromise do not bound and restrict the endless lusts of the unconscious; rather the 'id' encircles that small area of reason which represents all that man can and should know of the world. There are, in a sense, no doubts in Lovecraft's work: the world *is* a force of persecution, the faces that appear below the pavement are really there, there indeed with a greater degree of reality than we can comprehend.

One might regard such certainties as these as neurotic. Colin Wilson compares Lovecraft to Kafka in terms of his importance as a 'psychological case-history' (*Strength to Dream*, p. 27); whatever we may think of this judgement, Lovecraft's texts certainly demonstrate a remarkable set of psychological displacements. There is displacement at the verbal level, the continual inability to rely on the force of the individual word and the corresponding need to buttress it up with a vocabulary of subjective adjectives; at its best, this habit turns into ceremony, ritual, incantation, at its worst the words 'overkill' and slide off the object. But there are also deeper problems than that: Lovecraft's terror-figures are never quite terrifying enough because, surely, they do not truthfully represent the sources of his fears, which appear, as far as one can tell, to have been racial and sexual. There are almost no sexual references in Lovecraft's own stories, but there is an interesting one in Derleth's imitative 'The Dark Brotherhood' (1966), which brings out a depth of anxiety which never even becomes manifest in Lovecraft's own work. The hero knows that certain aliens have the ability to manufacture perfect likenesses of human individuals (Poe among others!), but he does not yet know how they do it. He comes into a room which contains two large glass cases:

> in the one that lit the room with its violently pulsating and agitated violent radiation lay Rose Dexter, fully clothed and certainly under hypnosis – and on top of her lay, greatly elongated and with its tentacles flailing madly, the rugose cone-like figure I had last seen shrunken

on the likeness of Poe. And in the connected case adjacent to it – I can hardly bear to set it down even now – lay, identical in every detail, *a perfect duplicate of Rose!*[16]

Derleth, steeped in the works of his master and devoted to extending his fame, has here performed a greater service than he knew or intended. It is all here: the blocked repetition of 'violent', the insistence on 'fully clothed', the carefully placed 'certainly' which absolves the woman of all participation, the 'elongated' and 'cone-like' alien, the hesitation about the possibility of setting down the account, and the shock and amazement that such a thing as reproduction should be. Much the same constellation of factors can be derived from an examination of the letters, and from such facts as are available about Lovecraft's brief and curious married life. The important thing is that the crude power of the fiction comes directly from Lovecraft's need to go on beating endlessly on the same wall, while its occasional tenderness and nostalgia derive from the haunting knowledge that there is another world on the other side of the wall, *not* a world of terror but a world in which unnamed fears can be named and thus brought under control. One of the strange primal cities of Lovecraft's mythology is called 'Irem'[17]; little could be clearer than the foreshortening of 'I remember', evidence of the impossibility of unblocking the path back to the past, or of thus reducing the hostility of that past.

Perhaps little more needs to be said about Lovecraft: his writing is crude, repetitive, compulsively readable, the essence of pulp fiction. Most of the time he reduces Gothic motifs to a kind of mechanism; his place in the tradition is not as an innovator or even modifier, but more as a latter-day reinvoker of past horrors. Yet, occasionally, there is something else in Lovecraft, a half-resigned, half-amused tone which is the nearest we ever come to discerning an interesting narrative voice. One might compare two rather similar passages, the first from Bulwer Lytton's 'The Haunted and the Haunters' (1857), the second from *The Dream-Quest of Unknown Kadath*:

monstrous things . . . larvae so bloodless and so hideous that I can in no way describe them except to remind the reader of the swarming life which the solar microscope brings before his eyes in a drop of water, – things transparent, supple, agile, chasing each other, devouring each other, – forms like nought ever beheld to the naked eye.

Shoals of shapeless lurkers and caperers in darkness, and vacuous herds of drifting entities that pawed and groped and groped and pawed; the nameless larvae of the Other Gods, that are like them blind and without mind, and possessed of singular hungers and thirsts.[18]

Lytton locates his image by suggesting the analogy with the bloodstream, whereas Lovecraft is dealing with 'interstellar spaces' with characteristic grandiosity, but more to the point is the ironic note in the Lovecraft passage, the suggestion that the fear is not of slaughter but of a kind of trivialisation, that the role of the 'Other Gods' is simply to giggle at human posturings. The phrase 'singular hungers and thirsts' is similarly ironic (and seems to be an adaptation of a habitual phrase of James Branch Cabell's) and marks perhaps a rare moment in Lovecraft's fiction when he becomes aware that mere weight and accretion do not of themselves construct a terror-symbol.

There are two things one needs to point out in conclusion about this particular branch of Gothic and its fate. The first is its increasing inability to sustain length: as we shall see, there are other kinds of recent Gothic which are still able to do so, but that kind which deals direct with horror and the 'supernatural' moves in Poe, Bierce, Chambers and Lovecraft increasingly in a world of fragments and momentary perceptions. The second point is connected with this: precisely as the form atrophies and crystallises, there is a series of attempts to construct a belief system or embracing myth which will sustain narrative length – Bierce's Carcosa, Chambers's King in Yellow, Lovecraft's Cthulhu, all try to recreate a situation in which a stable set of images of evil can inform a body of fiction. On the whole, they fail: in cultural terms, their power is nothing compared with that of Frankenstein and Dracula. There are several possible reasons for this, to which we will return, but one at least is that these culturally central myths of terror still embody particular historical fears in such a way that they do not need to be superseded, that there is little space for the 'Cthulhu mythos' and others to occupy. However, in looking at this group of American writers, we have moved far ahead, mainly in order to provide a location for Lovecraft's obvious archaism; it is time to turn back to other aspects of the Gothic in the late nineteenth and early twentieth centuries.

Notes and references

1. All the Bierce stories discussed can be found in *Ghost and Horror Stories of Ambrose Bierce*, ed. E. F. Bleiler (New York, 1964).
2. See **Jay Martin**, *Harvests of Change: American Literature 1865-1914* (Englewood Cliffs, N. J., 1967), p. 124.
3. See **Mary E. Grenander**, *Ambrose Bierce* (New York, 1971), pp. 106–14.

4. **Constantin François Volney** was the author of *Les ruines, ou méditations sur les révolutions des empires* (1791), a politically influential work with clear Gothic affinities; see also *The Complete Works of Percy Bysshe Shelley*, ed. Roger Ingpen and Walter E. Peck (10 vols, New York, 1963), II, 62.

5. See **Edmund Wilson**, *Patriotic Gore: Studies in the Literature of the American Civil War* (London, 1962), p. 628.

6. All the Chambers stories discussed can be found in **Robert W. Chambers**, *The King in Yellow and Other Horror Stories*, ed. E. F. Bleiler (New York, 1970).

7. See **Fred Lewis Pattee**, *The New American Literature 1890–1930* (New York, 1930), p. 243.

8. **Colin Wilson**, *The Strength to Dream: Literature and the Imagination* (London, 1962), pp. 27, 29.

9. **Edmund Wilson**, 'Tales of the marvellous and the ridiculous', in *Classics and Commercials: A Literary Chronicle of the Forties* (London, 1951), p. 288.

10. See Colin Wilson, *Strength to Dream*, p. 26.

11. See **H. P. Lovecraft** and **August Derleth**, *The Lurker at the Threshold* (St Albans, 1970), pp. 135–6, 103.

12. See, e.g. **L. Sprague de Camp**, *Lovecraft: A Biography* (New York, 1975), pp. 89–95, 249–56, 266–7.

13. 'The dreams in the witch-house', in **Lovecraft**, *At the Mountains of Madness and Other Novels*, ed. Derleth (London, 1966), pp. 249–50.

14. 'Nyarlathotep', in **Lovecraft**, *The Doom that Came to Sarnath*, ed. Lin Carter (New York, 1971), p. 60.

15. See *Mountains of Madness*, pp. 378–82.

16. **Lovecraft** and **Derleth**, *The Shuttered Room and Other Tales of Horror* (London, 1970), p. 165.

17. See **Lovecraft**, 'The lamp of Alhazred', in *Shuttered Room*, p. 127.

18. **Bulwer Lytton**, *The Caxtons; Zicci; The Haunted and the Haunters* (Boston and New York, 1849), pp. 316–17; **Lovecraft**, *Mountains of Madness*, p. 383.

CHAPTER 3
The ambivalence of memory

Henry James and Walter de la Mare

In talking of first Machen, and now Lovecraft, we have begun to raise questions about the fate of the Gothic in the twentieth century. By doing so, we have bypassed one of the most important of all the works influenced by the Gothic tradition, Henry James's *The Turn of the Screw* (1898). The reason for this is that James's novella represents a decisive moment in the history of the Gothic, and of the ghost story, in terms of which Machen and Lovecraft seem, archaic; I want now to turn back to it, and in doing so to place James in rather odd company, that of the mystical poet and story-writer Walter de la Mare.[1]

The central point I want to bring out can be put in a number of ways. It might be seen as a question of materialism. The dark forces of the mind which Machen and Lovecraft describe are attached to an objective correlative: a past history which is delivered as real, typically the prior existence of races of non-human beings which persist in secret. For both of them human fears are justifiable, insofar as they approximate to perceptions of a genuine threat; the heroes of their stories are romantic heroes, in that they are granted a power of imagination which breaks through everyday surfaces to a more 'real' account of the bases of life. Although there are books of Machen's – *The Hill of Dreams, The Three Impostors* – which move beyond this simple form, his main corpus, represented by *The Great God Pan* and *The Terror* (1917) among others, is a set of demonstrations of duality of perception, and a continuing vindication of that imaginative perception which seeks the real *behind* the surface; Lovecraft moves in the same direction, and the Cthulhu mythos serves as a connecting web which is supposed to provide additional evidence of the coherence of the imaginative vision. This question of the relation between surface and hinterland is precisely what is at stake in *The Turn of the Screw*, and it is also at stake in the best of de la Mare's short stories. The mode of existence which dark forces have in these works is, in one sense, clearly Freudian in structure: that is, it raises the paradox of the unconscious to our attention. That we cannot, by definition, *know* the 'unconscious' is a point of which Freud was perfectly well aware; his claim was that we *can* know that things 'rise to consciousness', and that it is therefore reasonable to hypothesise a hinterland whence these things emerge, even though its detailed topography may be a matter of great difficulty. *The Turn of the Screw* and de la Mare's stories assume this curious mode of existence for the unconscious; they also assume that, since the mode of transition from unconscious to conscious is, in some sense, selective, we cannot rely upon immediate perception to grant truth.

James and de la Mare share an intense concern with the past, but its focus is opposite to that of Machen and Lovecraft; they are preoccupied with the difficulty of access to that past, with the ways in which psychological processes may continually seek to rewrite it in a fashion acceptable to the conscious mind. This instability of memory is habitually conveyed by the merest of hints, the slightest verbal clues which throw doubt upon the texture of the whole. There are no grand or general mythological or historical schemes here, only vast areas of psychological doubt, on the brink of which individual narrative perches precariously. If James and de la Mare are preoccupied with childhood, it is not in any Wordsworthian sense: they do not look back to it as a time of true, instinctual perception, rather they are fascinated by it first as a time when lies may originate and control future development, and second as a symbol of the locked room of the unconscious. Nobody can be trusted in de la Mare, or in *Turn of the Screw*, but this is only marginally to do with malice; it has more to do with the customary tricks of memory, often with the also customary way in which memory distorts the past into a narrative centred on the self, recentres a general history on a personal one. Thus no two accounts of a past event are the same: in *Turn of the Screw*, we are presented with this clash in a complexly mediated form, in de la Mare's stories we often find ourselves trying to judge a single account against the probabilities of the world, but usually with insufficient evidence. One's feeling at the end of a de la Mare story is often curiously displaced; instead of satisfied interest, it is more often speculation, not so much on the events of the tale as on the 'real' nature of the teller.

The Turn of the Screw is one of the most extensively discussed works in modern literature; here I only want to bring out from it a number of points which relate to the Gothic, and particularly to the social concerns of Gothic. The bones of the story concern a governess – the narrator – who is appointed by a mysterious gentle-man to look after two children, Miles and Flora. She is granted a completely free hand, provided she under no circumstances troubles her employer. She finds a housekeeper on the premises, Mrs Grose, and encounters the children; her attempts, however, to settle into her position are hampered by a series of curious events and half-events which make her fear the children. In particular, they have been exposed in the past to the influences of the previous governess, a Miss Jessel, and a fellow servant named Quint, both of whom have disappeared, or died, under mysterious circumstances, and who, it seems, had an affair of which the children could not have remained ignorant. The governess suspects that this couple, even after their deaths, are continuing their influence over the children, and her apparent concern for them gradually turns into a bitter struggle for control, which culminates with the removal of Flora and the death of Miles.

Such supernatural apparitions and portents as there are are, of course, recounted solely by the governess, and even she is often doubtful of their reality; the whole story moves in a miasma of uncertainty, and most of the critical debate has effectually centred on one question: to what extent is the governess a reliable interpreter of the signals she claims to observe? That the matter should remain unresolved is, of course, a central part of James's purpose; his habitual subtleties of style interlock with this motif in such a way as to manipulate the reader into a situation of chronic doubt. This, however, does not prevent us from trying to identify a character-structure for the governess, and one which is not unfamiliar from earlier works. Briggs sensibly compares her with Radcliffe's Emily in *The Mysteries of Udolpho* (1794), with Jane Eyre and with Maud Ruthyn in Sheridan LeFanu's *Uncle Silas* (1864), all of them characters placed in situations for which they are unfit by reason of birth, expectation and training[2]: James's governess, whatever else she may do, clearly approaches her task with a set of preconceptions which make her handling of a delicate situation highly questionable.

Like earlier Gothic heroines, she prides herself on her 'sensitivity', yet in her actual dealings with the children and with Mrs Grose this sensitivity is hardly apparent. She claims to find Mrs Grose totally transparent, and considers herself justified in overriding the housekeeper's more experienced view of the situation at all points, even suspecting her of collusion with the children. The consequence of this – which flows, at least in part, from her assumption of Mrs Grose's social inferiority – is that she (the governess) becomes an isolated figure, relying solely on her own perceptions and confident of her skill in unravelling the 'mystery' – which in turn, of course, assumes that there is a mystery to unravel. Yet the skilful detective work which this might require is not helped by her habit of jumping to extreme conclusions; phrases like 'the strangest thing in the world' abound, suggesting very strongly her determination to place herself at the 'heart' of a highly charged emotional situation, whether such a situation already exists or not. Whatever this situation may be, the force of her narrative is to place herself at the centre of it, although we are given repeated suggestions that her importance to the children, in their eyes, is at best peripheral. It is precisely their self-sufficiency to which she continually objects: although the only mode of existence which Quint and Miss Jessel may have is as part of the children's private mythology (possibly, or possibly not, shared by Mrs Grose), she determines to read in the relationships between the four a perversion of natural order, and sees her role as keeping apart worlds which 'ought not to' meet. In this respect, her role as governess is clearly symbolic: if indeed she is less than sane, it is through an obsessive rationality which she is determined to instil in the children. The misty figures of Quint and Miss Jessel appear to symbolise several things to her: the tendency of the children to develop a private world of their own, their growing awareness of sexual and emotional life, their perpetually threatening independence and adulthood. She is in many respects a typified Victorian figure, totally self-righteous in her insistence on the necessary repression of children and in her confidence in her own approach to education. For her, Miss Jessel is a 'horror of horrors',[3] despite the fact that she knows next to nothing about her, and the even more damning fact that the little she does know derives from Mrs Grose, whose word she normally – that is, when it does not coincide with her own opinions – professes to doubt and even despise.

This obsessive rationality is emphasised in her habits of discourse: even at moments of apparently high drama, she is still able to use phrases like 'I completed my statement' (*TS*, p. 48), suggesting a degree of non-emotional control which should be belied by her vaunted concern for the children. When it comes to giving her opinion of Quint, however, she is bound by no such concern for precision. When she first forces the story of the two servants out of the housekeeper, she is much exercised over the fact that Miss Jessel was obviously of higher social rank than Quint. Mrs Grose admits that he was 'so dreadfully below', and the governess takes the opportunity to pigeon-hole him once and for all in her scheme of life:

> I felt that I doubtless needn't press too hard, in such company, on the place of a servant in the scale; but there was nothing to prevent an acceptance of my companion's own measure of my predecessor's abasement. There was a way to deal with that, and I dealt; the more readily for my full vision – on the evidence – of our employer's late clever, good-looking 'own' man; impudent, assured, spoiled, depraved. 'The fellow was a hound.'
>
> Mrs Grose considered as if it were perhaps a little a case for a sense of shades. (*TS*, pp. 48–9)

The phrase 'There was a way to deal with that' summarises her unquestioning and defensive conventionality; the catalogue of qualities going from 'impudent' to 'depraved' frighteningly demonstrates her willingness to generalise on insufficient 'evidence', and her psychological tendency to move towards extremes in her considerations of character. Because Quint and Miss Jessel transgressed, no evil deed can be beneath them; just as she needs to believe in the children's absolute purity and mistakes evidence of normal feelings for signs of incipient depravity, so she pushes her images of the departed pair to the furthest limits of imagination, thereby creating her own images of terror. Her insistence on keeping different worlds apart becomes self-feeding, while her need to rely on Mrs Grose is constantly thwarted by her stronger need to maintain the social boundaries between governess and housekeeper, a clash which makes some of her conversations with her 'companion' into exercises in controlled sadism. But the sneer in her comment on Mrs Grose's 'sense of shades' is characteristically ambivalent: is one, or is one not, correct to see within it a further comment by James on the governess's one-sided code of values?

While all around becomes increasingly chaotic, she is nonetheless able to derive 'two or three dim elements of comfort that still remained to me' (*TS*, p. 51). Her enumeration of them is revealing: basically, she is comforted by the knowledge that she has maintained the social hierarchy (by, as far as possible, severing the children from their 'polluting' contact with Quint and Miss Jessel), that she has thereby 'protected' the children, that she has maintained her own standards 'intact' and that she has pushed Mrs Grose about in a way suitable to their respective social positions. Yet her situation is curiously reminiscent of that of Blake's Urizen, who also devotes his entire energy to maintaining hierarchy and the semblance of order while the world around him falls apart, and who also ends up terrified by spectres of his own imagining. James's heroine creates her own objects of fear by exclusion: that which cannot be comprehended within her own limited apprehension is assumed to be evil, and is therefore credited with a power disproportionate to its actual effects.

The point is made very vividly in a conversation between the governess and Mrs Grose after the former has seen her first apparition, a man looking at her from a tower. 'What was he doing on the tower?', asks Mrs Grose:

> 'Only standing there and looking down at me.'
> She thought a minute. 'Was he a gentleman?'
> I found I had no need to think. 'No.' She gazed in deeper wonder. 'No.'
> 'Then nobody about the place? Nobody from the village?'
> 'Nobody – nobody. I didn't tell you, but I made sure.'
> She breathed a vague relief: this was, oddly, so much to the good.
> It only went indeed a little way. 'But if he isn't a gentleman—'
> 'What *is* he? He's a horror.'
> 'A horror?'
> 'He's – God help me if I know *what* he is!'
>
> (*TS*, p. 35)

There is nothing – nothing recognisable, that is, to the governess – between 'gentleman' and 'horror', between total convention and total disruption. What really appears to disturb her about the appearance of Quint is merely his anomalousness, his being where he is not supposed to be, and this, in one form or another, is in fact the source of almost all her fears. That the role of governess itself falls neatly into the abyss which she so carefully delineates is, of course, the heart of the multiple irony. As the story moves on, she comes increasingly to see herself in the principal agential role, as the one who is burdened with the responsibility of pushing the mystery to its final denouement: the role is entirely self-assumed, but it is also a response to the social ambivalence of the position which she occupies, as the mentor who is nonetheless not permitted answers from above to her own pressing questions. What she fears in Quint is the way in which he has escaped from his role as servant, and it is significant that on her third encounter with him she seeks to exorcise him through the exercise of her own sheer superiority:

> He was absolutely, on this occasion, a living, detestable, dangerous presence. But that was not the wonder of wonders; I reserve this distinction for quite another circumstance: the circumstance that dread had unmistakably quitted me and that there was nothing in me there that didn't meet and measure him. . . . I can't express what followed . . . save by saying that the silence itself – which was indeed in a manner an attestation of my strength – became the element into which I saw the figure disappear; in which I definitely saw it turn, as I might have seen the low wretch to which it had once belonged turn on receipt of an order, and pass, with my eyes on the villainous back that no hunch could have more disfigured, straight down the staircase and into the darkness in which the next bend was lost.   (*TS*, pp. 59–60)

There is an absolute contradiction between the clarity of vision which she claims on this occasion and the actual details which she picks out, the servile turn and the villainous back, which are evidence not of momentary accurate perception but of her own inability to see beyond the web of social stereotypes which comprises her world. Her final, lethal fury with the children is the frustrated rage of one who has failed to convince others of the validity of this mode of perception. Whether Miles or Flora 'see ghosts' may be a moot point, but it is clear that they do not see the world as the governess does, and that she fails in her struggle to make them do so. And as with so many Gothic texts, the roots of this frustration are convoluted: to say that she is herself deranged would be to discount the elements of derangement which exist in the situation around her, a situation in which she is expected to act as professional inductor into a world to which she is herself denied the key. There are suggestions in the text that she is infatuated with her employer, and this may be the case; at any rate, the possibility that she might be serves symbolically to strengthen the dislocation in her relationships with the children, and thus to underline the synthetic and displaced element in her emotional position.

To ask whether the ghosts in *Turn of the Screw* are 'real' is merely to run into paradox and to miss the principal points of the text. That text is given as the governess's account, and what it principally displays is a set of psychological problems in her position within the microcosmic society of the book. Within that society, she is called upon to fulfil all the duties of social reinforcement. She it is who is entrusted with the guardianship of the 'line', that is, with the production of 'suitable' successors for her employer, although she herself near the beginning of the book seems doubtful of her fitness for such a role. It is she who is responsible for educating the children into a sense of their 'station' in life, although she has little idea of what that station is, and even less of her own. She discharges these duties by conventional means, through the instilling of fear of 'tabooed' objects and relationships, and the attempt to redirect the children's affections onto herself. These tasks are incompatible: as she deploys all her strength to dissolve the children's world, she naturally renders their love impossible, and then condemns them for lack of feeling. And as she classifies their other relationships as impure, she sets herself an ideal of purity which is disabling and cold to the point of cruelty.

She either is given, or takes upon herself, an impossible task: to enter into a society, which she believes to have fragmented and reassembled in a 'wrong' form, and to reconstruct it with herself at the centre. To do this, her first and, in the event, only task is to impose control: in the name of this, she bullies, threatens and manipulates, but to little avail. She takes it upon herself to represent one kind of education, an induction into reason and order. There are indications that Quint and Miss Jessel had offered the children a different kind of 'education', less pure, perhaps, but also more 'real'; this has to be banished. And if the children themselves show more aptitude and affection for that other kind of education, and resist her attempts to redirect their development, then they too have to be banished. The fable of isolation and its paranoiac content are familiar; what is distinctive in *Turn of the Screw* is its minuteness of attention, its insistence on the apparent viability and coherence of different views of the same events. What takes place, perhaps, is a mutual struggle for exploitative power: moment by moment the governess and the children perceive, sometimes dimly, each other's weaknesses and move in on them when they are only half-formed. Within a single sketchy conversation the balance of power swings giddily as the rival participants gradually accept that the stake is getting higher and higher, and even that strength may lie eventually in their own ability to impose their individual fictions as the truth. Interpretation of events becomes pragmatic, particularly in the case of the governess who comes to wield her perceptions like weapons, weapons which attain in the end the power of life and death.

There is no transcendent truth *behind* interpretation; the psychology of *Turn of the Screw* is less romantic than dialectical, in that the 'real' is composed of the interrelations between event and account, and it is these interrelations which James insistently probes. And if this is the structure of reality, the 'ghosts' are neither more nor less real than anything else in the book; they are among the forms in which consciousness apprehends, and are elements in the process of psychological selection.

It is these ambiguities of memory which form one of the principal structural components of Walter de la Mare's short stories. Only a few of them are concerned with anything we can identify as 'supernatural', but then, the hinterland of recall in which many of his characters dwell is peopled with such insubstantial wraiths of a vanished past that the world itself takes on the lineaments of ghostliness. 'Perhaps I ought to tell you first exactly how the whole thing came about', says the story-teller in 'Missing' (1926): 'But – quite apart from the others – it's a relief to get things clearer even in one's own mind.'[4] The structure which is perhaps most typical of de la Mare involves an encounter with a story-teller of this type, a person who is engaged in a ceaseless but often hopeless attempt to sort out the past through reconstructing it in story. The actual narrator, often the figure who is buttonholed, generally finds himself in a state of greater and greater confusion as the tale proceeds and as the self-deluding quality of memory becomes increasingly apparent.

With few exceptions, de la Mare's ghosts manifest themselves as the very slightest of tremors in the fabric of the real, yet despite their lack of clarity, and even conviction, they owe a good deal to the ghosts of the Gothic. In 'All Hallows' (1926), the narrator visits an old and largely deserted cathedral, on a coast being eroded by the tides. As he nears it, it appears that he passes increasingly into a state of dream: he sleeps and loses his sense of time, as the building itself grows on him and begins to dominate him. Inside, he meets an aged verger, and is characteristically buttonholed. The verger's story is entirely a matter of hints and doubts: the Dean of the cathedral has had an inexplicable breakdown, curious inconsistencies seem to be appearing in the fabric of the building. 'There are buildings', says the narrator, 'that have a singular influence on the imagination. Even now in this remote candlelit room, immured between its massive stones, the vast edifice seemed to be gently and furtively fretting its impression on my mind' (*Connoisseur*, p. 266). The verger, who appears to need a witness to restore his confidence in his own perceptions, takes his visitor on a tour of the vast church; they end up in a 'coign of the southern transept', which is partly swathed in scaffolding and canvas, looking out over it:

> How long we stayed in this position I cannot say; but minutes

sometimes seem like hours. And then, without the slightest warning, I became aware of a peculiar and incessant vibration. It is impossible to give a name to it. It suggested the remote whirring of an enormous mill-stone, or that – though without definite pulsation – of revolving wings, or even the spinning of an immense top . . . .

I gazed and gazed, and saw nothing. Indeed even in what I had seemed to *hear* I might have been deceived. Nothing is more treacherous in certain circumstances – except possibly the eye – than the ear. It magnifies, distorts, and may even invent. As instantaneously as I had become aware of it, the murmur had ceased. And then – though I cannot be certain – it seemed the dingy and voluminous spread of canvas over there had perceptibly trembled, as if a huge cautious hand had ben thrust out to draw it aside. No time was given me to make sure.   (*Connoisseur*, p. 270)

De la Mare's extreme caution is strangely disturbing; no resolution is attempted, no judgement on the reliability of these minute perceptions. The verger's fear is that the cathedral is being attacked by diabolical forces, which are not trying to damage it, but rather to strengthen it for their own purposes; what the narrator concludes we are not told – except perhaps that the verger's view is at least one possible interpretation of the situation, and not to be discounted. The senses, for de la Mare, are constantly at the mercy of the imagination, constantly offering a surfeit of information from which we can only stumblingly attempt to select the most probable.

The psychological implications of his position are clearer in 'Out of the Deep' (1923), in which Jimmie, the protagonist, inherits a vast and opulent house from a hated uncle, a house, furthermore, in which he has himself suffered a variety of childhood traumas, mostly associated with a malicious butler named Soames. Jimmie tries to exorcise the ghosts of memory by selling off the house's riches and by keeping it in a constant blaze of candlelight. But his metaphorical attempt to bring light to the dark places of the mind is doomed: below his bright bedroom, the depths of the house begin to stir, and he starts to receive visitors from the empty servants' quarters whenever he dares to touch a bell-rope. One night he awakes to a curious mixture of comfort and threat:

The room was adrowse with light. All was still. The flitting horrors between dream and wake in his mind were already thinning into air. Through their transparency he looked out once more on the substantial, the familiar. His breath came heavily, like puffs of wind over a stormy sea, and yet a profound peace and tranquillity was swathing him in. The relaxed mouth was now faintly smiling. Not a sound, not the feeblest distant unintended tinkling was trembling up from the abyss. And for a moment or two the young man refrained

even from turning his head at the soundless opening and closing of
the door.[5]

But his attempt to retain his perspective is hopeless: once the creatures from below have been disturbed, their intrusions become more
frequent and less dependent on invitation. Mostly, they are visits
from a 'revenant' butler, a younger version of Soames: he appears
to have no particularly malicious designs on Jimmie, he is simply a
figure who has not been laid to rest, partly representing childhood,
partly Jimmie's unaccommodated hatred for his uncle. But then, in
response to one summons, a young girl appears, and Jimmie, who
has had enough, is far from polite to her. In a fit of anger, he
shouts down the stairwell for the inhabitants to send him more
congenial company:

> It had been a silly boast, he agreed – that challenge, that 'dare' on
> the staircase; the boast of an idiot. For the 'congenial company' that
> had now managed to hoof and scrabble its way up the slippery marble
> staircase was already on the threshold.
> All was utterly silent now. There was no obvious manifestation of
> danger. What was peering steadily in upon him out of the obscurity
> beyond the door, was merely a blurred whitish beast-like shape with
> still, passive, almost stagnant eyes in its immense fixed face. A perfectly
> ludicrous object – on paper. Yet a creature so nauseous to soul and
> body, and with so obscene a greed in its motionless piglike grin that
> with one vertiginous swirl Jimmie's candles had swept up in his hand
> like a lateral race of streaming planets into outer darkness.
>
> (*Riddle*, p. 258)

What causes the vertigo and claustrophobia in 'Out of the Deep' is
the knowledge that, whatever kind of reality these apparitions may
have, they are inextricably linked with Jimmie himself. There can
be no question of telling others about them: they are his and his
alone, and his failure to lay them to rest brings about his predictable
destruction. Neither Jimmie nor the verger in 'All Hallows' claim
any deeply true imaginative perception: what they see and hear is
true for them, and that is enough. They are both relatively asocial
beings, just as All Hallows itself, and Jimmie's house, are asocial
locations, cut off from the world, brooding on themselves. It may
be the humans who are dreaming and objectifying their dreams, or
it may be the buildings themselves which dream.

In other stories again, like 'Miss Duveen' (1923) and 'Miss Miller'
(1936), we are confronted with encounters with persons who are
clearly deranged: here again, their perceptions are offered to us as
they are, with a minimum of comment. It is true that in both stories
the 'mad-woman' is granted a certain degree of credence, but their

perceptions are not taken as advisable, or as applicable to the everyday process of life. Indeed, in 'The Nap' (1926) de la Mare jokes with the whole business of schizophrenia: he gives a dual account of Mr Thripp's Saturday afternoon, oscillating between the politeness and pleasantry which characterise his actual intercourse with the members of his awful family and the violence and fury which lies beneath. De la Mare is not at all saying that Mr Thripp is unbalanced, or even unusual; on the contrary, these are the accommodations, the selections which comprise the transition of unconscious to consciousness, and they are in no way the object of moral blame.

What is unusual in de la Mare is partly the depth of his liberalism. Almost nothing is condemned, and there is more than a touch of fatalism in his emphasis on the necessity of people behaving in the curious ways they do. One principal reason for this is to be found in his almost obsessional concern with childhood, which impregnates so many of the stories. For adults, he often seems to be saying, it is too late anyway: Miss Duveen matters less than the small boy on whom she has such an impact. We are formed at a very early age, and after that it would take very strong pressure to jerk us off the tracks. Yet, as with James, this does not amount to a simple romantic insistence on the value of childhood purity and its recollection: it is more the intensity of childhood with which de la Mare is concerned, and this intensity can involve a gathering of dark forces as well as a source of brightness. The small boy in 'Miss Duveen' does not learn sweetness and light from his contact with her; on the contrary, he is conscious of a quite different feeling when she is locked away:

> I know now that the news, in spite of a vague sorrow, greatly relieved me. I should be at ease in the garden again, came the thought – no longer fear to look ridiculous, and grow hot when our neighbour was mentioned, or be saddled with her company beside the stream.
>
> (*Riddle*, p. 89)

The child in 'An Ideal Craftsman' (1930), again, is by no means an idealised creation: he is remarkable chiefly for the coolness and efficiency with which he attempts to disguise a murder which he has discovered, although his sang-froid breaks down at the end. The children of 'The Almond Tree' and 'Seaton's Aunt' (both 1923), like Jimmie in 'Out of the Deep', have been irretrievably scarred by their childhood experiences, traumatised by an uneven and painful transition into the world of adulthood. Seaton and Jimmie in particular are in the grip of fate, condemned to suffer from wounds which they cannot comprehend; his natal house survives Jimmie's death without difficulty, just as Seaton's appalling aunt metaphorically smothers him with the sheer weight of her continuous presence. As the narrator says when he thinks of going to look for Seaton's grave, 'there was precious little use in pottering about in the muddy dark merely to discover where he was buried . . . . My rather horrible thought was that, so far as I was concerned – one of his extremely few friends – he had never been much better than "buried" in my mind' (*Riddle*, pp. 140–1). This is a characteristically double-edged comment, partly a self-criticism but also partly a reflection on the way in which Seaton had been effectively prevented from ever making the jump into 'life' by his inability to escape from childhood trauma.

One of the most interesting of de la Mare's stories about children is 'Physic' (1936), in which Emilia has to cope simultaneously with the unexplained sickness of her son, William, and the threatened flight of her husband. The relation between the two is unclear: it might be that de la Mare is hinting at some supernatural awareness on the child's part of the imminent collapse of his home, for certainly his sickness and the security of the role it allows Emilia to play gives her the strength to overcome her other difficulties. 'Husbands may go, love *turn*, the future slip into ruin as silently and irretrievably as a house of cards. But children must not be kept waiting; not sick children.'[6] Yet there are also hints that this opinion of the supreme importance of children's demands is itself incorrect and harmful, that Emilia has already in some sense sacrificed her husband in favour of her companionship with William, hints which emerge most clearly near the beginning of the story, when mother and son sit down to a 'feast' in the father's absence:

> This, once fortnightly, now weekly, Wednesday-night feast had become a kind of ritual, a little secret institution. They called it their covey night. Not even Daddie ever shared it with them; and it was astonishing what mature grown-up company William became on these occasions. It was as if, entirely unknown to himself, he had swallowed one of Jack's bean-seeds and had turned inside into a sort of sagacious second-husband. All that Emilia had to do, then, was merely to become again the child she used to be. And that of course needs only a happy heart.
>
> (*Wind Blows Over*, p. 45)

It is difficult to tell just how extensive the irony is here; what is clear, though, is that William, like Nicholas in 'The Almond Tree' and like Miles and Flora in *Turn of the Screw*, is a child who is being called upon to discharge adult responsibilities. William's mother seems to be seeking in him a kind of complete satisfaction which verges on the sexual; Nicholas is called upon to figure as a go-between for his errant father; while James's governess is looking in Miles and Flora for an ideal which can never be found, and is willing to destroy them in her disappointment. All four, in fact, are in different ways being required to fill the role of their absent or partly absent fathers.

Thus although there is a nostalgic tone to much of de la Mare's writing, it is not simply a matter of nostalgia for childhood, for childhood too is represented as having had its store of bitterness. The nostalgia is wider and vaguer than that; in 'The Creatures' (1923), a rather crude symbolist tale, an almost programmatic statement is made by the recounter of the story when he is speaking about the 'far country' in which his adventure took place:

> You cannot guess there what you may not chance upon, or whom. Bells clash, boom, and quarrel hollowly on the edge of darkness in those breakers. Voices waver across the fainter winds. The birds cry in a tongue unknown yet not unfamiliar. The sky is the hawks' and the stars'. *There* one is on the edge of life, of the unforeseen, whereas our cities – are not our desiccated jaded minds ever pressing and edging further and further away from freedom, the vast unknown, the infinite presence, picking a fool's journey from sensual fact to fact at the tail of that he-ass called Reason? I suggest that in that solitude the spirit within us realises that it treads the outskirts of a region long since called the Imagination. I assert that we have strayed, and in our blindness abandoned— (*Riddle*, pp. 276–7)

As in so much earlier Gothic fiction, psychological trouble originates in the attempt to superimpose a rational framework on the free life of the imagination, to repress the unexpected by binding it within the categories of conventional thought. In 'Missing', the story-teller says, with regard to a woman who has caused him much difficulty, 'I'm a great stickler myself for law and order, for neatness, I mean. I had noticed it before: it irritated me; in spite of all her finery, she was never what you would call a tidy woman' (*Connoisseur*, p. 85). Yet it is his need to organise his experience into 'neatness' which continually defeats him; by attempting to make 'sense' out of his story, he only succeeds in further puzzling himself and horrifying his auditor. In 'Miss Duveen', de la Mare suggests that 'madness' is itself the product of trying to acquiesce in half-understood social rules and conventions: 'it is a rule of conduct', says Miss Duveen at one point, 'and everything depends on them. What would Society be *else?*' (*Riddle*, p. 79). The irony is bitter, for this is the 'Society' which has turned her out, made her into an outcast and an object of anxiety and fear. For the result of unthinking acceptance of convention and reason is the devaluation of one's own instincts and impulses. Seaton's acceptance of his aunt's domination means that he loses all faith in his own worth, and in that of other people: 'it always seems to me', he says, 'that, after all, we are nothing better than interlopers on the earth, disfiguring and staining wherever we go. I know it's shocking blasphemy to say so; but then it's different here, you see. We are further away' (*Riddle*, p. 120). Literally, the 'further away' is geographical; metaphorically, Seaton has himself lost his grip on life because he has allowed his aunt's presence to intervene between him and his experience. He believes his aunt to be in league with ghosts and spirits, but it is he who is haunted by lack of achievement and understanding. At the end of 'Physic', a doctor is called to examine William, and he concludes the story with an alarming statement: 'As a general rule ... it's wiser never to wake *anybody* up, merely to give them physic – even mere doctor's physic' (*Wind Blows Over*, p. 71).

There is an alternation in tone here, as elsewhere in de la Mare's stories, between an idealist vaunting of the freedom of the imagination and an almost sardonic awareness of individual human limitations. There may be a freer, more various world out there beyond the scope of our enfeebled senses, but if there is, most of us are never going to know it; it therefore behoves us to be charitable towards our fellow suffers and fellow self-deluders. In the meantime we are all haunted, to a greater or lesser extent, because we are all unfulfilled. As in James again, the absence of a groundwork of truth means that we have to suspend our judgement about individual characters; and de la Mare's characteristic device for ensuring this suspension is his extraordinary manipulation of his story-tellers and narrators.

As we have seen from several examples above, it is often the case that these two roles are separated: that is to say, the narrator is he *to whom* the story has been told, and we receive both the story and the narrator's reactions. Often we are required to fill in for ourselves our pictures of both story-teller and narrator. An example is 'Mr Kempe' (1926), which is basically the story of an encounter with an elderly and very odd clergyman, who is engaged upon a lifetime's study of 'the soul', and who, in order to gain insight into his subject, appears to take pleasure in observing people in distressing and dangerous situations. This tale is told by a man who claims to be an unemployed schoolmaster to two strangers in an inn, one of whom is the narrator, the other, the 'man in leggings', appearing at first glance to have no function at all. In fact, at a decisive point in the schoolmaster's rather unlikely story, the man in leggings, coughing 'derisively', leaves, thus presumably signifying his lack of faith in the schoolmaster's reliability. After he has gone – the tale being by this time virtually finished – the narrator, who thus finds himself in the position of being the schoolmaster's only audience, becomes aware of certain pressures upon himself; questions occur to him, but he cannot ask them. He looks out into the rain outside:

> The spectacle depressed me beyond words – as if it had any more significance than that for its passing hour a dense yet not inbeneficent cloud was spread betwixt this earth of ours and the faithful shining of the stars.
> But I did not mention this to the schoolmaster. He seemed to be lost in a dark melancholy, his face a maze of wrinkles. And beyond him – in a cracked looking-glass – I could see his double, sitting there upon its stool. I was conscious that in some way I had bitterly disappointed him. I looked at him – my hand on the door-handle – waiting to go out . . .   (*Connoisseur*, pp. 42–3)

There are many possible interpretations. Perhaps the 'schoolmaster' is himself in search of certainty in the same way as the clergyman, and the narrator has failed to offer it. Perhaps the whole tale has been a parable, and the narrator has failed to understand – or even to query – its meaning. The schoolmaster himself is a fragmentary and dislocated person – symbolised in the 'maze of wrinkles', the 'cracked looking-glass', the double – and the narrator, again perhaps, has offered no healing. Or again, perhaps the man in leggings was right: perhaps the whole tale has been a farrago, designed to attract sympathy and attention. Each of the characters reveals defects in the course of the account: the schoolmaster claims that there seemed to be not one Mr Kempe but three, yet he himself divides in two, and there are suggestions that the man in leggings may be the narrator's own suspicious double. The reader feels strongly the eventual sense of disappointment, but the problem is with whom: with the schoolmaster for failing to press and clarify his point, or with the narrator for wilfully or otherwise refusing to draw out the implications of the story?

We have already mentioned the similar structural ambiguity in 'Seaton's Aunt', where two possible interpretations are maintained: that Seaton's fate is the result of his subordination to the powers, supernatural or otherwise, of his aunt, and that the narrator himself, by declining to treat Seaton's problem with real attention and sympathy, has in fact precipitated the denouement. De la Mare goes further in 'Missing'. Here, the narrator finds himself being talked to in a café by a man named Bleet, who tells him the story of his dealings with one Miss Dutton. He and his sister, who is a little 'weak in the intellects', have taken in Miss Dutton as a lodger; after a while, it appears that Miss Dutton's motives are to marry Bleet. When he turns her down, she disappears, taking his car with her; later the sister dies. Put like that, the story is simple, but in fact the interest is centred on an entirely different situation, that between Bleet and his auditor. The latter experiences a growing resentment of Bleet's story, of his imposition on his time, which is complicated by the fact that Bleet appears to be attempting to defend himself against various insinuations which were made about the time of Miss Dutton's disappearance. As Bleet can all too clearly see, the evidence looks pretty damning, especially as Miss Dutton's will benefited his sister considerably, and her own later demise presumably means that such money as there was has passed to him. When he talks about Miss Dutton, he is agonisingly aware of the unconvincingness of all he says:

> I advised her about her investments and so on, though I took precious good care not to be personally involved. Not a finger stirring unless she volunteered it first. That all came out too. But it was nothing to do with me, now, was it, as man to man, if the good lady took a fancy into her head to see that my poor sister was not left to what's called the tender mercies of this world after my death?
>
> (*Connoisseur*, pp. 67–8)

What Bleet is presumably trying to do is manage to tell his story in a way that will release him from the bondage of the evidence; his listener senses this, and fears being drawn into Bleet's private problem. When the story of Miss Dutton has been told, he enquires for the first time about the fate of the sister:

> 'She isn't "missing" too, I hope?' As I reflect on it, it was a vile question to have put to the man. I don't see how anything could have justified it. His face was like a burnt-out boat. The effect on him was atrocious to witness. His swarthy cheek went gray as ashes. The hand on the marble table began to tremble violently.
> 'Missing?' he cried. 'She's dead. Isn't *that* good enough for you?'
> At this, no doubt because I was hopelessly in the wrong, I all but lost control of myself.
> 'What do you mean?' I exclaimed in a low voice. 'What do you mean by speaking to me like that? Haven't I wasted the better part of a Saturday afternoon listening to a story which I could have picked up

63

better in your own county newspaper? What's it all to me, may I ask?
I want to have nothing more to do with it – or you either.'

'You didn't say that at the beginning,' he replied furiously, struggling
to his feet. 'You led me on.'

'Led you on, by God! What do you mean by such a piece of
impudence? I say I want nothing more to do with you. And if that's how
you accept a kindness, take my advice and keep your troubles to
yourself in future. Let your bygones *be* bygones. And may the Lord
have mercy on your soul.'

(Connoisseur, pp. 93–4)

The suggestion here is that, beneath his apparent reasonableness,
the narrator is to blame for this unpleasant conclusion, is unable
to bear Bleet's intrusive company in a balanced enough way to
evaluate the rights and wrongs of what he is saying. In 'Crewe'
(1930), the situation is reversed: here the button-holer, an ex-butler
named Blake, tells his story in a station waiting-room. It concerns
his employment by an elderly vicar, in which situation he found
himself in the company of 'a young fellow of the name of George'
and a gardener – 'Mengus he called himself, though I can't see *how*,
if you spell it with a z'. According to Blake, the gardener began to
drink heavily; Blake tried reprimanding him, but to no avail. In the
end, instead of confronting the gardener, he sends the luckless
George to do so; the result is a fight, after which the gardener is
sacked. It emerges that he has been worried about his family, and
this blow is too much for him; he hangs himself. Shortly after this,
Blake and George see a series of manifestations in the form of a
scarecrow, dressed in the gardener's clothes, getting progressively
nearer to the house. On the pretext of protecting their employer
from disturbance, Blake decides that this must be investigated; 'that
night there came something sounding about the house that wasn't
natural and no mistake'. Instead of investigating himself, he rouses
George, and divides the task up in a singularly unfair way:

'George', I said, 'you mustn't risk a chill or anything of that sort' –
and it had grown a bit cold in the small hours – 'but it's up to us –
our duty, George – with the Reverend at death's door and all, to know
what's what. So if you'll take a look round on the outside I'll have a
search through on the in. What we must be cautious about is that the
old gentleman isn't disturbed.'[7]

But Blake does not initially bother to look round the inside of the
house:

As for myself, I didn't move for a bit. There wasn't any hurry that I
could see. Oh, no. I just sat down on the bed on the place where
George had sat, and waited. And you may depend upon it, I stayed

pretty quiet there – with all that responsibility, and not knowing what might happen next. And then presently what I heard was as though a voice had said something – very sharp and bitter; then said no more. There came a sort of moan, and then no more again. By that time I was on my way on my rounds inside the house as I'd promised; and so, out of hearing; and when I got back to my bedroom again everything was still and quiet. And I took it of course that George had got back safe to his . . .   (*On the Edge*, pp. 113–14)

It comes as no surprise to learn that George was found dead in the morning, and still less that Blake stood to inherit by this strange series of events. Here the doubleness of the narrative is relatively clear, and Blake's guilt is further established by the revelation, at the very end of the story, that he is an obsessive frequenter of the waiting-room. What is startling in the story is the extent of its injustice; even the gardener's ghost is presumably fooled by Blake, and mistakenly visits its vengeance on the wrong man.

The central point of comparison which I want to emphasise between James's *Turn of the Screw* and de la Mare's stories is their insistence on the connection between fear and self-delusion. Where their narrators and story-tellers profess to see the world as haunted, we as readers are being constantly required to reassess these hauntings in terms of the deficiencies of the narrators themselves. De la Mare, like James, is helped by a highly elliptical and mannered prose style, and by a similar ability to register conversational misunderstandings in minute detail. Gothic traces abound: enclosed and archaised settings, situations of chronic isolation, doubtful attributions of persecution. Indeed, *Turn of the Screw* and many of de la Mare's stories – 'Out of the Deep', 'Mr Kempe', 'Physic' – hinge on precisely the problems of overdeveloped sensibility which can be found in Radcliffe.

But the psychological sophistication of these two writers places them apart from most other developments in the Gothic, in that they refuse to reside in either an acceptance or a dismissal of the supernatural. The texts are scaffolds for us to clothe in our own interpretations – and, to shift the metaphor, on which we can detect the ghostly shadow of the hanged man. The levels of consciousness and the unconscious interpenetrate as we come to see that everyday interpretation of situations and events is riddled with ambiguity and self-deception. Another way of putting the point might be to say that James and de la Mare do not need to be more than vestigially concerned with the historical past, since for them the immediate personal past is sufficiently problematic: certainty of memory is itself a mode of repression, and as such, of course, so is the fixity of narrative itself. The very process of putting into words is a matter of allaying and redistributing fear, a matter of trying to provide an acceptable organisation for the doubtful and terrifying facts of experience.

Notes and references

1. I should here acknowledge a debt to Briggs, esp. pp. 182–7.
2. See Briggs, p. 152.
3. **Henry James**, *The Turn of the Screw and Other Stories*, ed. S. Gorley Putt (Harmondsworth, Middx, 1969), p. 47.
4. **Walter de la Mare**, *The Connoisseur and Other Stories* (London, 1926), p. 79. (Dates given for stories refer only to the collections.)
5. **De la Mare**, *The Riddle and Other Stories* (London, 1923), p. 252.
6. **De la Mare**, *The Wind Blows Over* (London, 1936), p, 54.
7. **De la Mare**, *On the Edge: Short Stories* (London, 1930), p. 112.

CHAPTER 4
Formalism and meaning in the ghost story

Arthur Conan Doyle, H. G. Wells, Algernon Blackwood,
M. R. James, David Lindsay

I have suggested how, in *Turn of the Screw* and the stories of de la Mare, we can see Gothic fiction taking on a new psychological sophistication and deploying for this purpose a masterly range of literary ambiguity. Also, earlier on, we looked at a group of works from the late nineteenth century – *Dr Jekyll and Mr Hyde*, *The Island of Doctor Moreau*, *The Picture of Dorian Gray* and *Dracula* – in which various elements of the Gothic tradition proved still capable of acting as conductors for a range of new anxieties and attitudes, both historical and scientific. Yet the two more recent figures to whom we have so far given any attention, Lovecraft and Machen, both in different ways demonstrate a falling-away in originality, a kind of hardening of stylistic and thematic arteries, and in this they are not alone. In moving now more fully into the twentieth century, I want to depict what seems to me an important bifurcation. On the one hand, some of the more important constituents of Gothic – the exploration of paranoia, the fear of the intrusion of the barbaric, the alienation accompanying divisions between social groups and between areas of knowledge and feeling – appear to me to have recently received very considerable attention, and to have generated a range of very important fictions, some of them recognisable as Gothic in the traditional sense, some not. Most of these works belong to the last three or four decades, and I want to postpone discussion of them to a later chapter.[1] In this chapter, I intend to follow a different tradition, the highly mannered phase of Gothic which is represented in the ghost story of the early twentieth century, a mode which has been, and in some ways still is, immensely popular despite lack of originality and a constant repetition of themes and images which we have come across before.

I want to start with some comments on the horror stories of two of the most popular writers of the early century, looking again at Wells, and at Arthur Conan Doyle. In both cases, of course, they are best known for work which is quite outside this area, although there is a certain interpenetration of feeling and style between the horror stories and the body of more important work. I then want to look at two writers who are both highly representative of the later development of the ghost story, Algernon Blackwood and M. R. James; finally, I want to talk about one of the very few twentieth-century ghost stories which seems to me to have something of the power of the older Gothic, the power, that is, to use the supernatural as an image for real and carefully depicted social fears: David Lindsay's *The Haunted Woman*, which was written in 1922 and which, in many respects, brings us round again to a recollection of the purposes and themes of Radcliffe and her contemporaries while not sacrificing an intense and accurate perception of the historical dimension of terror. The principal interest of this whole development is concentrated on a single dialectic, which culminates in the shockingly bland tones of M. R. James, the dialectic between disturbance and comfort. Briggs writes that 'the combination of modern scepticism with a nostalgia for an older, more supernatural system of beliefs provides the foundation of the ghost story, and this nostalgia can be seen as inherently romantic' (Briggs, p. 19), and this is true as far as it goes; but it is also worth pointing out a further twist in this situation, whereby the tendency of the ghost story to reside in the trappings of the historical past has itself become reduced to a formula, a formula no doubt still capable of interesting variation, but nonetheless altering our reactions to the fiction from fear towards a more reassured awareness of the self-conscious fictionality of the works. Part of the terror to be derived from Conan Doyle or M. R. James arises not from ways in which the stories overturn our predictions, but precisely from the way in which they conform to them, the way in which, from the very first sentence, from the first act of settling into an armchair, or from the first intrusion of the surprise visitor, we know in advance the intention and approximate structure of what we are reading. If, of course, the writer can in fact exploit precisely this sense of security to any effect, then the achievement may be considerable, and all five of these writers seem to me at times able to do so; but for every one of them there are ten other writers of ghost stories for whom Gothic accessories have become a trap, and in whose works they merely conjure up for us a secure atmosphere of suspended disbelief.

In the case of Conan Doyle, the element of the formulaic was a large part of his popular success as a writer, particularly of course in the Sherlock Holmes stories. Some of these, especially the later ones, could themselves very reasonably be considered as horror stories, but here I want only to talk about some of those tales which were republished in 1922 as *Tales of Twilight and the Unseen* and *Tales of Terror and Mystery*.[2] Their structural predictability can be gauged from one of the early paragraphs of 'The Brown Hand' (1899), in which the protagonist is approaching a country house to which he has been summoned:

> It was through this weird country that I approached my uncle's residence of Rodenhurst; and the house was, as I found, in due keeping with its surroundings. Two broken and weather-stained pillars, each surmounted by a mutilated, heraldic emblem, flanked the entrance to a neglected drive. A cold wind whistled through the elms which lined it, and the air was full of the drifting leaves. At the far end, under the gloomy arch of trees, a single yellow lamp burned steadily. In the dim half-light of the coming night I saw a long, low building stretching out two irregular wings, with deep eaves, a sloping gambrel roof, and walls which were criss-crossed with timber balks in the fashion of the Tudors.

Such a passage is perhaps so deeply embedded in our expectations of the ghost story that in reading we pass over it without thought, but in fact the literary derivations are very clear: from Wilkie Collins and from LeFanu, both of them immediately relevant ancestors in the broad field of popular literature, but of course most of all from Poe and specifically from the 'House of Usher'.

The question of Poe's influence on Conan Doyle has been much discussed, especially the obvious connections between Poe's detective stories and the Holmes cycle, but in fact the influence is wider than that. Pierre Nordon, for instance, says that for Poe, Conan Doyle 'felt unqualified admiration',[3] and a case in point is 'The New Catacomb' (1898). Here Conan Doyle unashamedly adopts wholesale the structure of 'The Cask of Amontillado', while imposing upon it, to its considerable detriment, a moralistic 'explanation'. An archaeologist named Burger, a steady, plodding and obviously morally upright fellow, comes to see a colleague named Kennedy with news of a new catacomb he has discovered. Kennedy has a slightly soiled reputation as a man of the world; Burger offers to share his professional secret if Kennedy will let him in on the details of an affair which he, Kennedy, has just concluded amid some public opprobrium. Kennedy does so, and comes off far from well in the account. They descend together into the catacombs, which are vast in extent, whereupon Burger blows out the candle and leaves him there, mentioning as he goes that the person who had played the part of the unfortunate third party in the affair was himself.

If the plot is a moralistic elaboration of Poe's situation, the technique is also clumsy replication, in that Conan Doyle tries to make Kennedy to a large extent the author of his own doom. 'I hope you left no clue as to where we are going', says Burger, playing on Kennedy's fears of being professionally upstaged; 'Not such a fool!', replies the other, sealing his own fate. But the reader experiences none of the heady oscillation between fear and exhilaration which Poe manages to conjure up in his perfect wish-fulfilment: Burger is in no way interesting, and there is a diffuseness to the conversations which prohibits them from establishing the ironic doubleness of discourse on which 'Amontillado''s success rests.

In other ways too Conan Doyle delves into the corpus of available myths and themes without adding anything to them. 'The Ring of Thoth' (1890) concerns an encounter with an Egyptian who proves to have survived the centuries through a magic elixir, which he has come to loathe; the relation to the Wandering Jew theme is clearly underlined in his speeches to the protagonist:

> How can you understand how terrible a thing time is, you who have experience only of the narrow course which lies between the cradle and the grave! I know it to my cost, I who have floated down the whole stream of history. I was old when Ilium fell. I was very old when Herodotus came to Memphis. I was bowed down with years when the new gospel came upon earth. Yet you see me much as other men are, with the cursed elixir still sweetening my blood, and guarding me against that which I would court.

And the theme of the Wandering Jew was old even when Maturin dealt with it, and is indeed very old in 'The Ring of Thoth', which is much as so many other stories are . . .

In thinking, however, about what is interesting in Conan Doyle's stories, it is, as in so many cases, to that which is repressed beneath the smooth surface that we have to turn. Ronald Pearsall mentions and dwells on his 'preoccupation with the weird and the hideous', and usefully points out that they are 'stable-mates to his intense interest in the gory side of war',[4] which calls to mind the association of interests in the work of Bierce, also a stoical believer in empire. Pearsall also mentions an 'interest in sadism' which 'could result from suppressed sexuality', and it is this element which seems to provide the *raison d'être* for stories like 'The New Catacomb'. But the most outstanding example of sexually related sadism in Conan Doyle is the remarkable story called 'The Case of Lady Sannox' (1893), which must surely be one of the most unpleasant tales ever written. An eminent surgeon falls passionately in love with Lady Sannox, who is notorious both for the number of her affairs and also for the inexplicable complicity of her husband. One night when Stone, the surgeon, is about to pay her a customary visit, he is himself visited by an apparently wealthy Turk, who offers to pay him handsomely if he will immediately perform an operation on his wife, who has cut her lower lip on a poisoned dagger. The Turk points out that, as a strict Muslim, the lady is not allowed to use anaesthetic, but that she is in any case asleep as a result of the poison.

Stone has some doubts, but, largely because of the money, agrees. He points out that 'the disfigurement will be frightful'; the Turk replies, 'I can understand that the mouth will not be a pretty one to kiss'. The operation is swiftly performed, upon which the wife awakes in agony, tears off her yashmak, and reveals herself as Lady Sannox; the Turk unmasks himself as her husband; and not surprisingly Stone goes mad. Or, as Conan Doyle breezily puts it, he is 'found in the morning by his valet, seated on one side of his bed, smiling pleasantly upon the universe, with both legs jammed into one side of his breeches and his great brain about as valuable as a cap full of porridge'.

This tone of submerged sexual violence masquerading as jocosity seems to me, however, to be rare in Conan Doyle: the dialectic of comfort and disturbance seems to take place more frequently around the problems of empire and around the problems of history and civilisation. A very revealing comment occurs, apparently somewhat unwontedly, near the beginning of 'De Profundis' (1892), a simple story of the reappearance of a corpse which has been given a sea-burial:

> So long as the oceans are the ligaments which bind together the great, broadcast British Empire, so long will there be a dash of romance in our minds. . . . But for this a price must be paid, and the price is a grievous one. As the beast of old must have one young, human life as a tribute every year, so to our Empire we throw from day to day the

pick and flower of our youth. The engine is world-wide and strong, but the only fuel that will drive it is the lives of British men. Thus it is that in the grey, old cathedrals as we look round upon the brasses on the walls, we see strange names, such names as they who reared those walls had never heard, for it is in Peshawur, and Umballah, and Korti, and Fort Pearson that the youngsters die, leaving only a precedent and a brass behind them.

In 'The Brazilian Cat' (1898), in 'The Brown Hand', in 'Lot No. 249' (1892), it is something brought back from over that ocean which causes disturbance, some foreign intrusion which refuses to accept the domination of its imperial masters. In 'The Ring of Thoth', the point is made even more clearly in a description of the museum in which the action takes place:

> What though the outer city reeked of the garish nineteenth century! In all this chamber there was scarce an article, from the shrivelled ear of wheat to the pigment-box of the painter, which had not held its own against four thousand years. Here was the flotsam and jetsam washed up by the great ocean of time from that far-off empire. From stately Thebes, from lordly Luxor, from the great temples of Heliopolis, from a hundred rifled tombs, these relics had been brought.

The Brazilian cat and the mummy in 'Lot No. 249' refuse to acquiesce in their subjugation; they are capable of being reactivated by fifth-columnists in our midst, although they are then laid to rest, typically by stoical resistance on the part of Conan Doyle's heroes.

Many of the stories centre precisely on the unthinkability of terror intruding upon the polished life of England. The hero of 'The Terror of Blue John Gap' (1910), meditating on the possibility that an acquaintance of his might have been destroyed by a monstrous cave-bear, rather sympathetically ejaculates: 'What an inconceivable fate for a civilised Englishman of the twentieth century!', although in this case the visitant comes not from abroad but from below, from a region of caves connected in different ways with the caverns of 'Kubla Khan', the underground realms of Jules Verne, and Machen's land under the hills:

> All this country is hollow. Could you strike it with some gigantic hammer it would boom like a drum, or possibly cave in altogether and expose some huge subterranean sea. A great sea there must surely be, for on all sides the streams run into the mountain itself, never to reappear.

The oceans of empire, the sea of time, the caverns and rivers of the unconscious, against all these security is to be found in contemporary England. In 'The Leather Funnel' (1903), the protagonist sleeps next to an instrument of torture, and experiences a terrifying dream, from which he awakes sweating:

> Oh, what a blessed relief to feel that I was back in the nineteenth century – back out of that medieval vault into a world where men had human hearts within their bosoms. I sat up on my couch, trembling in every limb, my mind divided between thankfulness and horror. To think that such things were ever done – that they *could* be done without God striking the villains dead. Was it all a fantasy, or did it really stand for something which had happened in the black, cruel days of the world's history?

To feel the tone of passages like this is to see very clearly how Conan Doyle was able to act as an ideological comforter despite his ostensible subject-matter; nonetheless, there are points at which this tone is at least partly undercut by something more genuinely worrying. There is, for instance, his insistence on doubleness of character structure. Kennedy in 'The New Catacomb', although he is not a hero-figure, shares certain traits with a number of Conan Doyle characters, outstandingly Holmes himself: he 'had often been seduced by whim and pleasure from his studies, but his mind was an incisive one, capable of long and concentrated efforts which ended in sharp reactions of sensuous langour'. The relation between Kennedy and Burger is not unlike an upended version of that between Holmes and Watson, and both Holmes and Kennedy also contain within themselves a Jekyll-and-Hyde alternation, partly explained, of course, in Holmes by drugs. In a story like 'Lot No. 249', Conan Doyle makes it plain that the decent plodder is by definition morally superior to the 'unsound' man who is 'too clever by half'; but then, perhaps it is precisely the doubts cast on this simple diagnosis by the Holmes stories that render them surprising in their context. And if this emphasis betrays a less than complete faith in the monolithic English character, there are also stories, notably 'Blue John Gap' and 'B.24' (1899), which revert to the wider but related Gothic problem of evidence. After his ordeal, the hero of the former finds that there was left 'no sign of the creature, and no bloodstain which would show that my bullet had found him as he passed. Save for my own plight and the marks upon the mud, there was nothing to prove that what I said was true.' 'B.24' is a more interesting story, which has nothing to do with the supernatural, but poses an almost metaphysical detective problem: it concerns a petty criminal, trying to go straight, who nonetheless decides, for reasons of poverty and rejection, to burgle a large country-house. Once inside he is met by the lady of the house, who is only too ready to help him in order to spite her husband. She also comes up with the interesting suggestion that he, the burglar, might like to do something about the husband while he is there, but he rejects this. They are disturbed by the appearance of the husband himself: the burglar hears their conversation, and subsequently hears her murder him. Somewhat shocked, he takes the valuables and leaves, whereupon the lady has him arrested before he leaves the grounds and accuses him of the murder. The story is cast as his last plea for mercy:

> I told my story when I was taken, and no one would listen to me. Then I told it again at the trial – the whole thing absolutely as it happened, without so much as a word added, I set it all out truly, so help me God, all that Lady Mannering said and did, and then all that I had said and done, just as it occurred. And what did I get for it? 'The prisoner put forward a rambling and inconsequential statement, incredible in its details, and unsupported by any shred of corroborative evidence.'

This perhaps is one of the few points at which we are shocked by Conan Doyle's *narrative*. His imagination was fertile in producing objects of terror – most notably in stories like 'The Horror of the Heights' (1913), in which the upper air is conceived of as populated by strange, beautiful but malignant beings – but the matter-of-fact recounting, the armchair atmosphere which is the essence of the Holmes tales replaces disturbing effect by the cruder mechanism of grinding inexorability. The same is partly true of Wells's horror stories, but to a lesser extent since Wells often introduces an element of tension between the narrator and the teller of the story which casts doubt upon the reader's interpretation.[5] The extent to which this tension is itself an ironic reflection of Wells's divided status as realist and imaginative writer can be gauged from the introductory sentences of 'The Temptation of Harringay' (1895): 'It is quite impossible', says the ostensible narrator, 'to say whether this thing really happened. It depends entirely on the word of R. M. Harringay, who is an artist.'

The most typical of Wells's stories take this framework of doubt and apply it to a set of thematic preoccupation which we have already seen at work in *The Island of Doctor Moreau*: the problems of the justification of empire, of the nature of the bestial, of the uprising of the rebellious unconscious. In 'The Empire of the Ants' (1911), Wells summarises his doubts about the unique value of human civilisation as Holroyd journeys towards a place where, it is rumoured, a new insect 'empire' is arising:

In a few miles of this forest there must be more ants than there are men in the whole world! This seemed to Holroyd a perfectly new idea. In a few thousand years men had emerged from barbarism to a stage of civilisation that made them feel lords of the future and masters of the earth! But what was to prevent the ants evolving also? Such ants as one knew lived in little communities of a few thousand individuals, made no concerted efforts against the greater world. But they had a language, they had an intelligence! Why should things stop at that any more than men had stopped at the barbaric stage? Suppose presently the ants began to store knowledge, just as men had done by means of books and records, use weapons, form great empires, sustain a planned and organised war?

Similar doubts are expressed in 'In the Abyss' (1897), in which an exploration of the sea-bed reveals the existence of a race of underwater bipeds – who, interestingly, are only aware of humans in much the same way, says Wells, as we might be aware of angels: as beings from above who shower their realm with inexplicable signs and artefacts. In 'The Sea-Raiders' (1897), a story about the sudden appearance of a wave of marine monsters reminiscent of fast-moving octopi, he underlines the extent to which the apparent human domination of nature has, particularly in the 'civilised' world, rendered us unsuspecting with regard to the continuing dangers and inexplicabilities of nature. When the protagonist first sees the monsters in the distance, feeding, it gradually appears, on a human corpse, he fails entirely to read the signs of danger:

He approached his mark with all the assurance which the absolute security of this country against all forms of animal life gives its inhabitants. The round bodies moved to and fro, but it was only when he surmounted the skerry of boulders . . . that he realised the horrible nature of the discovery. It came upon him with some suddenness.

These stories, however, in which danger is represented by a gallery of curious 'natural' creatures, are comparatively crude. In 'The Valley of Spiders' (1903), internal and external worlds are more closely connected, for the appearance of the monstrous – in this case represented by fleets of giant spiders cocooned in floating webs – is directly precipitated by a disturbance of the psychological order. The story's symbolic nature is underlined by the facts that the three central figures are identified only as figures in a landscape – 'the man with the silver bridle', 'the gaunt man with the scarred lip', 'the little man on the white horse' – and that their situation and fate is supposed to be caused by an unmotivated surrender to autocratic passion on the part of their leader. Within the basic structure of pursuit and flight is an allegory of the corrupting nature of power, seen, as one might expect in Wells, from the viewpoint of the 'little man': 'Why should it be given to one man', he muses,

'to say "Come on!" with that stupendous violence of effect. Always, all his life, the man with the silver bridle has been saying that. If *I* said it—!' thought the little man. But people marvelled when the master was disobeyed even in the wildest things. This half-caste girl seemed to him, seemed to everyone, mad – blasphemous almost. The little man, by way of comparison, reflected on the gaunt rider with the scarred lip, as stalwart as his master, as brave and, indeed, perhaps braver, and yet for him there was obedience, nothing but to give obedience duly and stoutly . . .

Yet the eventual revelation of the master's cowardice makes no difference to this situation; he loses his silver bridle, but escapes at the cost of his companions' lives to meditate further vengeance on the 'mind-forged' spiders who have sought to thwart his absolute power.

Another group of stories – 'The Crystal Egg' (1899), 'The Remarkable Case of Davidson's Eyes', 'The Flowering of the Strange Orchid', 'The Moth' (all 1895) and 'Pollock and the Porroh Man' (1897) – concern various aspects of hallucination and obsession. 'The Crystal Egg' and 'Davidson's Eyes' are, in a sense, morally neutral stories, concerned only with the positing of extrasensory perception and with the invention of pseudo-scientific explanations to account for it. In 'The Strange Orchid', we are again in the realm of rebellious nature; but there is a strong suggestion that Wedderburn brings about his own fate by attempting to substitute a single obsessional interest for a more rounded engagement in life – an engagement from which he is in fact prevented by his psychological and social position, as a 'shy, lonely, rather ineffectual man, provided with just enough income to keep off the spur of necessity, and not enough nervous energy to make him seek any exacting employment'. In Wells, it is often to these ineffectual, displaced men that the horrors of the natural world get the chance to display themselves, presumably because of the tenuousness of their association with the body of civilised convention which would normally hold off the power of nature's nastier manifestations. In 'The Moth', however, the hallucination which afflicts and finally maddens the 'hapless' Hapley is directly the result of his other obsession, with demolishing the reputation of his fellow entomologist, Pawkins. Hapley knows full well that the moth which comes to blight his life is the dead Pawkins's reincarnation, but the terror of the story derives from the way in which every move he makes to reveal this to others only demonstrates his madness more clearly. Towards the end, he breaks his leg in pursuit of the hallucinatory moth:

> He knew he was a lost man if he did not keep himself in hand. But as the night waned the fever grew upon him, and the very dread he had of seeing the moth made him see it. About five, just as the dawn was grey, he tried to get out of bed and catch it, though his leg was afire with pain. The nurse had to struggle with him.
>
> On account of this, they tied him down to the bed. At this the moth grew bolder, and once he felt it settle in his hair. Then, because he struck out violently with his arms, they tied these also. At this the moth came and crawled over his face, and Hapley wept, swore, screamed, prayed for them to take it off him, unavailingly.

But the best of these tales – that is, the one in which Wells's dislike of the crueller aspects of imperialist and technological domination and his perception of the distorting power of obsession find their most adequate image – is 'Pollock and the Porroh Man', in which the unpleasant Pollock, on an African expedition, offends a witch-doctor, apparently by attempting to seduce his woman, and is thereafter pursued by a series of curses. A Portuguese trader he meets as he flees for Europe and safety is amusingly open-minded about the whole business: 'Den dere's dis – infernal magic', he says, 'Of course, I don't believe in it – superstition – but still it's not nice to tink dat wherever you are, dere is a black man, who spends a moonlight night now and den a-dancing about a fire to send you bad dreams . . . Had any bad dreams?' Pollock indeed has bad dreams, and he also develops a continuing hallucinaton of the head of the Porroh man – whom he has had murdered by a hired assassin – which eventually induces him to cut his own throat. That Pollock has brought this upon himself by his arrogance and dishonesty is left in no doubt; as soon as the curse becomes known,

> there was a disposition on the part of the expedition to leave Pollock to himself, and Pollock became, for the first time in his life, anxious to mingle with blacks. Waterhouse took one canoe, and Pollock, in spite of a friendly desire to chat with Waterhouse, had to take the other. He was left all alone in the front part of the canoe, and he had the greatest trouble to make the men – who did not love him – keep to the middle of the river, a clear hundred yards or more from either shore.

'The Moth' and 'Pollock' are similar in structure in that they both set up situations wherein outside opinion and internal obsession converge at the point of insanity or suicide. The reality of hallucination is left more skilfully in doubt in the well-known 'The Door in the Wall' (1911), in which a successful public figure recounts his childhood experience of passing through a door into a land of wonder beyond, and his several adult rejections of further opportunities to pass through that door, which only presents itself to him when he is at his most totally absorbed in practical affairs. In the end he is found dead, having apparently passed through a door which led only to an excavation site in East Kensington. The story ends with the narrator puzzling over the significance of his own tale:

> There are times when I believe that Wallace was no more than the victim of the coincidence between a rare but not unprecedented type of hallucination and a careless trap, but that indeed is not my profoundest belief. You may think me superstitious, if you will, and foolish; but, indeed, I am more than half convinced that he had, in truth, an abnormal gift, and a sense, something – I know not what – that in the guise of wall and door offered him an outlet, a secret and peculiar passage of escape into another and altogether more beautiful world. At any rate, you will say, it betrayed him in the end. But did it betray him? There you touch the inmost mystery of these dreamers, these men of vision and the imagination. We see our world fair and common, the hoarding and the pit. By our daylight standard he walked out of security into darkness, danger, and death.
>   But did he see like that?

In this play on the world of 'the hoarding and the pit', Wells calls to mind the nostalgic fantasies of de la Mare, particularly perhaps 'The Creatures'; and it is one of the few stories in which he transcends the normalising influence of his stereotyped frameworks, with their doubtful but reasonable narrators and their naturalistic physical settings.

He does so again, it seems to me, in two other stories, in very different ways: once by taking the entire Gothic apparatus and twisting it slightly, once by moving into a wholly different and more modern vein. To take the latter first, 'The Cone' (1897) is a story in which terror is conveyed against the background of that industrial landscape which is generally so carefully avoided by latter-day Gothic writers. It opens with the suggestion of an affair between one Raut and Mrs Horrocks, the wife of an ironmaster; which is to culminate on the following day with their flight. Horrocks, however, appears, and seems to have overheard at least part of their conversation. He offers to fulfil a promise which he has made to Raut, to show him a new kind of beauty, the effects produced by moonlight interacting with the lights of his own realm of blast-furnaces and rolling-mills. He takes Raut on a guided tour of the ironworks, which culminates in a visit to the largest of the blast-furnaces. They mount to the top of it, and Horrocks shows Raut the giant metal cone which is used to block its mouth and prevent wastage of energy.

> Raut gripped the hand-rail tightly, and stared down at the cone. The heat was intense. The boiling of the iron and the tumult of the blast made a thunderous accompaniment to Horrocks' voice. But the thing had to be gone through now. Perhaps, after all . . .
>
> 'In the middle', bawled Horrocks, 'temperature near a thousand degrees. If *you* were dropped into it . . . flash into flame like a pinch of gunpowder in a candle. Put your hand out and feel the heat of his breath. Why, even up here I've seen the rain-water boiling off the trucks. And that cone there. It's a damned sight too hot for roasting cakes. The top side of it's three hundred degrees.'

The ending is predictable, as Horrocks swings Raut over the edge and drops him onto the cone, shouting, 'Fizzle, you fool! Fizzle, you hunter of women! You hot-blooded hound! Boil! Boil! Boil!'

The story is based on an extended metaphor about the heat of passion and the heat of the ironworks, the boiling up and the boiling away of blood and energy. Like Holroyd in 'The Lord of the Dynamos' (1895), Raut is a sacrifice to the might of the machine, although unlike Holroyd his crime seems somewhat venal to warrant his ghastly fate. Here, as in most of Conan Doyle's stories, there is no real element of surprise; instead, the reader is fascinated by the steady working through to a predestined conclusion. The same is true for 'The Red Room' (1896), Wells's most significant direct contribution to the Gothic tradition. Here the protagonist moves almost like a somnambulist through the realm of the traditional haunted house: he has come to spend a night in a famous haunted room, although the three aged caretakers seem unable to tell him the exact identity of the ghost. Despite the customary warnings, he proceeds to the room, and lights candles and a fire to ward off evil. After a time, the candles begin to go out; he becomes increasingly frenzied as he tries to relight them in time. When the fire also starts to die, he abandons himself to an unreasoning terror, and rushes from the room, injuring himself in the process. He awakes to find the caretakers regarding him; one of them speaks to him, 'no longer as one who greets an intruder, but as one who grieves for a broken friend', and asks him the nature of the ghost. He replies:

> 'There is neither ghost of earl nor ghost of countess in that room, there is no ghost there at all; but worse, far worse'—
>
> 'Well?' they said.
>
> 'The worst of all the things that haunt poor mortal man,' said I; 'and that is, in all its nakedness – *Fear*! Fear that will not have light

nor sound, that will not bear with reason, that deafens and darkens and overwhelms.'

The oldest of the caretakers seems to be brought to a kind of understanding by this:

'That is it,' said he. 'I knew that was it. A Power of Darkness. To put such a curse upon a woman! It lurks there always. You can feel it even in the daytime, even of a bright summer's day, in the hangings, in the curtains, keeping behind you however you face about. In the dusk it creeps along the corridor and follows you, so that you dare not turn. There is Fear in that room of hers – black Fear, and there will be – so long as this house of sin endures.'

'The Red Room' is in itself a commentary on the Gothic tradition; terror, says Wells, begets terror, according to its own irrational laws of collusion between mind and environment. Like the House of Usher, the house with the red room is haunted by the fears of its own past and present inhabitants.

As writers of horror stories, Conan Doyle and Wells both demonstrate the eclecticism of the consciously popular author, even though in Wells it could be said that there is beneath some of the tales a consistent ideological pattern, an exploration of the possibilities and limits of scientific progress. The stories of Algernon Blackwood are very different, in that they are generally informed by, and contribute to the formation and validation of, a single world-view. In Blackwood, the realm of the supernatural is accepted as existent, his stories are full of 'explanations' – particularly those which feature the 'ghost-hunter', John Silence – but they are explanations which presuppose belief. And the peculiar terror which he often exploits is at an opposite pole to the moralistic tenor of tales like Conan Doyle's 'The New Catacomb' or Wells's 'The Moth', in that his chief characters (here Grimwood in 'The Valley of the Beasts' (1921) is a notable exception) rarely bring upon themselves a deserved doom. The supernatural forces which he posits are fundamentally *indifferent* to man: the wendigo, the elemental forces in 'The Willows' (1907), the forests in 'The Man whom the Trees Loved' are not hostile entities, but if disturbed, for one reason or another, they are able to act in powerful and terrifying ways. They are generally induced to do so by invasion: a typical story is 'The Camp of the Dog' (1908), in which a party of campers on a Scandinavian island find themselves threatened as a direct result of their attempt to 'return to nature'. Nature is not necessarily benevolent, as Dr Silence points out when he describes how the environment influences events:

There's no life here. These islands are mere dead rocks pushed up from below the sea – not living land; and there's nothing really alive on them. Even the sea, this tideless, brackish sea, neither salt water nor fresh, is dead. It's all a pretty image of life without the real heart and soul of life. To a man with too strong desires who came here and lived close to nature, strange things might happen.[6]

What actually does happen in 'Camp of the Dog' is that a perfectly innocent character, who is nursing a secret passion, develops a werewolf-self, a liberated 'Body of Desire', which shows signs of being about to destroy the love-object – for the reason that, as Silence puts it with pleasing ambiguity, the repressed desire at stake is 'to bathe in the very heart's blood of the one desired' (*IJ*, p. 347). The structure of 'The Wendigo' (1910), based on American Indian legendry, is similar, in that it posits an invasion of the farther reaches of nature by a group, one of whom – in this case the French Canadian Défago – is by race and inclination 'deeply susceptible . . . to that singular spell which the wilderness lays upon certain lonely natures' (*IJ*, p. 243), and who therefore becomes innocently involved in the manifestation of the supernatural. Blackwood's 'explanation', transmitted through the views of a trainee clergyman, for the appearance of the wendigo and his capture of Défago is curiously reminiscent of Blake, and deliberately avoids a full resolution of the question of the kind of 'reality' which the legendary monster possesses:

Out there, in the heart of unreclaimed wilderness, they had surely witnessed something crudely and essentially primitive. Something that had survived somehow the advance of humanity had emerged terrifically, betraying a scale of life monstrous and immature. He envisaged it rather as a glimpse into prehistoric ages, when superstitions, gigantic and uncouth, still oppressed the hearts of men; when the forces of nature were still untamed, the Powers that may have haunted a primeval universe not yet withdrawn. To this day he thinks of what he termed years later in a sermon 'savage and formidable Potencies lurking behind the souls of men, not evil perhaps in themselves, yet instinctively hostile to humanity as it exists'.

(*IJ*, p. 290)

The kinds of fear in these stories are odd partly for the simple reason that Blackwood does not here deal in claustrophobia, so often the obvious image for the repressed and dislocated psyche, but in quite the reverse, in anxieties about being not so much destroyed by nature as dwarfed into insignificance by it. In 'The Willows', a setting of similar wildness, this time an island in the

Danube, forms the background to a tale which involves beings who 'have absolutely nothing to do with mankind':

> We had 'strayed', as the Swede put it, into some region or some set of conditions where the risks were great, yet unintelligible to us; where the frontiers of some unknown world lay close about us. It was a spot held by the dwellers in some outer space, a sort of peep-hole whence they could spy upon the earth, themselves unseen, a point where the veil between had worn a little thin. As the final result of too long a sojourn here, we should be carried over the border and deprived of what we called 'our lives', yet by mental, not by physical, processes.
>
> (*IJ*, p. 50)

Man here is the intruder into a world which works by quite other laws, a world which may choose at any moment and for arbitrary reasons to rise and crush him, and in the context of which scientific progress looks laughable and toy-like. There is a dialectic of barbarism and the civilised in Blackwood, but it is not didactic or necessarily progressive: the barbaric exists in all its power alongside the commonplace, yet there is no sharing of laws or predictabilities.

Furthermore, as we see from another group of Blackwood's stories, the barbaric has its own inexplicable kinds of beauty. 'The Trod' is the story of a moorland path on which the fairies are said to appear from time to time; anyone who strays onto it is liable to be carried off, for the fairy pageant is 'just too lovely to look at – and keep your senses'. The heroine, Diana, is attracted to the life of the fairies, which is portrayed as filled with beauty and pleasure but totally static, beyond the rule of change; the hero, Norman, makes a due attempt to save her from this ambiguous fate, though not without his own struggle: 'two passions seized and fought within him: the fierce desire to possess her in the world of men and women, or to go with her headlong, recklessly, and share some ineffable ecstasy of happiness beyond the familiar world where ordinary time and space held sway'. Norman manages to pull her away from the Trod in the very act of succumbing, a consummation which appears to the reader to be wholly satisfactory until one reads the magnificently bitter final twist of the knife:

> and in due course he married her; he married Diana ... a queer, lovely girl, but a girl without a soul, almost without a mind – a girl as commonplace as the radiant nonentity pictured with shining teeth on the cover of a popular magazine – a standardised creature whose essence had 'gone elsewhere'.[7]

Far more heartening on the old romantic theme of beauty and terror is 'May Day Eve' (1907), which deals basically with a Machen-

like transmutation of the hills and with the revelation of the con-
cealed animism which lies behind the visible universe:

> increasingly, all the time, it came to me how the cries of the sea-birds
> sounded like laughter, and how the everlasting wind blew and drove
> about me with a purpose, and how the low bushes persistently took
> the shape of stooping people, moving stealthily past me, and how the
> mist more and more resembled huge protean figures escorting me
> across the desolate hills, silently, with immense footsteps. For the
> inanimate world now touched my awakened poetic sense in a manner
> hitherto unguessed, and became fraught with the pregnant messages
> of a dimly concealed life.   (*IJ*, p. 173)

The awakening of this sense, the 'expansion of consciousness' as
Blackwood also referred to it, is revelatory only to a point: the hero
is shown into a room filled with spirits, but those spirits have veiled
eyes, 'and my terror became simply a terror that the veils of their
eyes might lift, and that they would look at me with their clear,
naked sight'. As in 'The Trod', there is little compromise here: the
two worlds cannot be matched, they are different in essence, and
crossing from one to the other can only be achieved as a total,
and potentially irreversible, act. Beauty and terror are in dreadful
proximity, as in the bizarre 'Pikestaffe Case' (1924), where Thorley
and Pikestaffe disappear, having been involved in various experiments in the 'higher mathematics'. Some time after their disappearance, Thorley's landlady looks into a mirror which has previously
been turned to the wall, and receives a surprise:

> her own reflection was not visible, no picture of herself being there ...
> Thorley and a boy – she recognised the Pikestaffe lad from the
> newspaper photographs she had seen – were plainly there, and ...
> books and instruments in great quantity filled all the nearer space,
> blocking up the foreground. Beyond, behind, stretching in all
> directions, she affirms, was empty space that produced upon her the
> effect of the infinite heavens as seen in a clear night sky. This space
> was prodigious, yet in some way not alarming. It did not terrify; rather
> it comforted, and, in a sense, uplifted. A diffused soft light pervaded
> the huge panorama. There were no shadows, there were no high lights.
>   (*TUS*, p. 344)

Among other things, this strange vision of an alternative universe
sounds very much like a drug experience – and in various stories
Blackwood tackles that issue head-on – an impression which is con-
firmed by the descriptions of the landlady's euphoria whenever she
enters Thorley's room, and also by the description of Thorley himself before his 'translation':

> His walk was peculiar, she noticed at once; he did not walk in a straight

line. His tall, thin outline flowed down the pavement in long,
sweeping curves, yet quite steadily. He was not drunk. He came nearer;
he was not twenty feet away; at ten feet she saw his face clearly, and
received a shock. It was worn, and thin, and wasted, but a light of
happiness, of something more than happiness indeed, shone in it.
He reached the area railings. He looked up. His face seemed ablaze.

(*TUS*, p. 332)

There is much more that one could say about Blackwood, and
many more of his stories which it would be worth discussing. There
is 'Max Hensig' (1907), which in its interplay of everyday life and
obsession, and in its setting in a world of newspapermen and alcohol,
is very like Robert W. Chambers at his best. There is 'The Insanity
of Jones' (1907), in which the reader is made to feel throughout
that Jones's intended 'revenge' on his mortal enemy is justifiable in
terms of the visions he experiences of tortures he has suffered at
this enemy's hands in a previous incarnation, until the moment of
revenge actually occurs in a welter of violence so sickening that one
realises that one has been tricked into accepting a paranoiac's view
of the world. In the end he is taken away by a mixed guard, of a
policeman on each side and a 'veiled figure moving majestically in
front of him, making slow sweeping circles with the flaming sword,
to keep back the host of faces that were thronging in upon him
from the Other Region' (*IJ*, p. 215). And there is 'The Glamour of
the Snow', in which the hero, on holiday in a ski resort, meets
one night a girl who invites him to accompany her on a night ski
run, and leads him on to dizzying heights. She remains always
tantalisingly out of reach, until they reach the frozen peak of the
mountain:

> The girl stood in front of him, very near; he felt her chilly breath
> upon his cheeks; her hair passed blindingly across his eyes; and that
> icy wind came with her. He saw her whiteness close; again, it seemed,
> his sight passed through her into space as though she had no face. Her
> arms were around his neck. She drew him softly downwards to his
> knees. He sank; he yielded utterly; he obeyed. Her weight was upon
> him, smothering, delicious. The snow was to his waist . . . She kissed
> him softly on the lips, the eyes, all over his face. And then she spoke
> his name in that voice of love and wonder, the voice that held the
> accent of two others – both taken over long ago by Death – the voice
> of his mother, and of the woman he had loved.
>
> He made one more feeble effort to resist. Then, realising even while
> he struggled that this soft weight about his heart was sweeter than
> anything life could ever bring, he let his muscles relax, and sank back
> into the soft oblivion of the covering snow. Her wintry kisses bore him
> to sleep.   (*TUS*, p. 252)

It is, perhaps, these moments of death, or near-death, and con-summation which Blackwood handles with most assurance, and also with a degree of tenderness which is rare in the horror story. He is constantly reworking traditions, in order to capitalise on the reader's previous knowledge: his vision of 'The Dance of Death' (1907) is predictable from the title onwards, and yet there is still power in his depiction of a young man, suffering from a weak heart, who goes to a dance and there meets his heart's desire. ' "It won't hurt your poor heart to dance with *me*, you know", she laughed. "You may trust me. I shall know how to take care of it" ' (*IJ*, p. 224). And of course she will, for she too is a death figure: as he looks at her, 'a great pain ran swiftly through his heart', the pain of desire and the pang of death interlocked. And again in 'The Man whom the Trees Loved', there are no surprises in David Bittacy's dilemma: he has worked all his life with trees, and now the trees want and need him, to the despair of his wife. But their kind of wanting is, again, total: 'their love for you, their "awareness" of your personality and presence involves the idea of winning you – across the border – into themselves – into their world of living. It means, in a way, taking you over.' The mysterious life of the forest is frightening, yet genuinely attractive, especially when during a great storm the trees make their desires felt:

> For, unmistakably, the trees were shouting in the dark. There were sounds, too, like the flapping of great sails, a thousand at a time, and sometimes reports that resembled more than anything else the distant booming of enormous drums. The trees stood up – the whole beleaguering host of them stood up – and with the uproar of their million branches drummed the thundering message out across the night. It seemed as if they all had broken loose. Their roots swept trailing over field and hedge and roof. They tossed their bushy heads beneath the clouds with a wild, delighted shuffling of great boughs. With trunks upright they raced leaping through the sky. There was upheaval and adventure in the awful sound they made, and their cry was like the cry of a sea that has broken through its gates and poured loose upon the world. (*TUS*, p. 143)

The insistence on the importance of the sexual elements in terror in Blackwood's work is part of a larger and more general concern with the psychology of fear. In this area he is in strong contrast with the other major figure of the later ghost story, M. R. James. Briggs speaks of James's total lack of interest in the workings of the mind, saying that 'psychology is totally and defiantly excluded from his writings' (Briggs, p. 135), but this is perhaps not quite true: what James *is* uninterested in is the psychology of his *characters*. Blackwood displays to us the operation of fear within and upon particular minds: James, on the other hand, constructs minute and intricate working models which have as their end product fear in the mind of the *reader*. If his characters are not very interesting, complex or even concrete, this is precisely because he does not want them to form a veil between us and the terror. Other writers have tried to achieve the same end by making their characters so 'like us' that we locate our own feelings within them: James, instead, makes his characters totally cardboard and concentrates on the direct flash of terror between the event on the printed page and the reader. His characters are rarely provided with interesting motivations for the dangerous activities in which they indulge: in 'The Treasure of Abbot Thomas', for instance, although the structure of the plot looks conventional in that a search for treasure produces dreadful effects, the protagonist is moved not by greed or ambition but merely by intellectual curiosity; the fact that he ends up face to tentacle with the treasure's obnoxious guardian is in no way organic to him, and thus the breach in the natural order is all the more horrifying. Then again, there is perhaps a general connection, but it is very long-range: if the only motivation of most of James's characters is curiosity, then behind all curiosity, according to Freud, lies the displaced sexual urge, and James's characters do move in an entirely bachelor world.

Although James conjures up strange beasts and supernatural manifestations, the shock effect of his stories is usually strongest when he is dealing in physical mutilation and abnormality, generally sketched in with the lightest of pens.[8] In 'The Rose Garden', Mrs Anstruther, unwisely pressing on with her horticultural plans, perceives within her shrubbery what at first glance appears to be 'a Fifth of November mask':

> It was not a mask. It was a face – large, smooth, and pink. She remembers the minute drops of perspiration which were starting from its forehead: she remembers how the jaws were clean-shaven and the eyes shut. She remembers also, and with an accuracy which makes the thought intolerable to her, how the mouth was open and a single tooth appeared below the upper lip. As she looked the face receded into the darkness of the bush. The shelter of the house was gained and the door shut before she collapsed.

Almost all of the stories are structurally identical in that they proceed steadily through a series of prefigurations towards a single moment of revelation or encounter. Sometimes the prefigurations are at a distance, as with the appearance of the mutilated children in 'Lost Hearts', or the fate of Anders Bjornsen in 'Count Magnus', who 'was once a beautiful man, but now his face was not there, because the flesh of it was sucked away off the bones'. But some prefigurations and the final encounters are generally marked by an intensely rendered proximity, as in the well-known nightmarish sequence in 'Casting the Runes', when Dunning puts his hand under the pillow to find his watch, 'only, it did not get so far. What he touched was, according to his account, a mouth, with teeth, and with hair about it, and, he declares, not the mouth of a human being'; or in the subtler form of 'The Stalls of Barchester Cathedral': 'I was pursued by the very vivid impression that wet lips were whispering into my ear with great rapidity and emphasis for some time together.' In most of these cases, it is the very indefiniteness and incompleteness of the images that accounts for a large part of their effect: they are momentary glimpses, imprinted on the brain, as it were, by flashlight.

But thus far, one might say that there is nothing very unusual in James's presentations of terror; and in fact it is curiously difficult to find within his texts the exact grounds of his effectiveness. Partly, it has to do with another aspect of proximity, with the fact that James is constantly affirming that he is presenting his tales just as they were told to him. In this way he seeks to assert a continuity between the events and the reader, with himself as mediator: in 'Number Thirteen', he passes between high points of the action with the offhand comment that the protagonist 'had nothing to tell me (I am giving the story as I heard it from him) about what passed at supper'. In 'The Treasure of Abbot Thomas', he languidly discusses the possibility of himself making a visit to the scene of the story:

> It has not seemed to me worth while to lavish money on a visit to the place, for though it is probably far more attractive than either Mr Somerton or Mr Gregory thought it, there is evidently little, if anything, of first-rate interest to be seen – except, perhaps, one thing, which I should not care to see.

But more importantly it has to do again with predictability, with the fact that from the very first moment of the story a physical and literary background is established which promises precisely the mixture of the comforting and the disturbing on which this kind of ghost story thrives. A typical opening is that of 'An Episode of Cathedral History':

> There was once a learned gentleman who was deputed to examine and

report upon the archives of the Cathedral of Southminster. The examination of these records demanded a very considerable expenditure of time: hence it became advisable for him to engage lodgings in the city: for though the Cathedral body were profuse in their offers of hospitality, Mr Lake felt that he would prefer to be master of his day. This was recognised as reasonable. The Dean eventually wrote advising Mr Lake, if he were not already suited, to communicate with Mr Worby, the principal Verger, who occupied a house convenient to the church and was prepared to take in a quiet lodger for three or four weeks. Such an arrangement was precisely what Mr Lake desired. Terms were easily agreed upon, and early in December, like another Mr Datchery (as he remarked to himself), the investigator found himself in the occupation of a very comfortable room in an ancient and 'cathedraly' house.

The approach is reminiscent of the fairy-story, with its self-conscious anecdotalism, its terseness of description and the halo of suspense surrounding apparently mundane detail. And James, of course, also builds up his own norms: to read basically the same opening to four or five different stories is to learn the markers by which he invests the everyday with a sense of anticipation. Already in these brief sentences one can feel the haste to get the story moving, the almost impatient brushing aside of setting and even character so that the events themselves can take the forefront of the stage.

James is an intensely mannered writer, both in the local matter of his scholarly style – 'An Episode of Cathedral History' ends, and makes its point, with the untranslated phrase, *Ibi cubavit lamia* – and also in his insistence on self-conscious fictionality. 'The Tractate Middoth', ' "Oh, Whistle, and I'll Come to you, my Lad" ', 'The Ash-Tree', 'Mr Humphreys and his Inheritance' all hinge on ludicrous coincidences which are left happily unexplained even in terms of the supernatural. The coherence of the stories is not a matter of 'real' probability, but of literary probability: the probability, which he partly inherits and partly establishes within his own range of texts, that stories to do with ancient cathedrals, decaying towns, old manuscripts will 'naturally' move in a world of terror. Unlike Blackwood, he makes no attempt whatever to explain why this should be so: it is simply assumed as a convention. James is often regarded as a master of understatement, and this is true, but the understatements only work because of their context, because he establishes a dialectic of the predictable. He is thus able continually to maintain a pose of reticence, typically at the end of ' "Oh, Whistle . . ." ', where he appears to be about to describe the figure which appears in response to Parkins's whistle:

Parkins, who very much dislikes being questioned about it, did once describe something of it in my hearing, and I gathered that what he chiefly remembers about it is a horrible, an intensely horrible, face *of crumpled linen*. What expression he read upon it he could not or would not tell, but that the fear of it went nigh to maddening him is certain.

Or at the end of 'Number Thirteen': 'That same afternoon he told me what you have read; but he refused to draw any inferences from it, and to assent to any that I drew for him.'

But fundamentally, James's stories work through irony, and it is an irony of a particular kind in that it depends entirely on a prior acquaintance – not necessarily conscious – with the assumptions of the Gothic. There is the constant use of the device whereby, early on in the stories, the character becomes aware of the presence of something which *he* assumes to be perfectly natural, but which we already know not to be. Mr Humphreys is irritated one night by seeing in his garden an Irish yew which is so placed as to upset the order of his view. The following night:

The Irish yew came to his mind again as he was on the point of drawing his curtains: but either he had been misled by a shadow the night before, or else the shrub was not really so obtrusive as he had fancied. Anyhow, he saw no reason for interfering with it. What he *would* do away with, however, was a clump of dark growth which had usurped a place against the house wall, and was threatening to obscure one of the lower range of windows. It did not look as if it could possibly be worth keeping; he fancied it dank and unhealthy, little as he could see of it.

Again in 'Count Magnus', when Wraxall says that he would dearly like to see the deceased count, we are in little doubt as to the inadvisability of such an interest. James's settings – his isolated country houses, his Oxbridge colleges – are Gothic stereotypes, albeit his favourite style of architecture is Queen Anne: and he underlines his place in the tradition with references to Radcliffe, Coleridge and the Gothic Revival itself.

What he further does, however, is take this traditional background and ironise it to exploit his readers' fears. 'Number Thirteen' hinges on a mysterious hotel room, lit with unearthly light and apparently occupied by a dead occultist, which appears and disappears. Eventually certain floorboards are dug up: 'you will naturally suppose that a skeleton – say that of Mag. Nicholas Francken – was discovered. That was not so.' In this case, what actually is discovered is somewhat less terrifying; more frequently, however, this kind of knowingness renders the outcome all the more horrific. In 'The

Ash-Tree', he undercuts the consecutivity of his own narrative, assuming his readers' familiarity with the obvious kinds of terror:

> Next day Sir Matthew Fell was not downstairs at six in the morning, as was his custom; nor at seven, nor yet at eight. Hereupon the servants went and knocked at his chamber door. I need not prolong the description of their anxious listenings and renewed batterings on the panels. The door was opened at last from the outside, and they found their master dead and black. So much you have guessed. . . .

Where most writers of horror stories have followed Radcliffe in showing some respect for their readers' weaknesses, James follows Matthew Lewis, and openly gloats over their gullibility. In his stories the Gothic has become a habit, and displays the repetitive power which habits possess. The kinds of basic fear which he exploits – fear of the archaic, the irruption of chaos into an ordered world – are precisely those of the Gothic writers, but his stories are perfected forms drained of content. They *work* well, but they *mean* almost nothing, because they are not independent: they are extended foot-notes, further examples of a kind which, it is assumed, we already know. In this sense, James represents a final decay of the Gothic into formalism.

Essentially, in James the Gothic is no longer a mode for dramatis-ing problems: there are no points of hiatus or contradiction in his ghost stories. In David Lindsay's *The Haunted Woman*, however, one can still sense the pressure exerted on the form by the material with which it is trying to cope – issues about the relations between the sexes, about the power of social convention, about the possible balefulness of the past. Lindsay is best known, perhaps, as the writer of *A Voyage to Arcturus* (1920), an uneven but powerful fantasy which has recently re-emerged as an object of cult attention, and the style of the two books is in some ways similar: Lindsay was not a good writer, and it is often obvious how hard he has had to struggle to achieve a reasonably flowing narrative. But despite this, *The Haunted Woman* commands attention, rather as *Frankenstein* does, because the issues raised spread far beyond the author's conscious attempt to control them.

The story concerns Isbel Loment, who is at the start of the book engaged to be married to an upstanding young man, Marshall Stokes. She is, in ways unclear even to herself, dissatisfied with this situation, feeling herself to possess sensibilities which can scarcely be subdued to a conventional marriage. Stokes has met an elderly businessman named Judge, the owner of an ancient and mysterious house, Runhill Court; Isbel's aunt becomes interested in buying it, since the impending marriage will mean that she is to be left on her own. Isbel and the others go to visit the house, and she meets Judge. Runhill's main peculiarity is that at times a staircase appears where no staircase should be: this is connected in legend with a set of rooms called Ulf's Tower, no longer existent but rumoured to have been carried off, with Ulf himself, the Saxon builder of the original house, by trolls. Unfortunately for the verification of the legend, nobody who climbs the stairs can afterwards recollect anything of their trip.

Isbel feels a strange affinity for Judge, and the basic structure of the book concerns the disparity between their encounters in 'real life', which are conventional though puzzled, and the burgeoning and passionate relationship which develops between them in the realm above the stairs. The associated processes of memory and forgetting are complicated, but Lindsay handles them well, as they both become increasingly baffled by their attempts to reconcile their double life. The situation is further complicated by the presence of one Mrs Richborough, whose attempt to blackmail Isbel ends in her own death. The complex culminating scene is one in which Isbel, led on by Mrs Richborough's ghost, visits the grounds of the house for the last time and encounters Judge: but the world which Judge is seeing is no longer the same as hers, and there is a moment of genuine dislocation when he says, 'I *have* been up that staircase to-day, and I have not yet come down again.'[9] The principal feature of the 'other world' is a Saxon musician, presumably the missing Ulf, whose music serves as a harbinger of revelation. In a desperate attempt to convince Isbel of the reality of this alternative world, which he alone is still seeing, Judge awakens him and sees his face: what he sees is not described, but it kills him. Isbel, securely back in the real world with almost no memory of what has gone on, but knowing herself in some way compromised by the whole episode, breaks off her engagement to Stokes, but Lindsay leaves us with the strong hint that, once matters have 'settled down' again, the engagement will be resumed and Ulf's world will fade away from memory – even though at one point Isbel has realised a horrified fear that she and the other members of *her* world may be merely figures in Ulf's dreams.

The principal interest of the book lies in the way in which its hesitations and inconsistencies evidence a genuine attempt to dramatise a set of social and psychological problems, and also the difficulty of that attempt. The heart of the matter is clearly sex: like *Dracula, The Haunted Woman* is an elaborate eve-of-wedding fantasy of liberation. There is something in Isbel which sees marriage as bondage, and it may be an attempt at freedom on the part of this repressed self which sets the whole process in motion: the strength of her half-hidden resentment operates to open a latent breach in the natural order. Confusions in sexual stereotyping occur from the beginning, particularly in connection with the women: Isbel's aunt is described as 'one of those eccentric women who ought to have been born men' (*HW*, p. 4); Isbel herself experiences constant conflict between her wish to appear attractive and her contempt for the sexual exploitation which follows from acquiescence in a 'feminine' role; and the blend of voluptuousness and calculation which marks this socially sanctioned 'femininity' is personified in the flesh of Mrs Richborough:

> Her tall and lovely form was attired as usual in the rich, soft furs and velvets which she so much affected. She moved charmingly, and her gracefully-swaying waist was that of a quite young woman, but Isbel no sooner saw the angular, witchlike face than her old feelings of repugnance and distrust returned. (*HW*, p. 120)

But the fact that Mrs Richborough is present to fulfil the role of villainess does not mean that Lindsay wishes us to see Isbel herself as transcending stereotyping; on the contrary, he leaves us in considerable doubt as to her own self-apprehension, implying that even the passional side of the psyche is distorted by pressures towards social conventionality. Like Radcliffe's heroines, Isbel prides herself on her 'sensibility', but she can find no real correlative to this in the outside world. This is partly the result of her social position; she is wealthy, leisured, idle, and her alienation from the world in which she habitually moves finds no alternative relief in nature, which merely emphasises for her her inability to liberate her own instincts and desires:

> Streets, shops, crowds, any form of human activity, enabled her to forget herself, but natural surroundings threw her back on her own mental resources, and then the whole emptiness and want of purpose of her life loomed up in front of her. (*HW*, p. 15)

In the real world, she is able to perceive rationally the lack of justice in the social position of women: she wants money in order that her position within her impending marriage can have a kind of independence – 'After all, why *should* a married woman be a parasite? It makes her out to be a kind of property' (*HW*, p. 6). But it is only in the world of Ulf's Tower that she can admit her deeper desires to herself, and from this world she can bring nothing back.

In a mirror beyond the staircase, she sees a vision of herself as she would like to be: powerful and serious, yet *not* therefore desexed:

> Either the glass was flattering her, or something had happened to her to make her look different; she was quite startled by her image. It was not so much that she appeared more beautiful as that her face had acquired another character. Its expression was deep, stern, lowering, yet everything was softened and made alluring by the pervading presence of sexual sweetness. (*HW*, p. 49)

Yet the book produces, for the reader and for Isbel, only a sad awareness that the conditions for this kind of blend of characteristics do not exist. As Isbel ironically says, 'girls get all sorts of queer fancies in their heads, and that's because they don't live in the real world' (*HW*, p. 65); the response of the so-called real world to the revelations of the unconscious is only a forgetting and a residual sense of loss, well portrayed in the scene where Judge desperately tries to make Isbel cling to her fading vision.

Around this vision plays the full apparatus of 'dreadful pleasure', as Isbel admits things to herself that otherwise only baffle her: her hearing of Ulf's music is a combination of pleasure and a terrible fear of the consequences of release:

> when I was listening to that weird sound in that passage, it suddenly seemed to strike a very deep string in my heart, which had never been struck before. It was a kind of *passion*... It *was* passion. But there was something else in it besides joy – my heart felt sick and tormented, and there was a horrible sinking sensation of despair. But the delight was there all the time, and was the strongest... (*HW*, pp. 40–1)

Isbel hovers continually on the brink of freedom, yet in the end convention holds her back with its promises of acceptance and safety. She seems very near to a realisation when, looking round the house for the first time, she comes across the room which had been occupied by Judge's late wife, a room which Lindsay makes into an image of the female psyche:

> Quite evidently it was the sanctum of the late lady of the manor – no man could have lived in that room, so full of little feminine fragilities and knick-knacks as it was, so bizarre, so frivolous, so tasteless, yet so pleasing. And underneath everything loomed up the past, persisting in discovering itself, despite the almost passionate efforts to conceal it. (*HW*, p. 26)

The use of 'passionate' here seems hardly accidental: the Blakean tragedy which Lindsay is depicting is the way in which that mental and physical energy which could be used for personal integration is displaced into the service of repression and conventionality.

The Haunted Woman is one of the clearest statements of the importance of sexual roles as a motif in Gothic fiction; Lindsay comes out with comments that would not be out of place sixty years later. 'History', says Isbel, 'has been written by men, and men aren't the most enlightened critics where women are concerned. All that will have to be re-written by qualified feminine experts some day' (*HW*, pp. 62–3). The book uses the form of the ghost story to suggest the sexual revolution which Isbel herself fails to achieve on a personal level: 'henceforward', she claims, 'men are going to exist for us, not we for them' (*HW*, p. 76); but that, clearly, is a long way in the future. In the meantime, there is only the distorted glimpse of liberation, a life haunted by dreams of possibility.

This is, of course, not the only modern work of the supernatural in which Gothic is made over again into the service of real social commentary, but it is one of the most wholehearted; the remarkable thing, perhaps, is that the apparatus of haunted houses, mysterious staircases and distant music can still be made to say anything at all. During the last eighty years, although Gothic has continued to exert an influence – and indeed in many ways an increasing one – it has usually been only a partial one, with particular elements of the tradition being adapted to new purposes, as we shall see later; what is rare about *The Haunted Woman* is that, despite the draining of content which we have seen particularly in Conan Doyle and M. R. James, the entire ageing skeleton can still be made to dance. The other major arena in which, apparently, a similar feat can still be achieved is that of a different medium altogther, film; and it is to film that we must now turn to investigate further transmutations of Gothic imagery and themes.

Notes and references

1. See below, pp. 119–44.
2. All the Conan Doyle stories discussed can be found in *The Conan Doyle Stories* (London, 1929), pp. 447–876.
3. **Pierre Nordon**, *Conan Doyle*, trans. Frances Partridge (London, 1966), p. 79.
4. **Ronald Pearsall**, *Conan Doyle: A Biographical Solution* (London, 1977), p. 134.
5. All the Wells stories discussed can be found in **H. G. Wells**, *The Complete Short Stories* (London, 1927).
6. **Algernon Blackwood**, *The Insanity of Jones and Other Tales* (Harmondsworth, Middx., 1966), p. 336; subsequent references are to *IJ*.
7. **Blackwood**, *Tales of the Uncanny and Supernatural* (London and New York, 1962), p. 212; subsequent references are to *TUS*. Where a date is given in the text for

an individual story, this refers to its first inclusion in a volume of Blackwood's; where not, the story is most conveniently available in *IJ* or *TUS*.

8. All the James stories discussed can be found in M. R. James, *The Collected Ghost Stories* (London, 1931).

9. **David Lindsay**, *The Haunted Woman* (London, 1922), p. 179; subsequent references are to *HW*.

CHAPTER 5

Gothic in the horror film 1930–1980

The international history of the horror film to 1980 may be seen in three principal phases: the German masterpieces of the silent era; the developments in America between 1930 and the late 1950s; and the largely British-centred product of the 1960s and 1970s. In this chapter, I want, as with the fiction, to restrict myself to American and British work, but it is worth noting from the outset that behind all subsequent horror films there lurks, in a curiously resonant parallel with eighteenth-century Gothic fiction, a German presence. It manifests itself in theme, in content, in a specific set of photographic styles, indeed in an entire *mise en scène* which runs from the range of Universal Studios films of 1931 and 1932 to the Hammer cycle of the 1960s. The horror film thus has a complexly twisted provenance: out, originally, of a body of legendry which owes much to real or fake German and central European sources and 'Transylvanian' settings, via English nineteenth-century fictional developments, but then mediated again through the directorial styles of the great German directors, Wegener, Wiene, Murnau and Lang.

This is by no means to assume that all horrifying films are Gothic; but at the same time it is true that the fundamentally formulaic model which is conventionally known as 'the horror film' has indeed many Gothic aspects. In order to investigate these, I intend to examine briefly six different areas of the horror film, treating each through one or two specific examples. First, there are the 1930s American films, mostly out of Universal Studios, mostly again making use of previously existent horror plots, and relying heavily on both the directorial talents of such men as Tod Browning and James Whale, and even more on the acting presence of Boris Karloff and Bela Lugosi, still the forgers of the most culturally prominent images of Frankenstein's monster and Dracula respectively. A period of comparative infertility, relieved only by the undoubted but minor-key successes of the Lewton/Tourneur production team, is followed by an upsurge in the 1950s, typically of horror films with a science-fiction bias and an all too obvious political content; here a succession of extended images emerges in which are encoded arguments about the Cold War, about fears of invasion from the East, and about the dangers of technologisation. The 1960s are marked by two rather divergent developments: the emergence, in America, of Roger Corman as a horror *auteur* of enormous significance, more specifically identified as a major reinterpreter of Poe; and in England the prominence of Hammer Studios, which give rise to a whole series of further reinterpretations of the classic myths, and also to a less well-known but equally important series of examinations of psychopathology (*Taste of Fear* (1960), *Maniac* (1962), *Paranoiac* (1963), *Fanatic* (1965), *The Anniversary* (1967)). Historically alongside the work of Corman and Hammer there runs a rather different emergent tradition, superficially very much outside the Gothic formulae and represented in the work of such diverse directors as Hitchcock, Polanski and Michael Powell: films which might be described as revelations of the terror of everyday life, which prise apart the bland surfaces of common interaction to disclose the anxieties and aggressions which lie beneath. And finally we have the 1970s and the coming of a new range of films, of which one of the most prominent examples is *The Exorcist*, films which have been widely condemned as exploitative, yet which, if we are to follow through any argument about the social significance of the forms of terror, must be considered in a more detailed way.

In one sense at least the horror film is very similar to eighteenth-century Gothic fiction, in that, while being a popular form, it demonstrates on closer inspection both a surprisingly high level of erudition, actual on the part of its makers and also imputed to its audience, and also a very high level of technical virtuosity. Films like *Freaks* (1932), *Invasion of the Body Snatchers* (1956), *The Masque of the Red Death* (1964), the Hammer *Dracula* (1958), and *Peeping Tom* (1960) (to name only one film from each of the first five categories listed above) all demonstrate in different ways both the amount of technical care and ingenuity lavished on horror films and also the degree of psychological sophistication possessed by many of their makers. In fact, it would be fair to say that the whole development of the horror film is closely interlocked with the rather belated spread and reception of Freudian theory.

The prolificness of horror films in the years 1931 to 1933 is extraordinary; these two years saw the appearance not only of Browning's *Dracula* and Whale's *Frankenstein*, but also of Rouben Mamoulian's splendid version of *Dr Jekyll and Mr Hyde* (to date the most frequently filmed of Gothic fictions); Schoedsack and Pichel's *The Most Dangerous Game*; Erle C. Kenton's *Island of Lost Souls*; Victor Halperin's *White Zombie*; Karl Freund's *The Mummy*; and of course *King Kong*, a key twentieth-century myth, also directed by Schoedsack and Pichel. One obvious feature which connects many of these films is their dependence on Gothic literary sources; but there are other, more important aspects which justify defining them as a sub-genre. First, there is the genuine complexity of their attitudes towards the monstrous. In *Frankenstein* and *King Kong*, of course, we are now all too familiar with the ambiguous emotional effects which these early directors proved so unexpectedly adept at producing; but there are also strong veins of unexpected sympathy running through the Mamoulian *Jekyll and Hyde*, largely because of the sensitive playing of Fredric March, through *The Most Dangerous Game*, a 'tightly constructed, literate horror film'[1] which brings to the screen a fresh and important image of the displaced, anachronistic and bloodthirsty aristocrat, and through *White Zombie*, with its languorous style and sharpness of social perception.

Allied with this is the photographic inventivenes of the films. Real or unreal as the settings may supposedly be, they are linked by an air of doom, whether it be evidenced in the first graveyard sequence of *Frankenstein* or in the endless revolution of the zombie-powered mill-wheel in *White Zombie*. And the monsters themselves, whatever form they may take, are allowed the same grace, are allowed frequently a shadowiness, a half-seen quality which effectively permits a space for the complex interplay of audience emotions. To connect the thematic and the technical, one might perhaps say that what the 1930s horror films essentially possessed was a rare seriousness, of tone and feeling; their directors were content to be unrushed, to allow space and time for their conceptions to emerge on the screen, and in doing so they managed to create a series of works which possessed a genuinely tragic quality, at least insofar as they realised a sense of powerful forces, forces of destiny, operative in human life.

Whale's *Frankenstein* is, in fact, not one of the more consistently tactful of these films, and this is largely reflective of the conflict within the film between fidelity to the original story and an attempt, interesting in its details, at updating. The laboratory in which Frankenstein's experiments take place, for instance, is an odd blend of early nineteenth-century scientific paraphernalia and more advanced apparatus based on electricity. There is also the much criticised story change which resulted in the monster being given a madman's brain. Whale, a remarkably sophisticated director, was clearly attempting to suggest further ways, technical and psychological, in which the Frankenstein myth might be explored and recast for our times, and to a considerable extent he succeeded. If part of the essence of the Gothic is an insistence that it is possible to take melodramatic forms and conduct within them a complex and contemporary psychological argument, then Whale's *Frankenstein* is indeed a Gothic film at a deeper level than merely in terms of the portrayal of settings.

Much of the complexity of Mary Shelley's text remains present in the film. The obsessional nature of Frankenstein's motives, the monster's thwarted groping towards understanding, the emphasis on the contradiction between 'correct' family life and isolation, the arguments about natural evil, all persist in Whale's hands; and what is improved above all else in the film, due to Karloff's participation, is the presence of the monster himself. His acting is poised precisely on the edge of the monstrous, never degenerating into the clodhopping vulgarity with which he is sometimes parodied; the creature may have a preternaturally beetling brow, but beneath it is a face capable of a sensitive and moving range of expressions; the figure itself may initially appear mechanical and robot-like, but Karloff's sense of movement endows it with an uncanny fluidity which keeps our doubts about what is and what is not human ever open. Mary Shelley's over-compensatory denunciations of her creation are absent, which renders the scenes between the monster and the uncomprehending villagers all the more poignant.

In wider terms, *Frankenstein* and its sister films represent a strange collection of social and cultural forces. Schoedsack and Pichel made the social point apparent in the plot of *King Kong*, with its film director out to provide bread and circuses for the masses of the Depression; yet these films, like the Gothic novels, are not mere pot-boilers, and for an exactly identical reason: because they spring not only from social roots but also from the logic of internal technical development within culture. They are the first interesting product of the sound revolution, and of the accompanying situation in which film therefore stood poised on the brink of becoming a popular medium. And just as the expansion of the reading-public in the late eighteenth century led to a series of experiments in popular fiction, so the potential expansion of the film-watching public in the late 1920s generated a field in which directors could remain imbued with the excitement of the medium while attempting to provide popular filmic fare.

Kenton's *Island of Lost Souls*, a film version of *The Island of Dr Moreau*, is another example of this. Here, in fact, directorial intention considerably outstripped public response: the theme of miscegenation was pushed out into the open and personified in the form of an all too seductive panther-woman, and the result was outrage. Yet in terms of actual violence, *Island of Lost Souls*, like almost all the horror films of the early 1930s, was extremely reticent; it is greatly to the credit of both Whale and Kenton, in these particular films, that they used the possibilities of visualisation not to emphasise lurid situations but for quite a contrary purpose: to illumine further the conflicts of aspiration and doom which are at the heart of the Gothic.

For Moreau, as played by Charles Laughton, is just as complex a monster as Frankenstein or his creation. He is a splendid mixture of the diabolical and the gentlemanly, his whole being seemingly pivoted around the ambivalent connotations of his whip: is this a matter of life, death and pain, or merely, like hunting, another way for the bored upper classes to pass the time? Laughton manages to oscillate between venom and joviality in a way which at times surpasses the potential of the tale itself, strongly assisted by the settings, encapsulations of colonialism. One of the finer points of both *Island of Lost Souls* and *Frankenstein*, in fact, is a use of shadow, inherited from the German cinema, which serves as a direct intensification of the Gothic mood: both Moreau and the monster, in crucial scenes, are accompanied by a larger-than-life-size shadow which is a direct visual equivalent of both the transcendence of human life which they variously represent and the doom which consequently awaits them.

To concentrate on directors and production company styles in the early horror film is, of course, to beg an obvious question: clearly many of the films were vehicles for particular stars. Lugosi, at the high point of his career, was receiving as much fan-mail as any more conventional male romantic lead, and the whole history of the horror film, like the history of the Gothic novel, can be read as the evolution of a series of types of the hero/villain. *Frankenstein* and *Island of Lost Souls*, like many other horror films then and since, end in the same way (with some literary justification in the latter case, precious little in the former): with an uprising of the repressed

– angry villagers or beast-men – and the ritual purgation of the disordering element, but without leaving the audience feeling that all the relevant moral issues have thereby been solved. It is easy to scorn the horror-film convention whereby the hero/villain lives to fight another day and reappears in endless sequels, and clearly this device has some of its roots in the box-office, but it also reflects a genuine difficulty, native to the Gothic, with allaying the fears which these powerful figures represent. In the context of the long series of *Frankenstein* and *Dracula* films which have followed the originals, the problem of the undead gains an added dimension.

One of the most depressing features in the evolution of the horror film is the way in which, after the Second World War, these complexities of response seemed to come for a time to be systematically eliminated from the genre. The typical product of the 1950s lies on the edge of horror and science fiction: it confronts order with disruption in a simplistic fashion, usually by allowing some kind of generalised human society to stand as unquestioned and by throwing against it an alien being or species which never stands a chance. The beast may come from the stars or from 20,000 fathoms, from Mars or from beneath the earth, from the moon, Venus, the ocean floor or the black lagoon (*Flying Disc Men from Mars* (1950), *Radar Men from the Moon* (1952), *War of the Worlds* (1952), *The Beast from 20,000 Fathoms* (1953), *It Came from Outer Space* (1953), *Invaders from Mars* (1953), *Killers from Space* (1953), *Creature from the Black Lagoon* (1954), *The Monster from the Ocean Floor* (1954), to name but a few), but wherever it comes from generally it might as well not have bothered: the moral virtues of the clean-cut American hero, sometimes backed up by clean-cut American tanks and guided missiles, prove far too strong – or unattractive – for it to withstand. It is easy to read in this phenomenon a new American defensiveness, a Cold War paranoia, a continual acting-out of physical, mental or moral invasion and of strategies for resistance. Yet even here, in a most unpromising field, there were considerable achievements.

Perhaps the most imposing still remains Don Siegel's *Invasion of the Body Snatchers*, with its solid evocation of small-town America and its uncompromising insistence on vulnerability. Here there is no question of a direct battle between hero and invaders; the invaders have come not to wipe out the human race but to replace it with exact duplicates, and the hero's problem is to convince anyone that this is happening before the authorities themselves are taken over. The last scene of all, where his story is finally beginning to be believed, is rather a letdown; but that immediately preceding, in which, fleeing from the invaders, he arrives at a busy highway and wastes several minutes in a hysterical attempt to persuade someone to stop and take notice before being knocked down, has a nightmare power.

The *mise en scène* of films like *Invasion of the Body Snatchers* is a very long way from the 1930s films: settings are contemporary and normative to the point of deliberate banality, photography is mostly clear and flat, although Siegel in this respect produces a more inventive film than most. The great practical virtue of his plot-line, of course, is that he is able to raise the issue of the human and the non-human without having to call on a special-effects department: the only way of telling the supplanters from the supplanted is by their lack of emotion, which is a matter for acting skill rather than heavy machinery. This stylistic naturalism, however, becomes in Siegel's hands, an appropriate way of exploring contemporary social anxieties, not about the inability to understand but about the inability to communicate the understanding which has been forced upon one.

Yet in the end, *Invasion of the Body Snatchers* remains a conservative film. The invaders represent a possible order based on pure reason, the excision of the messiness of emotion, and there is no doubt that this alternative is held by the director in low esteem, but the psychological conflict is displaced: instead of being between ego and id, between reason and the uncontrolled, it is merely between two different kinds of conventionality. The hero and his fiancée – before she is herself taken over – do not represent any form of emotional life dominant enough to engage us in real choices: the change which would be involved were they to succumb would not, we feel, be particularly large anyway. Yet the film manages to haunt, to linger in the mind: largely because of the sense of a closing circle which it powerfully conveys, the sense of impending isolation against which succumbing to the 'easeful death' which the invaders promise gains a certain concreteness.

A film on which it is worth concentrating more closely is the rather later *Night of the Living Dead* (1968), directed on a limited budget by George Romero and played by amateur actors. It might seem historically out of place to consider it at this point, but the film is a self-conscious comment on and extension of the 1950s mode, marking a circling back from science-fiction stereotypes into a Gothicism of setting and authorial attitude. Huss and Ross summarise it as 'underground cult film on zombies, now emerging above ground',[2] which is either a very unselfconscious or a very witty summary, its theme being precisely the return of the dead from their graves. Its immense yet offbeat popularity is certainly in need of explanation: made by a television crew, shot in unfashionable black-and-white and with acting which is patchy at best, it yet became one of the most frequently shown films on the university and film society circuit.

Basically, it works through a series of inversions, which can only be properly understood by an audience which already has a certain familiarity with the assumptions both of the zombie film and of 1950s science fiction. The plot is initially conventional: a 'representative' group of Americans gets holed up in an isolated house, and in attempting to defend it against the returning dead go through the usual gamut of hysteria, courage and leadership struggles. Precisely those clean-cut kids, however, whom one naturally expects to survive get rather satisfyingly killed. Several of the group reveal themselves to be so generally appalling that one starts to want the living dead to get on with the job. And the one apparent survivor, a competent black who manages to outlast the siege, eventually emerges from the house in such a state of exhaustion and personal disappointment that he is instantly gunned down by the sheriff's men as one of the walking dead.

Almost all zombie films reflect fears about de-individuation. In *Night of the Living Dead*, it is highly unclear where the state of zombiedom begins and ends: some of the inhabitants of the house are such withered creatures of convention that one supposes absorption into this inverted afterlife would make little difference. Romero takes advantage of the besieged house to conduct a very similar exploration to that which takes place in almost all 1970s disaster movies: an investigation into what happens to people under the dual stress of external danger and internal claustrophobia. But where disaster movies typically emerge with a Fascist answer (strong leadership, the dispensability of the weak), Romero's attitude is very different: danger usually brings out not the best but the worst in people, and where it does bring out the best, that best is generally unrecognisable to the world outside. One is reminded forcibly of the ending of *Lord of the Flies*, where matters which have seemed of vital importance are suddenly dwarfed by the reappearance of adult reality.

One of the more disturbing features of *Night of the Living Dead* is that Romero is content to reside neither within the expressionism of the 1930s nor in the naturalism of the 1950s, but moves between one and the other: the house is depressingly, flatly real and unexciting, but some of the shots of the slowly but inexorably approaching zombies are 'atmospheric' almost to the point of parody. The effect of this appears to be to deprive the viewer of a consistent perspective, which is perhaps one source of the film's power. A problem with it is that, because of the film's self-consciousness, any attempt at a discussion of it makes it sound as though parody is indeed an important element; yet this is very far from the actual effect of the film, which is intensely serious. It seems, in fact, almost like the product of a mood of exasperation: as if the people involved with making it had finally become irritated with the horror film's unwillingness to speak its name, to confess explicitly its psychological and social emphases, and had set about trying to rectify the situation by producing a film which *proved* that apparently melodramatic and outworn apparatus could still be profoundly disturbing, and not only at the sensory level.

Returning to the late 1950s, the commercial initiative in horror films passed decisively to Britain with the release in 1957 of Hammer Studios' *Curse of Frankenstein*. I want for the moment, however, to remain with America, and with the horror films of Roger Corman. It should be stressed that these are only a small and transient part of his whole output: the most prolific director/producer in the cinema of these decades, Corman turned his hand to horror most consistently between 1960 and 1964, very possibly precisely as a response to Hammer's demonstration of the further commercial possibilities of the field. During these years he made a cycle of seven films (*The House of Usher* (1960), *The Pit and the Pendulum* (1961), *The Premature Burial* (1961), *Tales of Terror* (1962), *The Haunted Palace* (1963), *The Masque of the Red Death* (1964), *The Tomb of Ligeia* (1964)), which are usually referred to, not without reservations, as the Poe cycle. The reservations are important in two specific ways: although in each of the films Corman adapts elements of Poe's stories (except in *The Haunted Palace*, which is in fact based on Lovecraft's *Case of Charles Dexter Ward* (1927–8)) he is forced, by the brevity of the stories themselves and by audience assumptions regarding narrative film, to add much to them, and he also makes little attempt, except in *The Tomb of Ligeia*, to invoke the drowsy, opiated tone of Poe. To criticise Corman as an exploiter of Poe seems to be beside the point: Corman's cycle is surely very much a self-consistent set of horror films, with their own detailed and impressive *mise en scène*, within which elements of Poe are embedded.

What the films show is that Corman, as of himself, has a thoroughly distinctive Gothic vision. The intricate passageways, the creaking tombs, the wry but gleeful ironies of dialogue have more in common with Matthew Lewis than with Poe; indeed, Corman is probably the only contemporary director who could satisfactorily film *The Monk*. The films are a set of variations on a group of essential elements, not necessarily all present in any one film: a bravura use of colour and décor; a masterful if repetitive evocation of suspense; the inimitable acting of Vincent Price, which slides from high tragedy to high camp with no evident disruption of tone – perhaps Jacobean would be the best term for Price's style; a brilliant use of dream inserts; and an insistence on not simplifying or resolving the battle between good and evil which the films dramatise.

The two best films in the cycle are the last two, partly because Corman had at last a reasonable budget available, partly too because they contain Price's most extraordinary performances. With *The Masque of the Red Death*, it must have been apparent from the outset that there was not a great deal Corman could do within the bounds of the story, exiguous as it is: he bolsters it up with an insert adaptation of 'Hop-Frog', but even so the result bears little relation to Poe's world. What it does take from Poe, and put to excellent use, is the décor of Prospero's castle, with its single-colour rooms opening into each other in vistas of breathtaking magnificence. The Poe story, however, is essentially in a monotone, and this is a source of its power: the situation is imbued with doom from the outset, with Prospero's attempt to resist the Red Death by shutting himself and his friends in his castle and indulging in narcotic revelry resembling a Gothic act of divine defiance, and thus necessarily entailing its own defeat. Corman's film is far more various: the lusts and appetites of Prospero's curious 'court' and of Prospero himself are foregrounded, and suspense is created by Corman's ability precisely to enable his audience to forget the inevitable outcome for considerable periods of time. The ending has been much criticised: after the dance is finished, and Price has encountered a satisfactorily bloody death, the Red Death figure is seen meeting with other hooded figures and conferring with them on the success of their operation. It may be that the realisation of this scene is crude, but the purpose is important: first as a simple parody of the happy ending, but second as a demonstration of the smallness of the world in which we have just been absorbed. Like Chinese boxes, the ending of the film shows the tale of Prospero's doom only to have been one among others, and we are left still having to adumbrate a further level: in whose service do these various Deaths operate?

In a sense, it is an unusual role for Price: whereas he is usually constrained to act the part of a doom-laden and enfeebled aristocrat, here he is permitted the full range of Promethean defiance – again, most unlike any of Poe's more fully realised characters, but with a very close relation to Schedoni, Melmoth and those other more lusty and powerful rejecters of divine limitation. His role in *The Tomb of Ligeia* is more typical: in this film the elements of Poe are at their strongest in narrative terms, although again there is a vitality, even in some cases an ordinariness, to the characterisation which belies Poe's dream-tones even while giving added filmic bite to the intrusion of the supernatural into a world which at least has one or two features in common with our own. As in the Corman *House of Usher*, Price chooses to emphasise febrility (most notoriously by wearing dark glasses almost throughout), and admirably complements Corman's scenery of decaying grandeur.

The cycle gained a popularity similar in kind to that of Romero's film: critics were at best lukewarm, pointing reasonably to a *grand guignol* quality which inevitably lapsed into self-parody, yet there is clearly something about the films which transcends this danger. It could be hypothesised that their appeal may lie in their reflection of a crumbling adult world, certainly a possible way to appeal to a predominantly youthful audience.[3] It would seem, though, that perhaps the matter is more complex than this: certainly the conflagrations which terminate several of the films are satisfying in these terms, but they would not be so were it not for the loving care with which Corman chooses to portray the world which is passing. As with the Gothic, there are elements here of both attraction and repulsion. What is totally absent from the films is any kind of bourgeois moralism: usually one of the strongest audience reactions comes from the portrayal of the 'hero' in *House of Usher*, who is indeed a bourgeois character, trying to impose a schema of rationalism on the events with which he is confronted; naturally he fails at every turn, much to the intended and actual delight of viewers. In this sense the Corman cycle plays out yet again the problem of the bourgeoisie's relations with the aristocracy, and in doing so demonstrates the extraordinary fact that audiences in the 1960s and 1970s have not lost their taste for watching yet again a struggle which has been historically superseded for 150 years.

And this is perhaps the most curious fact about Corman's work – and, as we shall see, about the success of Hammer Studios: that both sub-genres demonstrate the extent to which our images of terror have become embedded in the endless recasting of a specific historical period. This is not to say that Corman's films possess intricate period accuracy, but that they accurately reflect what appears to be a received notion of period, and one which still occasions interest and indeed considerable excitement. In this sense, Corman works not so much *from* Poe as alongside him: both men express a fascination with the original Gothic, and in both cases it is mediated through a deliberate vulgarisation, which is presumably in itself a significant element of an attempt to deal with historical problems. To go further than this would be difficult without an extended discussion of the concept of 'camp';[4] but at least one can say that camp is a form of irony, and that Corman's films work through a dialectic of response. That is to say, they appear to be appealing to the terrible, and to a certain extent they are; but they are also appealing to shared assumptions about the limitations of terror, and thus are self-ironising in a way which earlier Gothic films were not.

Corman's films – and Price's acting – demand audience collusion, and it is in this structural sense, and not merely because of the extent of their appeal, that they can most fairly be called 'cult' films. They permit their audience to acknowledge its own intelligence and reasonableness before deliberately abandoning it. It has often been said that only a secure *avant-garde* can afford seriously to affront or abandon good taste, and certainly Corman's films afford intellectual relief – *not* escape – of a kind which cannot be far distant from the excitement ladies in the late eighteenth century derived from observing the wickedness of an Ambrosio. Corman's cinema is neither realist nor psychological: it is, in a sense, a cinema of pure formalism, and only *because* it is so reliant on fixed form can it afford the gross excesses of colour and dialogue which typify it.

Although Corman's work and the horror films, directed mostly by Terence Fisher and made by Hammer have often, quite reasonably, been contrasted, nonetheless there are similarities. The mingled audience response of fear and laughter which greets Dracula's fifteenth resurrection is the sure mark of 'cult', of a situation in which the rules are clearly known, and because they are, the filmmaker is free to move knowingly between the many variations possible on a theme. Yet in the long run what seems to be most remarkable about Hammer's films is, as David Pirie points out in *A Heritage of Horror*, their place in specifically British cultural life:

> It certainly seems to be arguable on commercial, historical and artistic grounds that the horror genre, as it has been developed in this country by Hammer and its rivals, remains the only staple cinematic myth which Britain can properly claim as its own, and which relates to it in the same way as the western does to America. . . . The rather striking truth is that in international commercial terms, the British cinema . . . has effectively and effortlessly dominated the 'horror' market over a period of almost twenty years with a series of films which, whatever their faults, are in no way imitative of American or European models but derive in general from literary sources.[5]

The reason for this, clearly, lies in the 'British-ness' of the sources with which the Hammer films deal; their international success, real as it undoubtedly is, would only have been possible under conditions where Hammer found itself – unexpectedly – able to reach a large home market with a product which, in 1957, already seemed to American film companies outmoded and preposterous.

A point from which to begin in trying to establish the nature of Hammer's contribution to the development of the horror film is that, just as it is deceptive to consider the Corman horror cycle as remakes of Poe, so it is deceptive to regard Hammer as indulging in remakes of American 1930s horror cinema. The roots of Hammer's treatment of the Frankenstein and Dracula myths, like the roots of Corman's films, lie not in nineteenth- or twentieth-century American adaptations of the Gothic, but more directly in the Gothic itself considered from the vantage-point of the 1960s. That is to say that Hammer horror is, again like Corman's, self-ironising; but this is only a similarity of means, and the ends of Corman and Fisher are radically different. Hammer's films do not on the whole embark on the tricky balancing of good and evil which Corman attempts, and nor do they strive so cheerfully to establish their own fictionality. Fisher is a moralistic director, not in any particularly strong sense, but in the simplicity of his demarcations between good and evil and in the way in which it is assumed that the moralism in some sense justifies the depiction of terror. It is not without symbolic significance that where Corman turned to the amoral nightmares of Poe, Hammer began its venture into horror with a version of *Frankenstein* which took with great seriousness many of Mary Shelley's more erudite arguments, or that in film after film they stress the nature/artifice contradiction which so beset a writer like Radcliffe.

When *The Curse of Frankenstein* first appeared, it was rapidly condemned on the grounds of explicit sadism, a criticism which seems to us now rather surprising, for the kinds of ritualised violence which occur in Hammer films seem very much bounded by assumptions of the form. What has been more shocking in Hammer films over their latter years has been the boldness and explicitness with which successive directors have dwelt upon the connections between violence and sexuality. Undoubtedly commercial pressures are partly responsible for this, but there again in the context of the Gothic tradition as we have tried to outline it, it seems hardly reprehensible for the film to bring into the open aspects of texts which are already present; and in fact one of the consequences of Fisher's moralism is that the fatal attractiveness of evil is inevitably undermined in all his films by his insistence on punishing the seductive. One can fairly see the Frankenstein cycle as a set of explorations of various sides of the multifaceted Frankenstein myth, informed by no little intelligence and discrimination. In *The Curse of Frankenstein*, for instance, the character of Frankenstein himself is deliberately altered in order to bring him more into line with the more charismatic Gothic heroes, with the consequence that the Faustianism of the original is brought closer to the surface; also he is considerably foregrounded at the expense of the monster, which provides opportunities for investigation of the psychological significance of the creator himself. In *The Revenge of Frankenstein* (1957), the scientist's character becomes more complex again, as Fisher shows him simultaneously capable of cruelty and disinterested kindness, and brings him into close proximity with the stereotype of the victimised pioneer. While *The Horror of Frankenstein* (1970), directed not by Fisher but by Jimmy Sangster, demonstrates Hammer's ability to parody itself: the very fact that the parody is far from successful underlines the complexity of approach which lies behind the better films, despite their apparent simplicity of appeal.

But clearly it is in the context of their Dracula films that Hammer has moved furthest into the realm of horror as sexual pathology. This is partly a question of character presentation: while Lugosi was well equipped to emphasise the shadowy foreignness and supernatural menace of the Dracula figure, he never made it quite clear what it was that his victims found so fatally attractive in a fate worse than death. Christopher Lee, on the other hand, has all the makings of an acceptable alternative to conventional life and sexuality: he has not only power but seductiveness, plausibility and a glint of knowing humour. Where Lugosi's posturings often seemed directed principally at the audience, and his films therefore suffered from a lack of internal psychological coherence, Lee's mesmeric effect on his usually nubile victims is readily appreciable as rooted in the obliging attractiveness of *noblesse*.

The strength of Hammer's Dracula films lies in an odd closeness to Stoker's text: not usually in terms of plot, but then *Dracula* was hardly remarkable for plot in the first place, but for a decadent poetic treatment of ancient legendry. The Hammer Draculas have a sense of historical depth: as in the Corman films, the fact that we as audience are assumed to be already fully conversant with the details of the legends frees the various directors Hammer have employed – Fisher being here again the most important – to weave free-floating poems of colour and allusion around the basic elements. In the later years, this took directions which seem entirely justifiable in terms both of passages from Stoker and also of other, later, literary treatments of vampirism: the transference of vampiric powers back from male to female, and the appearance of elements of both male and female homosexuality within the narrative. Stoker's *Dracula* becomes rightly blended with LeFanu's 'Carmilla' (1872) and Stevenson's sultry 'Ollala' (1886) in a hypnotic anthology of perversions. That all the vampires, male and female, in Hammer's films are sexually attractive, sometimes to the point of caricature, recalls precisely scenes in Stoker like that of the three female vampires, all long-drawn hisses and blood-red lips: that the breast into which the stake is plunged is invariably beauteous only brings out one of the principal arguments behind vampire fiction, that only for those who are in unfortunate possession of sexual attractions and urges which they are personally or socially incapable of expressing is vampirism a significant psychological danger.

Hammer's films are undoubtedly of variable quality, and they have committed some genuine disasters; nonetheless, the Frankenstein and Dracula cycles constitute a real attempt to accept, and even strengthen, the period bases of the literature while bringing out psychological implications in a way which has only more recently become permissible. Their other claim to fame may possibly come to rest on their series of psychological thrillers, from *Taste of Fear* on, in which various everyday psychopathologies are explored: here Hammer works the other way round, by taking precisely the contemporary and demonstrating within it the continuing presence of archaic fears and lusts. Both modes are varieties of melodrama, and both juxtapose past and present in such a way as to question the historical and social limits of reason.

With respect to this latter sub-genre, however, Hammer has neither the psychological sophistication nor the directorial talent to

rival the masters whom it attempts to imitate, and here I want
to glance briefly at three films which fall into the general field of
terror pathology: Alfred Hitchcock's *Psycho* (1960), Michael Powell's
Peeping Tom (1960) and Roman Polanski's *Repulsion* (1965). They
are all much written about, and I have no intention here of attempting any kind of detailed analysis: rather I want to bring out what
seems to me one important feature of them in relation to other
horror material, namely their relation to Gothic motifs and attitudes.
To start from simple premises: each of the three films is a study in
paranoia. Each of them posits a correlation between paranoia and
a thwarting in the relation between the ordered and the chaotic.
Each of them, in the search for a visual equivalent for a psychological state, finds a setting which relates closely to traditional imagery:
in *Psycho*, the house, with its cellars and mysterious doors, is pure
American Gothic, as Hitchcock of course intended; in *Peeping Tom*,
the film-processing laboratory which is a substitute for the hero's
homelessness, shot as it is in half-tones and impossible as it is
to discern its physical limits, is the laboratory of generations of
Frankensteins, in which the endless attempt is continued to discern
the secrets of (the hero's own) creation; Catherine Deneuve's apartment in *Repulsion*, albeit outwardly contemporary, is nonetheless
capable at times of sprouting supernatural apparitions worthy of the
direst secrets of Udolpho.

One of the most remarkable features of *Psycho* is Hitchcock's
determination and ability to involve the audience in complex ways
with the unfolding of the plot. The obvious example is the shower
murder of Janet Leigh, which requires us to find a whole new way
of engaging with what is left of the film, a moment which follows
on from our unwelcome realisation that we are being required to
participate in Norman Bates's unpleasant voyeurism. If one of the
principal strengths of Gothic fiction was its undermining of simple
processes of identification, its development of the intense ambiguities of persecution, then it is a strength which *Psycho* shares. The
most remarkable feature in this respect is the ending: since by then
we are being invited to take simultaneously two opposite views of
the putative inhabitant of Norman's body, we are effectively prevented from absolute moral resolution. We have, as Robin Wood
comments, been led into a complicity with Norman, and with the
film itself;[6] we are provided with no way out of the maze in which
this has trapped us. And the way in which Hitchcock achieves this
manipulation is shameless: subtle though he is in technical terms –
and the stabbing of Leigh is a supreme example of photographic

virtuosity and even reticence – in other ways his style is pure bravura. He is quite unashamed of coincidence; he is addicted to nasty jokes (for example in the film, there is the revelation of Mummy's 'mummy', and his general practical-joker reputation is always a necessary adjunct to reading the films); and he is overjoyed by the possibilities of sexual titillation of his audience, as in the entire treatment of Leigh's body. A film which can be referred to as 'balancing us, even at its most horrifying, on the knife-edge where there is almost no distinction between a laugh and a scream'[7] is once again elaborating the mixture of seriousness and grotesquerie which has always been a hallmark of the Gothic: like Matthew Lewis's writing, like Vincent Price's acting, Hitchcock's directing is to do with virtuoso spectacle. Both camerawork and acting are theatrical; the music which accompanies *Psycho* would not be out of place in a Victorian melodrama.

Psycho is not precisely a study of an obsession: it is an investigation of what effect viewing the outcome of an obsession has on an audience. It has often been remarked that the interpretation which the psychiatrist offers at the end is inadequate, and this is perfectly true, *not* because Hitchcock wanted it to be specifically so, but because it does not matter one way or the other. Hitchcock is interested only in the fact that reasonably similar obsessions do occur, and in the possibilities which this fact affords for cinema. Here again, as in the fiction, specific concern with narrative is intertwined with a concern for exploring the limits of the medium itself: terror is the clearest and most easily examinable of audience responses to attempt to provoke, the reaction which therefore gives most satisfaction to the virtuoso director of popular films. Just, again, as with the fiction, *Psycho* is at least partly an exploration of the potential of disruption of expectations, and its horror emerges from its form as well as from its content.

Many of the same things could be said about Powell's *Peeping Tom*, except that here the director has added important extra twists to the argument by making the paranoiac hero himself a film cameraman, and by rendering as the source of his disturbance a set of previous experiences – at the hands of his sadistic father – which also involved film. This complexity makes for a highly self-reflexive film; it has by no means the same power for instant shock as Hitchcock's best work, but its central thematics are far more tightly woven. Discussion of *Psycho*, so widely regarded as the most important modern exercise in filmic terror, may well suggest that there is indeed no such thing as a 'straight' horror film, and perhaps this is true: but *Peeping Tom* certainly comes very close to it. As hinted above, it is far from free from Gothic devices but these are put to use not as irony but as density; the fact that the audience is aware of the cultural provenance of motifs such as the discovery of a murder victim in a trunk does not undermine the intensity with which we are required to confront Carl Boehm's psychosis but reinforces it, since it is precisely through the power of film that he endures his repression.

Boehm acts a photographer and amateur film-maker whose principal obsession is with photographing moments of pure terror. To facilitate this task, he has an array of specialist equipment including a tripod the front leg of which is able to snap up and pierce the throat of its victim. As the film progresses, Powell reveals more and more of the origins of Boehm's situation: in particular he shows, through clips inserted from film supposed to be in Boehm's own possession, how his father, played by Powell himself, had sought to investigate his fear responses by such devices as releasing live lizards into his bed and filming his reaction. The father is supposed to be the author of a series of works on the psychology of fear, in respect of which the son was his guinea-pig. Where the psychological interest in *Psycho* is largely spurious or at best secondary, in *Peeping Tom* it is central: Powell is tracing the genesis and operations of a psychosis. Interestingly, this seems to make his actual horrors not more convincing to the audience but less: precisely because of the absence of forced suspense or melodrama, we lack equipment with which to deal with the film, and the result is often a great deal of nervous laughter.

To say, then, that Boehm's photographic laboratory bears a relation to Frankenstein's haunts is not to say that this is a device for directly alerting the audience's assumptions; instead, it is a further indication of the kind of grotesquely distorted world in which Boehm perforce lives – in which, as we come to realise, he has been effectively placed by his dead father. Similarly, there is a Gothic complexity to the narrative structure and to the unfolding of stories within stories, films within films, but this is not a mere device but an essential way of representing the induced tortuousness of Boehm's mind. Every sudden and apparently inexplicable cut, every narrative twist, every insertion of the past replicates the false channels of action and response which have been set up in his psyche. The father's investigations into fear, into what prevents us from confronting the world directly, have produced in the son a syndrome whereby methods of evasion have been honed to a fine point (the point of the bayonet tripod) and the world has ceased to appear real except insofar as it appears on a screen or through the lens of a camera. The implications for the nature of the horror film are vast: the whole issue is raised here of the dimming of responses through overexposure, of the moral ambiguity of confronting one's own fears in real or represented form, of the effects film may have when it takes it upon itself to experiment with emotional response. Psychological concerns and the concerns of the medium are elided in a brilliant series of metaphors: after all, all Boehm is seeking in his murderous procedures is a moment of recognition, a moment when he can perceive in another (momentarily) living being the basic configuration which has been made into the basis of his own personality. Through film he seeks a repetition, confirmation and explanation of previous experience, as do we all; the fact that film for him is film of terror means only that his own previous experience has been of a suffering too intense and too unintelligible for him to get past without the aid of cultural props. Aristotle's concept of the tragic is not very different.

Andrew Sarris says of Roman Polanski's *Repulsion* that it is 'the scariest if not actually the goriest Grand Guignol since *Psycho*', but in terms of tone it is very different from either *Psycho*, with its ironic black humour, or the seriousness of *Peeping Tom*. On the one hand, it was passed by the censor on release without cuts because of professional affirmation that it constituted an important study of a psychopathic condition; on the other, as Sarris goes on to say, 'Polanski is actually interested more in the spectacle of repression released than in the psychology of the repressed female'.[8] What Polanski appears at first glance to do in the film is invite us to share in distorted perception: Catherine Deneuve's obvious delusions are presented in an identical filmic texture to the rest of the events. The delusions themselves are extensions of environment: the heroine spends most of the film locked in her flat, which gradually becomes more and more menacing as walls crack, unused doors are forced open and hands appear where no hands should be. *Repulsion* is a study less of claustrophobia than of invasion, finding a series of visual correlatives for the rape anxiety which is the main form Carol's paranoia takes.

The repertoire of effects gains novelty only from its incorporation into a contemporary location in South Kensington: otherwise, they are traditional – the beauty parlour in which Carol works appears at first sight to be some kind of torture chamber; darkened corridors yield dire experiences; the entire flat at one point expands in Carol's mind to enormous proportions in which items of furniture are lost. Horror is present here even – and particularly – in the heroine's Gothic retreat. Furthermore, Carol's problem is partly presented as one of excessive sensibility, linked with a problematic urge towards excessive cleanliness and order which turns into chaos. Carol is unable to stand contact with the gross world: the presence of her sister's boyfriend, Michael, and his belongings in the flat provoke her to fury and eventually terror. Strangely, however, her sensibility does not actually produce much sympathy on the part of director or viewer; it is mostly presented as a profoundly irritating absent-mindedness and selfishness. Carol's world is one in which other people have ceased to exist except as intrusions into her privacy; when she realises her inability to keep them out, she abandons all attempt at order, allowing the flat to degenerate into filth and chaos.

Many critics have suggested that the importance of *Repulsion* is that it allows us entrance into the heroine's own perspectives on the world, and this is partly true, but there is also a further element of directorial presence which dialectically alienates us from her. The fact that we see her *delusions* as real does not encourage us to accept the view she has of other characters or of herself. The fact that we are able to share the manifestations of her paranoia carries with it the corollary that we remain aware that the actual extent of her persecution is minimal: the attempt to indicate an explanation by tracking into her family photograph at the end is perfunctory, certainly by comparison with the genuine attempts, ironic or serious, to introduce a level of explanation in *Psycho* or *Peeping Tom*. In terms of relations of repression, Polanski's treatment of Deneuve is more sadistic than Hitchcock's treatment of Leigh: he offers us an attractive but unobtainable heroine, and then proceeds to martyr her as a ritual punishment for her purity. In this context it is significant that when Carol is finally carried from the flat, it is by Michael. It has been suggested that this, and the curious look which he gives her, reflect a possibility that she has been in love with him all along, despite her apparent revulsion, but it seems more likely that Polanski is here reasserting a characteristic treatment of women in horror literature, leaving Carol passive and broken in the arms of the male who, through doing nothing at all, has emerged once more as successful, capable and dominant.

In these three films, then, we have a range of attitudes to the possibilities of terror for outlining and underlining psychopathology: in *Psycho*, a black irony which involves characters and audience in a playing-off of moods, attitudes and interpretations; in

Peeping Tom, a flat presentation designed to engage our sympathies by a well-rounded statement of the hero's plight; in *Repulsion,* a presentation of spectacle which involves us in the director's vindictiveness towards his heroine and the qualities which she symbolises. Fundamentally, these are three different balances of the dreadful and the pleasurable, three different relations between terror and psychological well-being. It is, of course, thoroughly understandable that alongside the development of the 'traditional' horror film there should have arisen a genre more designed to cope with specifically contemporary perceptions of terror: what is harder to understand is that in the 1970s both of these forms appear to have been temporarily supplanted at least in terms of commercial success by a third form, which returns to age-old themes of satanism and possession. Rather ironically, the first important exponent of the form was Polanski himself in *Rosemary's Baby* (1968), but a more typical example is *The Exorcist* (1973), directed by William Friedkin from a book by W. P. Blatty.

As Pauline Kael says, *The Exorcist* is a Gothic work in its trappings, and not a Gothic relieved with the ironic spice of comedy, as are *Psycho* and *Rosemary's Baby* in their different ways, but a film of 'gothic seriousness' which functions 'below the conscious level'.[9] In other words, and in sharp contrast with almost all the other works we have discussed in this chapter, it is a work which professes not knowledge but ignorance, ignorance of the psychological ambivalence of the vocabulary of Gothic images. Yet this ignorance is itself fake: clearly Blatty – who actually, as writer and producer, appears to have had most say in the shape of the film – is in fact all too well aware of the manipulative potential of film, but chooses to delude us into believing in his literal-mindedness. It is doctors and psychiatrists themselves who in the film recommend that the case of twelve-year-old Regan MacNeil be referred to the exorcists; thus the audience is put in the position, not of interpreting horror symbolism as commentary on psychological disorder, but of accepting it wholesale as the outward and visible sign-system of the Devil.

On the whole, immersion in Gothic fiction and film makes one very wary of using the term 'exploitation', and it is in any case a difficult term to justify objectively in the case of a highly popular work. Any work which attempts to provide a point of view can be judged in some sense as non-exploitative, whether that point of view be regarded as good, evil, valid, invalid or criminal. What makes it possible nonetheless to call *The Exorcist* a work of exploitation is precisely that it does not have a point of view at all. It is not the case that what ought to be disturbing about the film is its apparent spurious vindication of the Catholic Church and of the real existence of the Devil; the really disturbing feature is that this is clearly a matter of no importance whatever in the film, despite Blatty's own religious affiliations. *The Exorcist* is simply a sequence of special effects, its narrative submerged during the actual viewing experience, and deliberately so. Let it not be said that there is much wrong with the effects themselves: they work extremely well for the most part, and several of the images of terror which are called upon are also quite new.

What is good in the best horror films, from Hammer to *Psycho*, is their ability to use images of terror to provoke powerful tensions between different interpretations; this is a process which *The Exorcist* sets out to short-circuit. From the first moments, we are left in no doubt whatever as to the reality of the little girl's possession. The audience is thus reduced to a nadir of passivity: it is highly significant that one of the most appalling and horrifying scenes occurs when an attempt is made at medical treatment of the girl's condition, for what this demonstrates is that the film's makers were drawing throughout upon a single language and a single level of intensity with complete disregard of the film's narrative or thematic coherence. The object-lesson which one might draw from *The Exorcist* is not about a decreasing vitality in the horror film, or about the dangers of pop religion, but about a crisis in film itself, which is well outside the scope of this book, and which rests on recognition and exploitation of the extraordinary power of film to appear to make its audiences accept assumptions which in the cold light of day appear the most arrant nonsense; this crisis, which bears upon media proliferation, will be addressed more thoroughly in Chapter Seven.

This being said, *The Exorcist* nonetheless *is* a horror film, and as such it corresponds with the most uninspired Gothic magazine fiction of the 1840s in its literal-mindedness and lack of ironic tension. What makes it remarkable is only the technical skill – and 10 million dollars – which went into its making. It would perhaps be as well, however, to conclude on a more positive note. Despite the existence of *The Exorcist* and its numerous progeny, horror film has substantially, and to a rather surprising extent, continued in the Gothic tradition of providing an image-language in which to examine social and psychological fears. The idea that we have all become too sophisticated to watch the traditional horror film has been long belied at Hammer's turnstiles: of course the *way* in which we watch them is profoundly self-conscious and complicated, but this was certainly true for most early Gothic fiction. For it is not enough to say that horror motifs have lost their bite because we no longer 'believe in' them; we have never believed in them as simply existent, but more as valuable and disturbing fictional images which gain their vitality, when they do, from the underlying truth which they represent.

Notes and references

1. **Carlos Clarens**, *Horror Movies* (London, 1968), p. 123.
2. *Focus on the Horror Film*, ed. Roy Huss and T. J. Ross (Englewood Cliffs, N.J., 1972), p. 12.
3. See Clarens, p. 185.
4. The most interesting arguments are those in **Susan Sontag**, *Against Interpretation and Other Essays* (New York and Toronto, 1966), pp. 275–92.
5. **David Pirie**, *A Heritage of Horror: The English Gothic Cinema 1946–1972* (London, 1973), pp. 9–10.
6. See **Robin Wood**, *Hitchcock's Films* (London, 1969), pp. 112–23.
7. **John Russell Taylor**, *Cinema Eye, Cinema Ear* (London, 1964), pp. 197–8.
8. **Andrew Sarris**, *Confessions of a Cultist: On the Cinema, 1955–1969* (New York, 1971), pp. 208, 209.
9. **Pauline Kael**, *Reeling* (London, 1977), p. 250.

CHAPTER 6
Modern perceptions of the barbaric

Mervyn Peake, 'Isak Dinesen', John Hawkes, Joyce Carol Oates, James Purdy, William Burroughs, Thomas Pynchon, J. G. Ballard, Robert Coover, Angela Carter

The kinds of material discussed in the chapters on the ghost story and the horror film may well have suggested that the term 'Gothic' is becoming outmoded or, at the very least, descriptive of only a rather marginal and limited form of the imagination. It is curious, when surveying aspects of literary reception over the years between 1960 and 1980, to find that this is not at all the case. Indeed, the term 'Gothic' is more in use now as a description of kinds of writing than it has been since the 1790s, and in a far, far broader range of contexts. As the term has lost its more precise currency, it has acquired a new and extensive range of further meanings, some of them seemingly very different from its original usages. One central meaning, however, it has retained: Gothic writing is not realistic writing. And as non-realistic and broadly expressionist forms of fiction multiply in England and America, so has the use of the term 'Gothic' has become more prevalent. A list of some of the writers with whom I shall be concerned in this chapter may give some idea of the range of fiction at stake: Mervyn Peake, John Hawkes, Joyce Carol Oates, James Purdy, Thomas Pynchon, J. G. Ballard, Angela Carter have all found works of theirs greeted with the description 'Gothic', and this is entirely aside from various less visible modes of popular fiction which still flourish under the same title.

It would be hopeless to attempt a general survey of the field; it would also be misleading, for it is only by some sort of selection that we can get at the core of meaning which Gothic has recently had. In this chapter, I want instead to take a range of books, all of which have been described for one reason or another as Gothic, and to see whether, by connecting together some of their thematic preoccupations and stylistic features, we can arrive at some kind of 'landscape' of Gothic. Many writers, and many specific works, will inevitably be omitted, and I would not want to pretend that my own choice has been objective. I have selected works on two grounds: first, because they appear to me to be important and achieved works in themselves, and second, because they appear to me to make distinctive contributions to the field of contemporary Gothic.

Centrally, Gothic writing still bears a close relation to social fears and taboos, but enormous changes have occurred both in the nature and degree of consciousness of those fears, and also in the literary self-consciousness of the medium through which they pass. In a writer like William Burroughs, Gothic interlocks with the heritage of Kafka to produce a mode of fiction about bureaucratisation, institutionalisation, the alienation of the individual from power and control over his or her own life. In J. G. Ballard, the principal subject at issue is the conflict between the individual and a dehumanised environment; the fears of scientism which we have looked at in relation to Mary Shelley and H. G. Wells recur in terms of an exploration of incompatible geometries. In John Hawkes, fantasy landscapes are used to express and comment on mental disintegration and cultural decay. And in a number of modern Gothic writers, the insane narrators of Maturin and Poe reappear in fresh guises which threaten to overspill and create a new category in the social relations of fiction: the reader who is himself or herself assumed to be insane.

Most of the works within these general parameters, however, although in many cases – Ballard, Peake, Pynchon – they derive a substantial part of their energy from popular fictional modes, are themselves esoteric: they are the products of writers who typically have cult followings, where there are 'followings' at all. At a very different cultural level, there are still whole ranges of paperback fiction available which proudly style themselves 'Gothic romances' and which, presumably, appeal partly because of this label. To read through a few of these works is to be amazed at the persistence of a form which appears to have little intrinsic competence and still less sensational appeal. I will cite more or less at random. Joan Fleming's *Too Late! Too Late! The Maiden Cried* (1975) is a slightly muddled though readable tale of a half-mad American Indian villainess and her disruptive effects on a Hampstead family. The only recognisable 'Gothic' touch is a poltergeist, which she apparently generates, but which is singularly ineffectual. Considerably less literate in style though more so in its self-conscious exploitation of the Gothic tradition is a book we have mentioned before, *The Spectral Bride*, published under the pseudonym 'Margaret Campbell', which has an unintelligible plot and a remarkably unpleasant cast of slow-moving, half-crazy characters. The punctuation and dialogue are no more appalling than the authoress's inability to handle action, but the book abounds with proud backward references. There are many gestures towards spiritualism; Lytton receives a statutory mention; there is much Radcliffean emphasis on the corrupting power of 'romances'. Yet, for all this, there is no recognisable attempt actually to invoke terror, merely an exercise in a genre where the reader is apparently expected to know a kind of verbal shorthand from the outset.

More amusing though little better is *Castle Cloud* (1949), by Joan Grant, which owes its provenance to Wilkie Collins and his worse imitators. Rich but vulgar American girl marries archaic Highland aristocrat, and has to exorcise ghosts at his castle, which involves her in 'becoming' a character from the past. Impressions of villainy are supposed to be gleaned from, for instance, the amount everybody smokes. Underneath the slushy but coherent romance lies an unfortunate amount of pretentious 'psychologising' – everybody appears to have theories about personality fragmentation and 'second sight'. But the real emphasis seems to be mostly on description of interior décor, clothing styles, fashion and so forth; there is a great deal of wish-fulfilling wealth, and hints of *droit de seigneur* to satisfy a lower-middle-class audience.

What seems to have happened here is a cultural process akin to chemical precipitation, where a tradition of past works has generated a set of forms which are exploited by fast-working, pseudonymous authors almost regardless of originality or coherence of content; but there are many more important and fertile uses of Gothic. The logical place from which to begin an analysis of such uses and influences during these decades is surely within the field of fantasy itself, and here one text stands out, not least because it clearly has as its origin a partly traumatised attempt to deal with the Second World War and with the issues of social organisation associated with it: Mervyn Peake's trilogy, *Titus Groan*, *Gormenghast* and *Titus Alone*. Here I want to look at only the first of the volumes, because *Titus Groan* (1946) seems to me a work of a considerably higher standard than its successors, and this for a very concrete reason: that Peake, as several critics have pointed out, is not at his best in the portrayal of character or action, but in the depiction of environment and the claustrophobic and stultifying effects of certain types of environment on character itself. The heart of *Titus Groan* is Gormenghast, the final Gothic castle, an edifice without historical or physical limits, symbolising in its grandeur and decay the ruins of a civilisation, and in its ritualised modes of behaviour the persistence of rules and norms unintelligible to the post-war world. As in the early Gothic, the image of the castle is multifaceted: it is the established world conceived as enclosure and bondage, it is the retreat of the mind tortured by chaos, it is the sign of the failure of human aspiration, and it is the locale for the persistence of primal fear. And like the early Gothics, Peake is obsessed by barbarity: he is both attracted by its colourful pageantry and its rigid sense of hierarchy, and appalled by its reduction of human endeavour to dust and ashes.

The most vividly memorable parts of *Titus Groan* are the great set pieces, typically the fight between Flay and Swelter, which takes place in a curious slow motion. So all-enveloping is the atmosphere of the castle that even the moments of blood and violence become elements in a ritual: the castle itself, partly through its representatives and 'masters of ceremonies' Sourdust and Barquentine, predicts and determines all the action that takes place within it; and characters move as if through a sea of tradition and conditioned responses. Even the gradual emergence of Steerpike, the proto-capitalist revolutionary whose ambition shows signs of overturning the conventions of centuries, does not break the fabric: Steerpike, like everyone else, can use for his purposes only what comes to hand, the tainted resources of the dying castle itself. The castle *is* the world; it has subsumed nature and stands as a hollow mockery of the powerless natural realm.

> Autumn returned to Gormenghast like a dark spirit re-entering its stronghold. Its breath could be felt in forgotten corridors – Gormenghast had itself *become* Autumn. Even the denizens of this fastness were its shadows.
> The crumbling castle, looking among the mists, exhaled the season, and every cold stone breathed it out. The tortured trees by the dark lake burned and dripped, and their leaves snatched by the wind were whirled in wild circles through the towers. The clouds mouldered as they lay coiled, or shifted themselves uneasily upon the stone skyfield, sending up wreaths that drifted through the turrets and swarmed up the hidden walls. (*Groan*, p. 196)

Peake's fictional techniques have sometimes, to their detriment, been viewed alongside Tolkien's, but the difference is vital: at the end of *The Lord of the Rings* (1954–5) there is a map, but there can be no map of Gormenghast. Dimensions in *Titus Groan* flicker and warp: besides, the castle which Sepulchrave, the melancholy Earl, perceives and through which he moves as man and owl is not the castle as it appears to his daughter Fuchsia, whose room is the symbol of an atavism beyond repair. In *Titus Groan*, the dead do not need to rise up against the living, for the living already inhabit a world of the dead, like sleep-walkers: their rituals and the cobwebs of Gormenghast's remoter corridors both signal their imprisonment. The mental twistings of the more enlightened characters, as they endeavour to find a place for rational apprehension in an environment which has no space for it, are the twistings of Peake's own consciousness as he wrestles with two simultaneous fears, locked in static conflict: fear of the deadly embrace of the past, and a fear of what progress might entail in a world which has accepted the possibility of total war.

In a way which is ironically akin to the methods of those writers who saw in the aftermath of the French Revolution new possibilities for the exploration of the human capacity for self-degradation, Peake holds up before his own eyes and those of his readers a hideous microcosmic image, and is himself fascinated by it. There is an intractable contradiction at the heart of Gormenghast: the castle represents a world which is terrifying because its limits cannot be known, but the rituals which govern its occupants' everyday life are even more terrifying in that they represent a kind of knowledge, but a neurotic knowledge which is condemned to circularity. What cannot be known, or admitted, is change: the whole fabric is so intricately knotted together, and has been so for so long, that the minutest tremor would precipitate landslide.

Peake's use of the Gothic is eccentric by virtue of its very traditionalism; and the same could be said of the earlier *Seven Gothic Tales* (1934) of 'Isak Dinesen'. Dinesen's claims to inclusion here stem from the fact that she wrote in English and more importantly from the unique way in which her work continued in the twentieth century to foreground the connections between Gothic and the problems of the aristocracy. There is an irony in the very use of the term 'Gothic' for her, because she is concerned not with terror but with the gentle and debilitating nostalgia which has replaced it as the aristocrat – and the artist – has become increasingly rootless and homeless, no longer sustained by a relevant system of social relations and unable to form others without sacrificing those residual notions of honour and privilege which are all that remain of the feudal idyll. For many of her characters, displaced in class, in nationality or in even more fundamental ways, the emotion of fear is, like the other emotions, only now a distant memory from a time when feeling was possible in the world. Although the stories are various in time and place, their locale is rigorously consistent in one way: in its early eighteenth-century rejection and exclusion of the world of trade and commerce. 'The Dreamers' figures a 'retired' story-teller, Mira Jama, who 'specialised in such tales as make the blood run cold. Devils, poison, treachery, torture, darkness, and lunacy: these were Mira's stock in trade'. But now, he says, the springs of his gift have dried up:

> as I have lived I have lost the capacity of fear. When you know what
> things are really like, you can make no poems about them. When
> you have had talk with ghosts and connections with the devils you are,
> in the end, more afraid of your creditors than of them; and when
> you have been made a cuckold you are no longer nervous about
> cuckoldry. I have become too familiar with life; it can no longer
> delude me into believing that one thing is much worse than the
> other. . . . How can you make others afraid when you have forgotten
> fear yourself?[1]

One side of Dinesen's talent follows directly from the high idealism of the German romantics: Hölderlin and 'Novalis' particularly spring to mind as fellow practitioners of a literary mode in which characters exist largely to embody ideas and passions, yet in which there is no trace of allegory. Her attention to minute details of form, her insistence on elegance of behaviour and writing, render her archaic, 'Gothic' in her yearning to reside amid the colour and certainty of an idealised past; but alongside this, and interwoven with it, is an entirely different tone, and a connected but surprising set of preoccupations: for Dinesen is above all a feminist writer, in the sense that for her the problems of society are filtered through a pervading and ironic female self-consciousness. That is to say, feminism in her writing is not a question of attitude or opinion: it is the very fabric out of which her tales are woven, and it is present even when the apparent opinions being expressed are – as they frequently are – deeply and committedly reactionary. The old lady in 'The Roads around Pisa' mourns over the fate of her unfortunate granddaughter:

> God alone knows what has come over the generation of women who
> have been born after the Revolution of the French and the novels of

that woman de Staël – wealth, position and a tolerant husband are not
enough to them, they want to make love as we took the Sacrament.
(*Gothic Tales*, pp. 173–4)

As we have seen so many times, a preoccupation with sexual role is
an enduring characteristic of the Gothic; but for Dinesen there
is no easy attribution of blame, little sense of persecution, rather
an amused tolerance coupled with an astringent and bracing insistence on frailty as a *necessary* human quality, a chink in the carapace
of repressive reason.

Dinesen's use of the term 'Gothic' does not really connect her
to the earlier body of fiction, but direct to the wider cultural attitudes from which it sprang: centrally, to the ambiguous attempt
either to ward off the unpredictable future by celebrating past and
passing beauty, or, failing that, to derive a sense of glory from that
very passing. There is a constant scorn for standardisation and for
those individuals who succumb to the world's pressures and
demands, and a corresponding emphasis on destiny; but there is
also an amused awareness that the Gothic to which she refers was
itself a glorious fake, doomed to fail in the recapture which it
intended. She herself points out that she is referring only to 'the
imitation of the Gothic, the Romantic age of Byron, the age of that
man – what was his name? – who built Strawberry Hill, the age
of the Gothic revival';[2] forgetting Walpole's name seems curiously
symbolic, of the shifting sands of history against which her fiction
tries to stand, a baroque fantasia which constantly threatens, like
William Beckford's Fonthill, to collapse, not at all under its own
weight – Dinesen's tales are weightless – but because of its own vaunted and defiant inappropriateness to its cultural surroundings.

Peake and Dinesen, however, are mavericks, both of them writing
to an intense personal vision – although 'intense' seems in some
way too heavy a word to apply to Dinesen's stories – and both
without very much recent influence. In America, on the other hand,
a recognisable 'grouping' of Gothic fictions has appeared and been
hailed as 'New American Gothic'.[3] There are many works which one
could consider, but here I want to limit myself to three: John Hawkes's *The Cannibal* (1962), Joyce Carol Oates's *Expensive People* (1968)
and James Purdy's *Eustace Chisholm and the Works* (1967); and it is
worth mentioning before discussing them that in each case, and
especially in that of Oates, these particular works are not necessarily
typical of the writers concerned.

The Cannibal, Hawkes's first major novel, is a very difficult book
to summarise. It is set in Germany, and moves in time between 1914

125

and 1945. The actual plot chiefly concerns an attempt to overthrow the lone American soldier who has been left in charge of the area after the war, an attempt which is successful and leaves Spitzen-on-the-Dein, the village which is Germany in microcosm, on the brink of a new awakening under the political leadership of Zizendorf, the narrator. But the plot is extremely difficult to find: it is buried under layers of baroque language, and its development is deliberately thwarted by the extraordinary way Hawkes refuses to emphasise the important and pass over the trivial. Its experimentalism, in fact, almost demands a new way of reading, since it is impossible to guess the relative importance of particular events, images, characters from the way they are described: only retrospectively can one start to untangle at least the principle obsessions of the book.

Albert Guerard comments that 'the characters are passive somnambulistic victims of the divine or diabolic process (history)',[4] thus reminding us of Peake and, in a more cerebral way, Dinesen – although, as Guerard also says, the more important immediate comparisons to make are with Faulkner, Kafka, Djuna Barnes. They have no freedom of choice, partly because they are seen as the maimed products of a maimed world, but also because the whole book is a series of distorted and distorting memories. Sometimes even professed facts clash, but this is of no importance: facts are in any case somewhat shadowy to most of the physically and mentally crippled figures who make up the population of Spitzen-on-the-Dein, some of whom, like the Duke, appear to spend their entire lives endlessly repeating the same obsessive actions, not out of actual desire but as an attempt to conjure desire in a world from which it has disappeared.

The strongest grounds on which Hawkes has usually been seen as a Gothic writer are those put forward by Leslie Fiedler when he says that the vision which Hawkes offers is of a world in which not love but terror is the driving principle of life and action.[5] All the characters in *The Cannibal* are uncomprehending, driven by fears and lusts which obliterate the world around them. There is clearly a dialectic operating here: the actual terror of what the war has done produces a series of psychotic escape routes, but the consequences of these escape routes only compound the original terror. The Duke kills and eats small boys, but it seems that he sees them as foxes, so does that, Hawkes implicitly asks us, make it less serious? The Duke is only trying to find order in the world, to compensate for social chaos:

He would have preferred to have a light and a glass-topped table, to follow the whole thing out on a chart, knowing which muscles to cut and which to tie . . . He should have preferred to have his glasses, but they were at home – another mistake. . . . The very fact that it was not a deer or a possum made the thing hard to skin, the fact that it was not a rabbit made it hard to dissect; its infernal humanness carried over even into death and made the carcass just as difficult as the human being had itself been.   (*The Cannibal,* pp. 206–7)

For it is not that Hawkes is offering us a distinctive unitary perspective: he is offering instead a group of contradictory perspectives, pathological views of the past and the present, which clash and jar. It is impossible to know what Zizendorf is: whether his beliefs and intentions are honourable or dishonourable, sane or insane. In a new barbarian age, he might represent a move back towards civilised order, or merely a ratification of tribalism.

Stylistically, the 'Gothic-ness' of *The Cannibal* lies in its deep-rooted rebuttal of realism. There are plenty of appearances, plenty of perspectives, but behind them, one suspects, nothing whatever. Or rather, the structuring of the 'real' world, Hawkes claims, is arbitrary; as with the language he uses, so with the perceptions of his characters – whether we choose to see and dwell on the important or the unimportant is not a matter of some essential rightness or wrongness, but merely of inexplicable internal compulsion. In terms of theme, this extreme expressionism is used to demonstrate how, in a world rendered void by the breakdown of value, the gap will be filled by monstrous projections of ourselves: like many Gothic villains, Hawkes's characters are often rhetoricians of the self, devoting their time to convincing themselves of their own importance and destiny. One of the characters sees himself as an expert fencer, but he is, of course, merely incompetent and cowardly. The terror derives partly from the suggestion that the chaos of war may indeed prove to be liberating after a fashion: that it may remove those conventions which keep our essential inner perversions from emerging.

The Cannibal is a very threatening book in one way: in that one would expect any book written about Germany in 1945 to have to draw fairly clear ethical boundaries. Hawkes does not: the reader feels no particular objection to Zizendorf's activities because he seems no worse than anyone else – and yet of course he may well be a second Hitler. Uncertainty about the narrator is endemic to American Gothic: *The Cannibal* is in this respect unusually complex, the more frequent structure being one in which a simple oscillation between sanity and madness is at stake. Another of Hawkes's books, *The Blood Oranges* (1971), is structured in this way, as are many of Purdy's short stories and as is Joyce Carol Oates's most Gothic work, *Expensive People*. But the threat at the heart of *Expensive People* comes from a different source: it is a matter of being forced into hideous proximity with the narrator. 'One thing I want to do, my readers', he says at the beginning of the book, 'is to minimise the tension between writer and reader',[6] but of course this is ironic: the book thrives precisely on that tension, on the inexorable way in which Richard Everett insists on telling us the whole repulsive truth about his life and crimes.

And the irony is in fact double. 'I was a child murderer', says Everett, and indeed he was, spectacularly. But he appears to have become a murderer, a sniper, because he has been driven mad by the American Dream, a disposition towards which readers might be expected to feel some sympathy: the trouble is the difficulty of feeling sympathy for an obese, neurotic, self-pitying and in some ways retarded hero. Any move we try to make towards him is undermined by his own repulsiveness and his insistent lack of self-understanding. This lack of understanding, the locked psyche, is similar to that of the narrator of Joseph Heller's terrifying *Something Happened* (1974), in which also the American Dream figures in its alternative guise as a cloud of unknowing; the difference is that Heller's hero continues to function in society precisely on the basis of his self-deceits and tortured excuses, whereas Oates's hero has abandoned the struggle, 'disintegrated'.

As much as by anything else, he has been driven to extremity by a landscape; by the pretty, boxed-in gardens and terraces of expensive suburban America, symbols of the hidden pressures of conventionality:

> Imagine Fernwood like this: an odor of grass, leaves, a domesticated river (with ducks, geese, and swans provided by the village, and giant goldfish swimming gracefully), blue skies, thousands of acres of faultless green grass ... And mixed in with the odor of lawns being sprinkled automatically on warm spring mornings is the odor of money, cash. Fresh crisp cash. Bills you could stuff in your mouth and chew away at. My mouth is watering at the thought of that tart, fine blue-green ink, the mellow aroma of the paper! (*Expensive People*, pp. 37–8)

Everett is a victim of wealth, of over-consumption: his response is insane but logical – to bring a little chaos into order by gunfire, and then gradually to kill himself by overeating. For it is not easy to disrupt the carefully built-up fabric of middle America: one of his first manifestations of disorder is to go berserk in a flowerbed, but nobody minds very much: a policeman offers to help him find whatever he might have lost, and as he walks away nobody makes a move to stop him: 'it seemed incredible to me that they would let me go . . . but yes, they did, they let me go! And though many clean people in the village noted my filthy clothes and tear-streaked, mud-streaked face, of course no one said anything' (*Expensive People*, p. 262). After this kind of incident, it becomes increasingly obvious that, in order to get any kind of response from society in general and from his disastrous parents in particular, only something of the order of mass murder is going to suffice.

As in *The Cannibal*, a real locale is used as a skeleton on which to construct a fantasy landscape. But the horror of *Expensive People* is not really much to do with violence, it is rather a continuing nausea. As Everett himself says,

> Father said I was always sick and I want to defend myself. I wasn't always sick. There were many days when I was well, ordinarily well, and many other days when I was well enough to drag myself around. On other days I suppose I was 'sick', but not really ill. There is a
> difference. (*Expensive People*, p. 233)

This is a sickness we can find in Hawkes, Oates, Purdy: a dislocation which is associated with a creeping awareness of the insanity of social demands. This is not to say that Everett, any more than the inhabitants of Spitzen-on-the-Dein, knows *what* is wrong with himself or with Fernwood: he knows only that he is subject to contradictory pressures, and that the attempt to cope with them produces a thin film of distortion between himself and others. In *Expensive People*, as in *The Cannibal*, there is no conspiracy at stake, only the steady and intense horror of a world whose basic principles of organisation – war economy and/or suburban living – prevent the individual from even phrasing the necessary questions, let alone receiving answers to them.

James Purdy's *Eustace Chisholm and the Works* is not a first-person narrative: we are made aware, not of minds wrestling internally with impossible demands, but of characters who placidly and occasionally cheerfully accept the reality of perversion and violence. Chisholm, failed poet and voyeur, is slightly superior to his acquaintances because he *knows* that he is unpleasant, treacherous and cruel: since he is therefore considered by his friends to have some insight into the wider world, he becomes the focus of a neurotic whirlpool which ends predictably in torture and death. Amos Ratcliffe, retarded adolescent traumatised by his affair with his mother; Daniel Haws, fixated on the army and the possibilities for masochism which it involves; Captain Stadger, who finds in Haws the supernaturally willing victim for whom he has been longing all his life; Reuben Masterson, the American aristocrat fighting feebly against mother-domination and the social requirements of his class: Chisholm observes them eddying around him and responds with the aplomb which has given him his reputation for wisdom, by doing nothing at all. In this world, any attempt at help would only make things worse: as in *The Cannibal* and *Expensive People* there is a destiny to be worked out, and it behoves the 'wise' not to interfere with its workings.

Yet to describe the characters in these terms is to do the novel an injustice. One at least expects that a book about sadists, psychopaths and the ever-present Oedipus complex might present its characters as 'interesting', but this Purdy cleverly avoids doing. The people in Chisholm's world – and preeminently Chisholm himself – are not in the least interesting; they are inarticulate, self-deluding and without any particular signs of intelligence. The prevailing tone of the novel is sparseness: the world portrayed, the poorest part of industrial Chicago, has nothing going for it, not even the grandeur of starvation, and the principal common ground of the characters is their remarkable ineptitude, both in terms of survival and, more obtrusively, in the very language that they use. The fact that nobody understands each other is due not to any intensity of introspection, but to the fact that nobody is capable of expressing themselves with any degree of sense, and this also goes for the author himself. One central focus is the thwarted affair between Ratcliffe and Haws, thwarted by Haws's inability to bring to consciousness his somnambulistic drives and by Ratcliffe's fear of him, but we are not for a moment made to think that even if these barriers could have been overcome the situation would have been much different. There is a total absence of the conventional romantic conflict between frustration and depression: either possibility is equally absurd and destructive. When Ratcliffe is finally killed, it is not for any reason deriving from the principal events of his life, and when Chisholm's lengthy and continuing poem is finally burnt, it is by the merest of accidents, and of no particular importance to anybody.

What is distinctive about the book is its absolute refusal to imply alternative patterns. Purdy has created for it a prose style which is itself as stupid and incoherent as the dialogue of his characters, and which is distractingly inconsistent within itself. An event which is authorially viewed at one moment as important will be dismissed at another; matters which on one page appear to be highly serious will be treated as jokes a few pages later. 'The dreadful has already happened'; nobody in the book is particularly likely to break down, because life has broken down anyway. The perceptions which the characters have of each other are not interesting distortions, they are merely mistaken and not very useful. One thing which has caused Hawkes and Oates to be classified as Gothic writers is the sheer intensity of their focus; there is no intensity whatever in *Eustace Chisholm* about matters of importance to the plot, although horror does attach to some of the peripheral scenes, particularly to the lengthy description of an abortion. Violence is random: it may intrude at any moment, but there is little to be done about the threat. No specific actions or ways of behaviour will ward it off, because there is no way of understanding its provenance.

Hawkes and Oates are psychological novelists at root, although their versions of psychology are eccentric and fearsome. Purdy is not, at least in *Eustace Chisholm,* and to this extent he shares certain features with a rather different area of American writing, which seems to me best represented by Thomas Pynchon. What I am talking about is a kind of writing which shifts focus from individual character and psychology onto systems: systems of order, systems of behaviour, systems of oppression. Chisholm and his friends are mere nodes of action, locked into a system which they cannot even perceive, let alone understand. They have no free will; their behaviour is interesting only as evidence of wider social disorder, not in itself. Pynchon's fiction, however, is altogether more radical, partly because it is a sustained and highly self-conscious investigation of the connections between system and paranoia, but to understand it requires us to go back to a slightly earlier master of paranoid fiction, William Burroughs.

Burroughs seems to me to be considerably more 'Gothic' than Hawkes or Oates in several ways. He is concerned with the limits of the human, with the points at which man ceases to be man and becomes either beast or machine. He is concerned with vampirism, with the ways in which people feed off each other, but more importantly with the ways in which whole metabolisms may be changed and inverted. He is involved in an attempt to form a style of narrative which can offer a description of psychological and social processes without succumbing to simplistic laws of cause and effect. He is concerned with the various meanings of commerce, and with the atrophy and transformation of 'human' relations. And above all he is concerned with distortions of perception, with the point at which people begin to see the entire world arranged over against themselves, and with probing the validity or otherwise of this view of the universe. And the principal result of all this is a fine ambiguity: when Burroughs describes to us the world as it appears to the eyes of the junkie, a faceless and repressive syndicate, we never know whether he is undercutting this vision or offering it as a correct account of international capitalism.

He is, of course, doing both. The fate of the junkie is *neither* to escape from the pressures of the world to happier lands, *nor* to lose all grip on reality. The dreadful truth about the junkie's position is that, on the one hand, it reveals to him truth about the hideous operations of commerce, because junk is the ultimate commodity, but on the other it renders this truth useless and incommunicable because the junkie is precisely dependent on the world thus revealed to him. Burroughs's paradoxes are not unlike Marcuse's: the only way to perceive manipulation is through close proximity, but it may be impossible to escape from hell. His books are dreadful warnings, but they are double-edged: they warn against junk, but they also warn against ignoring what junk has to tell us. The junkie's life is reduced to the sheer structure of necessity: and down there, with everything stripped away, lies the essence of the system, the set of impersonal laws of trade and exchange which has usurped the role of God. Down there, on the streets, or shivering in the grey morning, the messages that come to the junkie from invisible radio sources are ones which we would all hear if we could cut out the interference: subliminal messages advising conformity and warning against resistance, nudging us into awareness of the dreadful penalties the system can exact for revolt. Junk knowledge is an inverted Faustianism, but this is because society is itself inverted: true knowledge is to be found not in divine realms, but in the hell which shudders and festers just below our feet, or in our veins. We cling to the illusion of free will, but we can only do so because we are allowed to by the manipulators of a scarcity economy. The junkie is an inverted Gothic hero: he searches for escape, but is condemned to find and live with a truth which he never wanted to know. His is the revelation of the arbitrariness of the moral law: he is cursed like the Wandering Jew, and like the Jew he bears the stigmata of the vengeance of an unjust god.

This view of Burroughs's fiction sounds rather like an attempt to displace the drug experience itself as the centre of attention, and this is partly the point. There have been plenty of 'drug odysseys', many of them consciously influenced by Burroughs, but almost none of them have achieved any breadth of reference, the one notable exception being John Rechy's magnificent *City of Night* (1963), in which extensive drug use and homosexuality are again assumed as experiential parameters. What is good in Burroughs and in Rechy relates very closely to Kafka, particularly to the Kafka of *The Castle*, which, like *The Naked Lunch* (1959) and *City of Night,* is not really a narrative at all but an attempt to conjure an expressionist view of the universe as nightmare. Thomas Pynchon's longer works, *V* (1963) and *Gravity's Rainbow* (1973), take this process one stage further: they are not primarily narratives but they take a diabolical pleasure in continually pretending that they are – starting stories which are never finished, suggesting causal explanations which are later undermined, implying progression where there is in fact only endless circularity. Pynchon's favourite tag is 'it seems'; the seeming is the way the mind attempts to interpret chains of incident in coherent ways, when in fact – and this is the heart of Pynchon's fiction – we never have the evidence to make such interpretations. There are always vital clues missing, clues which exist only in the world of The System, if indeed they, and The System itself, exist at all. The problem of the world as offered to consciousness is the problem of the Loch Ness Monster: we may choose to infer from the photographs that there is down there a unitary being of approximately regular shape, but what we are seeing might always be flocks of sea-birds or rafts of turtles, or, of course, a fault in the process of photography itself. Similarly, coherence to Pynchon, may just be a fault in the retina or in the brain.

Gravity's Rainbow, to limit the field of reference, is an achievement comparable in scope and in kind with *Melmoth the Wanderer* (1820), albeit informed by a vastly increased fictional self-consciousness. Like *Melmoth*, it is a tissue of stories and stories within stories, designed to vindicate a cosmic view in which individuals count for nothing beside the hidden plans and patterns of history. As in *Melmoth*, most of these individuals, exquisitely described as they are, exist to display forms of perversion, sometimes the extreme perversion of normalcy; and again as in *Melmoth*, this is a view which has almost nothing to do with the realm of the moral. The paradigm of *Melmoth* is the Wandering Jew taken as a symbol of the all-encompassing fallibility of humanity; the paradigm of *Gravity's Rainbow* is the Poisson Curve, which demonstrates that chance and purpose are the same thing seen from different angles. Neither Maturin nor Pynchon will have anything to do with 'justice', except to gloat over the manifold misfortunes of those who choose to rely on it to right their undoubted wrongs.

But *Gravity's Rainbow* is Gothic for our time, in that its apparatus is modern, its fictional tactics self-consciously and often ironically modernist. The problems of paranoia it sets up are insoluble because the conspiracy is so diverse and enormous that it takes in the whole of recorded history. The book is set in a Europe attempting to right itself immediately after the disaster of the Second World War, because it is only at such moments of turmoil and confusion that parts of the naked machinery of the world are occasionally laid bare, only then that some of the carefully hidden clues to the inner meaning of history can be found lying around on the battlefields before they are equally carefully cleared away or substituted by the mysterious agents of universal order. In a different age, the agents of *Gravity's Rainbow* would have belonged to the Inquisition or, more appropriately, to the Rosicrucians; now they work for a variety of organisations, known mostly only by their initials, and transcending national and diplomatic boundaries. Throughout the text, it seems as though the shape of the denouement will be for one of the many seekers after knowledge to find it, but this never properly happens; we have known all along, right from the very first pages, that the subject of the book is a vast, widespread and perhaps indifferently effective system of world domination, and that is precisely all we still know at the end; some of its elements, some of the historical patterns with which it has been associated have been a little more clearly defined, and a good many lives have been lost, but that is all.

In the meantime, what Pynchon has done, again like Maturin, is taken an apparently taut structure and used it for almost entirely paranoiac purposes, as a sustained and varied demonstration of the ways in which the apparently natural is under the dominion of the unnatural or supernatural. Some characters – the drug addicts, sadists, hopeless victims – occupy a privileged position, in that they have suspected this for some time; others, principally Slothrop, the transatlantic *ingénu* who rather unwillingly plays the role of protagonist, will probably never know. It is not that, during the history of civilisation, development of natural resources has permitted artifice: it is that nature is only kept in being, and in reasonably good shape, by artifice, and that at a high level. It is not difficult to see the connection between Pynchon's cosmology and a concept of the 'divine plan', but Pynchon's plan is a Gothic one in that it has nothing to do with justice and complacency, everything to do with the power of strength over weakness and with the terrible might of a god who 'passeth all understanding', even, probably, his own. For this is the other irony: if indeed the world is at the mercy of unknown manipulators, then are they competent? Or is it impossible to unravel the immediate evidence precisely because what they produce is only a series of more or less colossal mistakes? Have we the right to rail against this God, who or whatever it may be? And here, of course, the great railers against God, the great sufferers from divine injustice, in the literary tradition are the characters of the Gothic writers – Lewis's Ambrosio, Maturin's Melmoth, Coleridge's Ancient Mariner.

Pynchon's work is very far from the so-called American Gothic, and partly this is simply a matter of scope. Like few other works of the twentieth century, *Gravity's Rainbow* – and *V* – are attempts to come to terms with history, with the relations between its mechanisms and its ghosts. Pavlov lies explicitly close to the surface, but his most appropriate image is Roger Mexico, the mathematician who is always able to build a satisfactory graph from where the bombs have dropped, but is paralysed by his inability to predict the location of the next one. The closest parallel to Pynchon is the English writer J. G. Ballard, who uses the apparatus of science fiction to convey a view of the world as pattern and geometry. Ballard is the prolific writer of a long series of meditations around a single central group of obsessions; generally the success or failure of his books hinges on how fluently they are written, which has over the years been a rather variable factor, but what has not varied is an almost manic fertility of idea and form.

The prototype for his most interesting work is *The Atrocity Exhibition* (1970). Pynchon points out in *The Crying of Lot 49* (1966) that being paranoid does not stop one from being persecuted, and a similar irony is at the heart of *The Atrocity Exhibition*. As a novel, it makes even fewer concessions to conventional narrative than the other texts we have looked at: it is written in separate, headlined paragraphs, tailored to resemble brief newspaper articles; its principal 'character' changes in name and identity; in place of story there is a sequence of interlocking images, many of them drawn from the contemporary world, most of them to do with violence. The problem presented by the protagonist is that he is not in any full sense a 'person' at all; he is attempting to achieve identity in a world which appears to deny it. This he does through the reconstruction of situations, attempting to find the lines, curves, nodes which comprise history, in order to be able to situate himself among them.

Then again, it may be not that *he* is trying to do this, but that he is being used as an experimental 'subject'. A typical paragraph demonstrates the mixture of themes of violence and sexuality with a quasi-scientific discourse:

> *Indicators of Sexual Arousal.* During the interval when the reels changed, Dr Nathan saw Trabert peering at the photographs pinned to the windshields of the crashed cars. From the balcony of his empty office Catherine Austin watched him with barely focused eyes. Her leg stance, significant indicator of sexual arousal, confirmed all Dr Nathan had anticipated of Trabert's involvement with the events of Dealey Plaza. Behind him there was a shout from the camera crew. An enormous photograph of Jacqueline Kennedy had appeared in the empty rectangle of the screen. A bearded young man with an advanced neuromuscular tremor in his lower legs stood in the brilliant pearl light, his laminated suit bathed in the magnified image of Mrs Kennedy's mouth. As he walked towards Trabert across the broken bodies of the plastic dummies the screen jerked into a nexus of impacting cars, soundless concertina of speed and violence.[7]

Ballard is a self-conscious artificer, piercing together a book out of elements from newspaper reports, newsreel films, scientific documents: Burroughs's emphasis on casual violence, crossed with Robbe-Grillet's painstakingly alienated naturalism, crossed with Godard's *Weekend*. The book is a faulty rerun of obsessions, a search to find interconnections between apparently inexplicable phenomena. Trabert, Travers, Tallis, Talbot, in his various incarnations is obsessed by detail, both in terms of scientific perception and in terms of the body. At one point Dr Nathan diagnoses the problems of desire by which he is afflicted:

> Sex, of course, remains our continuing preoccupation. As you and I know, the act of intercourse is now always a model for something else. What will follow is the psychopathology of sex, relationships so lunar and abstract that people will become mere extensions of the geometries of situations. This will allow the exploration, without any taint of guilt, of every aspect of sexual psychopathology. Travers, for example, has composed a series of new sexual deviations, of a wholly conceptual character, in an attempt to surmount this death of affect.
>
> (*Atrocity Exhibition*, p. 97)

The horror of *The Atrocity Exhibition* is precisely to do with this death of desire, with the automatisation of feeling. As with Pynchon, everything in Ballard's world may signify, but what it signifies remains a mystery. The world of assassinations and high-speed car crashes which he depicts has ceased to be amenable to interpretation in terms of natural laws, and individuals have ceased to be able to hold themselves together either literally or metaphorically. New chains of connection are needed. The 'systems' with which Ballard is concerned are more sharply focused than those of Burroughs or Pynchon, for two reasons: because they are largely *physical* systems, systems of objects and shapes, and because they are not distorted by clearly psychotic perception. We are not tempted to devalue Travers's observation of the world, because he is himself merely part of the texture of that world, a fluid coalescence of forces and patterns. The 'radical decentring of consciousness' of which the structuralists speak is taken by Ballard as a fictional principle; *The Atrocity Exhibition* is an attempt to examine the conclusions of an extreme materialism in which minds exert no hold over matter but have to find spaces in the material to insert themselves into, so that they can be fixed into some semblance of coherence.

Pynchon and Ballard are both writing about a new kind of claustrophobia, the claustrophobia of excessive information and the corresponding breakdown of selective retrieval systems. The individual is submerged under a deluge of details, the victim of computerisation. Control has become the property of the machine and its servants, individual lives and perceptions merely the fuel which services the juggernaut. War and assassination are seen as evidence of a new barbarity, all the worse for the high level of hidden organisation at which it operates. I want to conclude this chapter by looking briefly at three other works in which the essential Gothic dialectic of civilisation and barbarism is central, Robert Coover's collection of short stories, *Pricksongs and Descants* (1969), and two of Angela Carter's novels, *Heroes and Villains* (1969) and *Love* (1971). These works fall neither within the tradition of dislocation and nausea represented by Hawkes and Oates, nor squarely within the domain of paranoiac fiction common to Burroughs, Pynchon and Ballard. They are also very different books in their own right, although in each case the emphasis on the irruption of the barbaric carries with it the old Gothic habit of dwelling on the awful demise of innocence.

One of the stories in *Pricksongs and Descants*, 'Morris in Chains', concerns the hunt through an almost entirely urbanised world for the mysterious Morris, a rough-and-ready Pan-like figure who represents the last vestige of the rural and uncivilised. The hunt is conducted by one Dr Peloris, who warns her troops of the dangers of Morris's insinuations thus:

we are ready, let us admit, to a degree corrupted. As much by our own

137

shaky starts as by Morris. We can nearly admit notes of savagery in
our parks, have not yet stifled the wild optimistic call. We might yet
be thrilled by the glimmer of disembodied eyes burning hot in the
dark forest, by the vision of bathing naiads' bared mammaries or of
nutbrown torsos with furry thighs, by the one-note calls of hemlock
pipes. In short, we are not yet freed from the sin of the simple. But it
is our children, to speak in the old way, whom we must consider.
There must be no confusions for them between the old legends and
conceivable realities. It is *they* who oblige us to grub up, once and for
all, the contaminated seed of our unfortunate origins.[8]

It is precisely the seed which continues to contaminate the sanitised
world which is the centre of Coover's attention in many of these
stories, which are nothing other than 'confusions . . . between the
old legends and conceivable realities'. 'The Door', 'The Gingerbread House', 'The Milkmaid of Samaniego' are all retellings of old
legends, either from an unusual angle, or with the accent subtly
changed towards the sinister; 'The Magic Poker' is more Coover's
own, but reads similarly. In many cases the stories are not coherent
within themselves: they are accumulations of sections of stories,
some of them sequential, some alternative, among which the reader
has to pick his way with care. One of the most impressive, 'The
Babysitter', takes a simple situation and works it out not to one
straightforward conclusion but to a number of different conclusions,
some of which are clearly developments of the fantasies of individual
characters. Coover has perfected a style of extraordinary simplicity,
in terms of both syntax and imagery: the book glows with the simple
primary colours of fairy-tale, with just a hint of dark shadow at the
corner of each page. As the children approach the gingerbread
house, 'the witch flicks and flutters through the blackened forest,
her livid face twisted with hatred, her inscrutable condition. Her
eyes burn like glowing coals and her black rags flap loosely.' But
they seem to arrive safely:

> The boy climbs up on the chocolate roof to break off a peppermint-
> stick chimney, comes sliding down into a rainbarrel full of vanilla
> pudding. The girl, reaching out to catch him in his fall, slips on a
> sugarplum and tumbles into a sticky rock garden of candied
> chestnuts. Laughing, gaily, they lick each other clean. And how grand
> is the red-and-white striped chimney the boy holds up for her! how
> bright! how sweet! But the door: here they pause and catch their
> breath. It is heart-shaped and bloodstone-red, its burnished surface
> gleaming in the sunlight. On, what a thing is that door! Shining like
> a ruby, like hard cherry candy, and pulsing softly, radiantly. Yes,
> marvellous! delicious! insuperable! but beyond: what is that sound of
> black rags flapping? (*Pricksongs*, pp. 58–9)

And in 'The Door', it is the aged grandmother/witch whom we hear reminiscing obscenely about her own past life and about the dangers which await her 'innocent' granddaughter in the forest:

> oh I know why she's late you warn her and it does no good I know
> who's got her giddy ear with his old death-cunt-and-prick songs
> haven't I heard them all my God and smelt his hot breath in the
> singin? yes I know him can see him now lickin his hairy black chops
> and composin his polyphonies outa dread and appetite whisperin his
> eclogues sprung from disaster croonin his sacral entertainments yes
> I know him well and I tell her but Granny she says Granny you don't
> understand the times are different there's a whole new –
>
> (*Pricksongs*, p. 11)

Coover's world has a neat, tidy, glittering surface below which bubble the old passions and fevers: much of his writing is self-consciously a form of repression, forming the world into neat, taut images but then suggesting the unreality and incompleteness of this process by setting the images alongside each other in impossible combinations. Against this are the discourses of, for instance, Morris and the grandmother: records of ancient evils and joys, long-suppressed but never to be killed.

One of the epigraphs to Carter's *Heroes and Villains*, which also has strong, and malevolent, connections with fairy-tale, is from Fiedler's *Love and Death in the American Novel*: 'The Gothic mode is essentially a form of parody, a way of assailing clichés by exaggerating them to the limit of grotesqueness.' The opening sentences establish the tone of fake innocence by means of which this particular kind of parody is to be achieved:

> Marianne had sharp, cold eyes and she was spiteful but her father
> loved her. He was a Professor of History; he owned a clock which he
> wound every morning and kept in the family dining-room upon a
> sideboard full of heirlooms of stainless steel such as dishes and cutlery.
> Marianne thought of the clock as her father's pet, something like her
> own pet rabbit, but the rabbit soon died and was handed over to the
> Professor of Biology to be eviscerated while the clock continued to tick
> inscrutably on. She therefore concluded the clock must be immortal
> but this did not impress her.[9]

The central convention of *Heroes and Villains* is certainly a cliché:[10] a world divided between tribes of new barbarians and the over-intellectualised relics of an effete civilisation, and Marianne's exploration of the realm of the barbarians; but it is a convention transcended by the authorial tone. Marianne is no innocent heroine: if she is sometimes shocked by the barbarians' worst excesses, this is not because they offend her purity but because they do not conform to her idea of the reasonable. Again, the barbarians are not quite the tough, colourful people they first appear, but a motley collection of incompetents and poseurs, admirable more for their reactions to the immense difficulties they continually face than for any particular innate heroism.

The scene where Marianne is raped by the barbarian Jewel is typical. She has run away and he pursues her, finding her up a tree; his behaviour is a bizarre blend of half-remembered *politesse* and not wholly convincing violence. Marianne is particularly incensed when, covered in amulets and charms, he points out in a managerial tone that 'we'd have to establish common ground to communicate as equals'. What she is upset by is both the reminder of her educated past environment and also, it seems, the *lèse-majesté* implied in Jewel's use of civilised forms of address. She springs upon him, but predictably loses the battle:

> Afterwards, there was a good deal of blood. He stared at it with something like wonder and dipped his fingers in it. She stared at him relentlessly; if he had kissed her, she would have bitten out his tongue. However, he recovered his abominable self-possession almost immediately. She began to struggle again but he held her down with one hand, half pulled off his filthy leather jacket and ripped off the sleeve of his shirt, as he had done before when he had treated her snakebite. This repetition of action would have been comic had she been in a mood to appreciate it. He held the rag between her thighs to sop up the bleeding, a bizarre piece of courtesy.
>
> (*Heroes and Villains*, pp. 77–8)

The conflict, here in particular and in the book in general, is a multivalent parody: of class relations, of relations between the sexes, of the battle between rational control and desire. And it is also a conflict within Marianne herself, but one which only becomes clear progressively. She has no conscious aims: indeed, her discourse is half-traumatised, not by her escape into barbarism but rather by the veneer of civilisation which she has acquired earlier. She is impressed by Jewel, but only in a limited way, and it gradually becomes clear why: because she is herself stronger than the barbarians, and has only to realise this to seize power for herself. They may play at being violent but Marianne grows, precisely through her female experiences, through her first-hand knowledge of repression, into a force far more effective than they, more pragmatic and less bound by ritual and superstition. In the end, both male-dominated worlds look like different aspects of the same nursery.[11]

There are, obviously, no heroes and no villains; only a set of silly games which men play. Thus to call *Heroes and Villains* parodic is not to say that it parodies the real world but rather that it exposes some of the ways in which the real world habitually parodies itself: some of the ways in which people exaggerate their own conflicts, attempt at all costs to construct a distinctive life-style even if it is radically inappropriate to the surroundings. Nor is the fact that Marianne is partially exempt from this process particularly encouraging: what protects her is not insight but psychological blockage. Carter ironically suggests that the Gothic vision is in fact an accurate account of life, of the ways we project our fantasies onto the world and then stand back in horror when we see them come to life.

This kind of horror, and the specific position of women in relation to it, are again the themes of *Love*, in which the large-scale fantasisation of landscape is rejected and the horror consequently comes closer to home. It is a truly chilling book, in the way apparent naturalism alternates with bland distortion. There is a point at which Annabel, one of the central figures, recalls a childhood experience (which itself may or may not be real):

> When she was two or three years old, her mother took her shopping. Little Annabel slipped out of the grocer's while her mother discussed the price of butter and played in the gutter for a while until she decided to wander into the middle of the road. A car braked, skidded and crashed into a shop front. Annabel watched the slivers of glass flash in the sunshine until a crowd of distraught giants broke upon her head, her mother, the grocer in his white coat, a blonde woman with dark glasses, a man with four arms and legs and two heads, one golden, the other black, and many other passers-by, all as agitated as could be imagined. 'You might have been killed!' said her mother. 'But I wasn't, I was playing,' said Annabel, no bigger than a blade of grass, who had caused this huge commotion all by herself just because she could play games with death.[12]

Annabel and the other characters are monsters, though not of their own choosing: monsters in that they are unable to perceive connections between action and consequence, because they fail to establish a dividing-line between game and life – or death. The childhood voice of 'all as agitated as could be imagined' and 'no bigger than a blade of grass' signifies a terrifying absence of responsibility, again a traumatised inability to perceive moments of transition: it is the voice of Oothoon in Blake's *Visions of the Daughters of Albion*, and of Esther in Sylvia Plath's *The Bell Jar* seeing herself in the mirror, but also a voice informed by the casualness of the 1960s, partly aware of its own lack of ethical values but skimming over the surface of the psychotic depths beneath. The characters do not struggle for self-realisation, or indeed for survival; they are much too far gone for that. Nor does Carter struggle to impose 'meaning' on the narrative: one of the central events occurs at a party, and is introduced thus:

> Afterwards, the events of the night seemed, to all who participated in them, like disparate sets of images shuffled together anyhow. A draped form on a stretcher; candles blown out by a strong wind; a knife; an operating theatre; blood; and bandages. In time, the principal actors (the wife, the brothers, the mistress) assembled a coherent narrative from these images but each interpreted them differently and drew their own conclusions which were all quite dissimilar . . .
> (*Love*, p. 52)

The description of the early stages of the party then proceeds with bland cheerfulness; there are tensions in the air but this, the authorial voice seems to say, is only usual, nothing to worry about. Annabel sees her husband in the act of deceiving her, and thinks about this a little:

> She let the curtain fall back into place and turned from the window. The party went on as if nothing had happened . . . She went immediately to the bathroom to kill herself in private. Fortunately it was unoccupied. After she locked the door, she remembered she should have borrowed one of Buzz's knives and stabbed herself through the heart. She was irritated to realise she would have to make do with an undignified razor blade but quickly cut open both her wrists with two clean, sweeping blows and sat down on the floor, waiting to bleed to death. She had always bled very easily.
> (*Love*, p. 54)

Again, it is the alternation between childishness and terror, between apparent innocence and actual violence which is so effective, and the parallel alternation between significant and insignificant detail. The characters in Carter's novels have not managed to assemble the world into any semblance of coherence, and nor do they see much point in trying to do so; instead they try on ways of being, never noticing the appalling consequences which are likely to flow from their actions. And the author persuades us too to enter into the fun: we are led to believe that in these worlds the truly dreadful cannot really happen, that the characters are somehow protected by some mysterious force of benevolence, which makes the actual moments of violence and dislocation paradoxically dreamlike in their intensity. Carter's voice is the voice of Red Riding Hood's wolf, and even though we all know it is a wolf really we remain helpless before its hypnotic seductiveness.

It is impossible to summarise so diverse a field as modern Gothic:

but what one can say is that most of its manifestations are closely related to perceptions of the failure of accounts of the world and the mind predicated on the supremacy of subjectivity. The Gothic world is one in which health, strength and moral well-being will not at all serve to get one by; on the contrary, they will prevent one from seeing the real sources of power and control, and thus make one's demise the more fitting an object for irony. Sensitivity of response is no more help to Pynchon's or Carter's characters than it was to Emily in Udolpho: again on the contrary, it is a hindrance, a burden to be borne in a realm where the only hope of escape lies in travelling light. Thus the rewriting of fairy-tales: the version of cosmic justice which they imply is not only not true but a splendid object for derision. The natural world is not benevolent, and indeed it is not merely organically 'red in tooth and claw', it is actively hostile and actively able to find interesting and tormenting ways of getting its own back. Similarly, childhood is not a pretty sight: it is the locale of the first traumatic encounters with experience, the place from which one is born into the world screaming. And there are really no ways out: the search for the true self, or for real knowledge about the forces of manipulation, is a quixotic journey towards a greater devastation. Any perception of truth comes too late, and usually all it demonstrates is the misguidedness of past action, or of action at all. And yet it is precisely here that so much of the energy of modern fiction lies: in the relentless exposure of the paucity and deception of traditional criteria of realism, in the portrayal of a world in which persecution is an iron law.

Notes and references

1. **Isak Dinesen**, *Seven Gothic Tales*, introd. Dorothy Canfield (New York, 1934), p. 274.
2. See **Curtis Cate**, 'Isak Dinesen', *Atlantic Monthly*, Dec. 1959, p. 153.
3. **Irving Malin**, in *New American Gothic* (Carbondale, Ill., 1962), discusses six writers: Truman Capote, James Purdy, Flannery O'Connor, John Hawkes, Carson McCullers and J. D. Salinger. Unfortunately, however, the view of Gothic which he puts forward is far too generalised to be helpful, and this view is itself further undermined by frequently specious argument.
4. **John Hawkes**, *The Cannibal*, introd. Albert Guerard (London, 1962), p. xi (Introduction).
5. See **Hawkes**, *The Lime Twig*, introd. Leslie A. Fiedler (London, 1962), p. xi (Introduction).
6. **Joyce Carol Oates**, *Expensive People* (London, 1969), p. 5.
7. **J. G. Ballard**, *The Atrocity Exhibition* (St Albans, 1972), p. 54.
8. **Robert Coover**, *Pricksongs and Descants* (London, 1973), pp. 38–9.
9. **Angela Carter**, *Heroes and Villains* (London, 1969), p. 1.
10. It is, in particular, one of the clichés, which lie behind the 'sword-and-sorcery'

fiction of Michael Moorcock and others. There is unfortunately no room here for discussion of this school of writing but it is worth noting as another fruitful offshoot from the central stem of Gothic; Moorcock especially demonstrates a considerable power in the manipulation of mythic and quasi-mythic materials, which is in no way harmed by the simple nature of his dualistic universe.

11. There are important comparisons to be made here with Bram Stoker: see above p. 21 in connection with the 'New Woman'.

12. **Angela Carter**, *Love* (London, 1971), pp. 85–6.

CHAPTER 7
Contemporary Gothic transformations

In the last twenty years, the cultural meanings and implications of Gothic have grown ever broader. In the 1980s, for example, it came to describe not only a kind of pop music, but also the whole swathe of fashion, dress, and indeed social behaviour and style associated with the music. Indeed, it has become increasingly apparent that changes in marketing and advertising strategy make it more and more difficult for the critic to separate out any one cultural strand, one cultural product from another, as new films, for example, are virtually overwhelmed by the vast industry which goes into producing associated accessories, clothing, children's and adult toys in a kind of systemic coagulation of production and consumption which Gothic itself predicts and reflects.

This process has been accompanied by vast alterations in the media and in information technology. The growth of the video industry has both spread film-watching to a wider swathe of the population, and at the same time threatened to render ridiculous any attempt at classification, control or censorship. The first novels available solely on the Internet are now appearing, novels which may never see any other form of publication and whose availability is controlled only by the cost of suitable hardware. At least one 'true neo-Gothic computer novel'[1] – which might equally accurately be described as an interactive video game – is currently available in a format which raises pressing questions about narrative structure and audience positioning – the question of whether Emily could *now* escape from Udolpho, in a constantly remade historical loop, now invites our attention.

In the light of these developments, selection of material for this chapter on the contemporary Gothic has proved particularly diffi-

145

cult, and I have decided to accept the overall title of the book, *The Literature of Terror,* as a provisional guiding principle. In other words, I propose to look at *narratives,* insofar as it is possible to isolate them from the surrounding culture; and, in accordance with a principle I have followed earlier, I have regarded film – and, by association, video – as within my remit, alongside the novel and the short story; within this field, I shall continue to explore the Gothic as it is being reworked around us.

The narratives I want to examine are all concerned with terror. (I should add here that I am not concerned at this point with traditional or modern distinctions between 'terror' and 'horror', which appear to me to be unsatisfactory and often misleading). They all also owe some allegiance to the previous traditions of the Gothic, albeit now mediated in an even greater diversity of forms than at any time previously. In the materials I have chosen there are enormous variations of cultural appeal and location; and they speak to many different parts of a complexly fractured audience. They also confront us immediately with a series of questions about the effects of terror, effects which, of course, we have seen discussed from the very earliest roots of Gothic, but which now have a highly specific cultural inflection as we watch the 'literature of terror' figuring in a string of legal cases, of which the question of the effect of a horror video on the killers of James Bulger is only one of the best-known; and also as we see the problems which a therapeutic culture is encountering as it struggles with the extreme complexity of child, sexual and satanic abuse and the ways in which narratives of fear may have effects in this sociopsychological arena. Questions of memory and reconstruction, which are at the heart of these legal and psychological arguments, are also germane to the whole area of the contemporary literature of terror, from Stephen King to the snuff movie, and they are ones to which I shall constantly return in this chapter.

I shall begin with a genre which has so far received little critical attention, despite its readerly popularity, the 'graphic novel'.[2] Graphic novels, it is often said, are no more than overgrown comics, a regressive and mindless form of entertainment; but this is certainly not true of the best of them. To see them clearly, perhaps we have to perform the critical action encouraged by W. J. T. Mitchell when he criticises Derrida's notion of 'grammatology' precisely for perpetuating the privileging of word over image and suggests substituting for it an expanded 'diagrammatology' which can approach the sign in ways as much visual as verbal.[3]

Watchmen (1987), by Alan Moore and Dave Gibbons, is one of the most remarkable achievements to date in this new form, and a highly sophisticated text in its own right, involving a type of 'syncopation' of word and image which slows and complicates the narrative thrust and makes for a genuine depth of reading. This is further enhanced by the way in which the text is a tissue of referentiality, taking us back to Blake, Nietzsche and the Gothic and romantic traditions as frequently as to Bob Dylan. The test of such a text might be: could what it does be done in any other way, is it merely hybridising existent forms? Here I think it is clear that *Watchmen* has evolved its own form; in the corners of the pictures there are always other narratives, other fragments of story, which are then continually picked up and rethreaded later in the text.

However, it could still be said that this display of technical virtuosity is expended on a topic of scant interest, since the story itself concerns precisely the question of comic-book heroes, especially when they are past their sell-by date. It could alternatively be argued that this is inevitable in the genre: that the question then becomes one of how the text recycles and adapts these preexisting materials, precisely in the way in which 'literary' texts prove themselves through their reuse and adaptation of the trace, through the way in which they can give added resonance to past texts, the 'manuscripts' of Gothic, which are, at the end of the day, precisely their subject matter.

The figure of the newsvendor who provides the common man's commentary on events in *Watchmen* is continually falling through the black holes of his own words as he tries to grasp the apocalyptic nature of the political background, which is the Soviet invasion of Afghanistan and the consequent fear of global war. 'Don't people see the *signs?*' he asks, 'Don't they know where this is *headed?*',[4] but the visual content makes it clear that we also have to see these 'signs' not merely as social portents but also as material signs and 'headlines', precisely the stuff of the newspapers which he is forever half-comprehendingly reading; and when he adds, '*See? Apathy!* Everybody escapin' into comic books an' TV! Makes me *sick.* . . . I mean, all this, it could all be *gone:* people, cars, TV shows, magazines . . . Even the word "gone" would be gone', then we glimpse an intensity of involvement with the spread of media influence in general which would be very difficult to achieve in any other form.

Self-referentiality, a concern with personal and social terror, the shameless exploitation of the exotic and the disastrous, all these give *Watchmen* a distinctly Gothic feel; this is even stronger in a 1994 graphic novel by the master of the genre, Neil Gaiman, called *Brief Lives*. Here we are in a world not of costumed heroes but of the gods, or rather, in a new mythology of the seven 'Endless' who lie even further back behind the gods, and perhaps their names can best give us an idea of the parameters of the world in which they move: Destiny, Death, Dream, Destruction, Desire, Despair and Delirium – although we also note that, at some previous time, before dislocation or before the Fall, Delirium's true name was 'Delight'. The action hinges on Destruction's abandonment of his quasi-divine tasks in the face of the far greater destructiveness unleashed on the world through human scientific and technological discovery, a remake of the Frankenstein myth. Again we have here the highly complex textuality typical of Gothic (these 'brief lives' are also, for example, John Aubrey's), looking back precisely to the Gothic masters, Blake, Coleridge and de Sade among others.

Much as in Blake's *Vala, or, The Four Zoas*, the disappearance, or rather dereliction of duty, of Destruction unseats the balance of the world. Delirium in particular, the youngest of the Endless, embarks on a search for him, and is assisted by Dream. Dream has his own reasons for embarking on his journey, for, as Morpheus, he has unfinished business with his son Orpheus, who exists now only as a severed head in a tiny Greek shrine: Dream knows that he has to complete the task of releasing Orpheus from his bondage, into life, into death, and the release of Destruction from the world enables him also to complete his task.

Brief Lives is a more violent text than *Watchmen*, and yet the stylisation of the artwork keeps this within strict boundaries. Certainly neither can be regarded as 'comic books', if the comparison is supposed to be either with children's comics or with the 1960s 'head comix', largely because they each owe a sombre allegiance to a far wider mythic tradition, and are largely free from the manic glee in destruction large and small which characterises so much of the 'comic' world. Neither are they in any sense lighthearted texts; on the contrary, one of the faults which both share is an unremitting solemnity which at first sits oddly with the form. At the end of the day, however, perhaps what they remind us of is that a culture which relies on the visual image at least as much as on the written or spoken word, and in which the majority of newspapers are themselves now given over to the image as the amount of newsprint in the tabloids shrinks year by year, is as much in need of applicable interpretation as the more traditional forms; and it is this serious work at the interface of word and image which the graphic novels, at their best, are performing, while at the same time they carry forward an expressionist tradition in which the extreme emotions are personified and thrown into violent interaction.

But of course the principal form today of the 'literature of terror', in terms of audience, is film; and it is also in film (through video) that the real problems with the portrayal of violence and its social effects are to be found. I have chosen to look briefly at four very different films, the first two of which can be seen as genre instances of terror, the latter two being far more sophisticated works although securely within the boundaries of the Gothic tradition: *Friday the Thirteenth* (1980), the first of a lengthy series, and *Freddy's Dead* (1991), which at the time it came out purported to be the last of the *Nightmare on Elm Street* series; Martin Scorsese's *Cape Fear* (1991); and the iconic *Basic Instinct* (1992).

The entirely vestigial plot of *Friday the Thirteenth* concerns a group of teenagers who arrive at Camp Crystal Lake (naturally known to the locals as Camp Blood) to set the camp up for incoming children. One by one they meet with violent deaths at the hands of an unseen killer, who is eventually revealed to be a woman, the mother of a child who died at the camp some while previously by drowning. This was supposedly as a result of the negligence of two counsellors who were engaged in suitably adolescent activities at a time when they were meant to be on duty. The mother is now pursuing an appalling revenge against camp counsellors in particular (which might appear forgiveable) and adolescents in general (which is less so).

The Gothic panoply is present in full force: the isolated campsite, the mysterious snake under the bed, the dead telephones, the jeep stuck in the swamp, most especially the lashing storm which rages with moderate conviction for the whole of the second half of the film. All the key moments involve a wandering hand-held camera, familiar from previous generations of Gothic film as representing the vantage point of the killer herself. To say that *behind* this lies a prurient sexual concern would be to overestimate the film's subtlety; the gloating shots of perfect young flesh, the scene in which one young lover lies murdered in a top bunk while her partner is innocently below, are in no way withheld from view but form, along with scantily dressed bodies, a running refrain to murder by axe, knife and arrow. Truly it is a veritable arsenal the wounded mother carries around with her, and it could be said that, given the woodenness of the acting and the indistinguishability of the teenagers, the only attempt at differentiation lies in the choice of mode of death.

What is surprisingly absent from *Friday the Thirteenth* is any real hint of the supernatural; the date of the title is finally revealed as significant only because it was the thirteenth of the month when the son died. The one chilling scene comes towards the end when the heroine, a somewhat older camp attendant who has managed to decapitate the vengeful mother with some kind of boathook (the search for appropriate weaponry goes on) and imagines herself safe, if a little tired, upon the lake which gives the camp its official name, is tipped into the water by the bloody revenant of the dead son; but this is revealed as only a shocked dream as she wakes up in hospital, albeit uncertain as to whether this ghostly presence will now continue to haunt Crystal Lake for ever, as we suspect he must do to ensure the continuance of the series.

The question naturally arises as to the role of adolescence in films of this type, which can be seen contentually as a kind of adult revenge on youthful sexual activity, the mark of a fantasised clampdown on maturation. One of the most interesting arguments about this is that of Donald Campbell, who has hypothesized that the root of the attraction of horror movies for adolescents lies less in bloody murder than in a prevailing atmosphere of disgust which provides duplicate images for the adolescent's disgust with the changes in his or her own emerging body, from acne to menstruation.[5] The body, we might say, is always rising up against the adolescent, a bloody, half-formed body, in which things which should be kept inside are always pressing to and out of the surface, while the things which beg for outer attention – emotions, self-images – have no means of outlet and must be kept down in an apparently permanent state of tension. Thus the bloody figure of Jason, and the contrast between his drowned, bloated flesh and the projections of perfection on which his mother's vengeance – which is perhaps his own – is expended.

A tension, then, between the body as leaky, full of unwanted holes, and the psyche as unable to find expression, unable precisely to become 'articulate': Camp Crystal Lake, the innocence of childhood, turning into Camp Blood, full of dark imaginings and premonitions, Gothic avatars of sexual complexity. These themes are also present in *Freddy's Dead*, although the tone of the film is quite different. *Freddy's Dead* is much faster; it is also much funnier; and it is also more disturbing.

If the plot of *Friday the Thirteenth* was vestigial, *Freddy's Dead* can hardly be said to have a plot at all; what it has instead is a weave of the imaginal and the real – as the black psychologist who is the film's main anchorman says with accuracy but without style, Freddy exists to 'fuck up the line between dreams and reality'. The accuracy runs deep. Freddy Krueger is an icon for our time; he is the ultimate bad father, and in this particular film of the series we even go back into his own history of abuse at the hands of *his* strap-wielding father-figure as we watch him in turn visit violence and mayhem on a range of children, almost all of whom have themselves been abused. The children concerned are inmates at a children's home set in a shabby near future, and in brief congested flashbacks we see their own terrors of father, fears in relation to which the manic, gleeful figure of Freddy comes as a kind of inverted fulfilment.

What is impressive about the portrayal of Freddy, and what also connects the series with the motifs of *Friday the Thirteenth*, is that the image of the bad father is not just a matter of blood and mutilation, but contains also a savage mockery: we are made to see how irony and sarcasm are major artillery in the war of the generations, in the battle for survival of the Primal Father, the Father-of-Enjoyment,[6] imaged of course in the razor blades which serve him for fingers, those same armed fingers we see used to such different effect in *Edward Scissorhands* (1991). For Freddy enjoys his work; translated into his own hell, at the controls of his own engine-room of the unconscious (an obvious comparison would be with the exploding boiler-room of *The Shining* (1980), although we might here also think of the mad 'father' Frankenstein setting his own galvanic machine in motion), Freddy laughs at the world of law and routine even while the fists and weapons of others turn his flesh into putty and distort his body through the spectrum of the monstrous.

Haunted houses, witches on broomsticks, they are all here, but are mere figments in the context of Freddy's paradoxically more 'real' dream presence. The other side of this continual, satyriatic abuse lies where we would expect it (or have now come to expect it after the death of religion and the consequent demise of earlier Gothic demonologies): in therapy and psychology, and each film in the series (a series which shows no real sign of ending) enacts the contest, no longer between Dracula and Van Helsing, but between the (in Freddy's case, supernatural) psychopath and a group of avatars of the psychological models which seek to explain and control him while providing succour to the orphaned, abused children who now become merely part of the film's *mise-en-scene*.

'Kids', Freddy agreeably reminds us towards the end of the film, 'these days have no respect'; one of them, therefore, meets his end (in an enactment of a fantasy no doubt entertained by parents throughout the Western world) by being translated into a video game, bouncing bloodily around a Gothic house like a creature at the other end of a vicious Nintendo, whether or not there are walls, floors or ceilings in the way. One of the great differences between this kind of material and the kind we find on display in *Friday the Thirteenth* and its many clones lies in the subject position. In *Friday the Thirteenth* there is no place to be except with the distraught adolescents; in *Freddy's Dead* the matter is not so simple, and the crazed zest which characterises Freddy takes us over the line to entertain not only the imaginal hypothesis of being savaged and abused, but also the pathological force of being oneself the abuser, possessed of powers which are supernatural if only in the sense that they have no clearly defined or authoritatively sanctioned limits. And then, of course, we also imagine the power we would need to survive this violence, the Superman into which we would have to grow, the carapace, the shield we would have to develop . . . and so a certain circuit of disavowal is set in motion.

Freddy is a figure who is dragged out of the realm of dreams, over and over again: he rises up laughing, grinning, flexing his razors, ready for another day's work. He is strictly blue-collar; his opponents – the black doctor, the caring woman, the tough girl who has survived abuse from her own father by killing him – all seem to lack what we can only call Freddy's social integration, they are, as again in *Dracula*, figures who have power and interest only as part of a team, whereas Freddy is a lone operator, the foul embodiment of individualism, fully adequate to whatever world, of his own creation, he inhabits. Significantly, both sides attempt to achieve their goals through dream: Freddy can only be freed through a kind of somnambulism, the effect, no doubt, of the sleep state into which he has himself been plunged by earlier trauma; therefore the psychologists and therapists who attempt *his* cure – of him, or from him? – can operate only by sending emissaries into the labyrinth of dream, there to do battle with the monster.

There is no doubt that we are here in the presence of a gleeful attack on the culture of therapy and social work, banal as that might sound in view of the film's Gothic and melodramatic excesses: but the brutal, inescapable and supremely important fact is that there is no ideological line separating the *Elm Street* films from the hard-hitting ethos of Thatcherism, or from the savage revitalisation of Freud's problems with seduction theory.[7] It is a battle in which a principal instrument has been turned against psychoanalysis itself, the instrument of dream: instead of being seen as a means, through interpretation, to potential enlightenment, it is here seen as the means by which the everpresent narrative of abuse will continue to be replicated down the centuries, so that, by a neat political inversion, the 'cure' can now be held responsible for the problems themselves.

With *Cape Fear,* we are in one sense on quite different terrain. Scorsese's film is a Gothic national parable, a version, like all Gothic as we have now seen so often, of history. At one point an ex-policeman brought in to try to contain the killer delivers a speech on the 'fear which saves', about how, for example, it was the fear of Indians that 'saved' the Union; the whole dialectic of barbarism and civilisation is here again, coupled, as in so many previous instances, with a class argument.

Nick Nolte plays a successful lawyer, in a marriage which is gradually revealed as sapped and empty, with a daughter with manifold problems evidently stemming from the violence of the situation between her mother and father. Nolte is revisited – haunted – by Cady, played by Robert De Niro, who has recently been released from a fourteen-year (the double of the biblical/magical seven) jail sentence for aggravated rape. Nolte was his defence lawyer; De Niro suspects (quite rightly) that Nolte suppressed a piece of evidence which, however dubiously, could have reduced this sentence. During his imprisonment De Niro has become something of a legal expert himself, but his pursuit of Nolte, first at his home and later on a houseboat at Cape Fear, is not designed to end in legal niceties but in murder, presaged by his violent rape of Nolte's mistress, his killing of the family dog, and other persecutory habits which drive Nolte, his wife and daughter to an extreme of terror.

Cape Fear itself figures in the film as a memory of a lost family happiness, symbolised in the 'house'-boat. But this lost happiness was, as it were, merely human; De Niro, while in jail, has had as his mission to become 'more than human', to survive and be resurrected from a living death in Superman form, and so he proves as he shows us how he has inured his flesh to burning and also survives death by water. Cady is a Gothic villain for our times, rising up impossibly against us just when we think we have reached the sunny uplands, tattooed with biblical messages, an incarnate prophet and himself the son of a family of preachers: as he says to Nolte's wife as he is about to rape her, 'Ready to be born again, Mrs Bowden?';

and by the end of the film, dying as he is, he is certainly also, and impressively, speaking in tongues.

His aim, as he expresses it, is curiously literary: he means to consign Nolte to the ninth circle of hell, the circle of traitors, although the pathological peculiarity about this is that the grounds for his claim of treachery seem so flimsy. After all, the suppressed document only said that his victim had been promiscuous; as Nolte uncomprehendingly says at one point, it was hardly likely that that would ever have got him off. However, the argument is quite other than this: it is about social privilege – Nolte may not be a Wall Street Master of the Universe,[8] but he moves in an analogous world – and about how the perspective of privilege can lead one to damn the underprivileged whether the reason for that is licit or merely an effect of a general belief in the villainy of the lower classes.

De Niro cannot, of course, win: after all, even though the director is Scorsese, this is still a particular kind of US cinema, and thus it cannot come about that any of the three central figures of righteousness get damaged, although the threat is always there. Abuse is certainly here, and in a very stark form: whatever De Niro is about to do to the daughter of the house, it will have to go a long way to contend with the everyday violence she has already suffered at the hands of her own father, which also serves to make her willing game for De Niro's curiously sexless advances.

If *Friday the Thirteenth* thought it kicked up a (Gothic) storm, the storm of the final scene of *Cape Fear* should put it to shame; here we have the mother and father of all Gothic storms, with the mad monk preaching to the last and eventually going down, beyond flames, but to a no less certain doom. What is dramatic about the ending, however, may have been unintended by the director; admittedly the nuclear family survives, Crusoe-like, washed up on a terminal beach, but the question surely in the audience's minds, considering the vicissitudes of this supremely dysfunctional family, is, what will happen then? Will it be, for any of them, worth carrying on, or have they received a Gothic revelation – of the ninth circle of hell, or of the pit – which will undermine their lives for ever?

In a way, the film provides us with part of an answer to this, as the daughter is given framing set speeches at beginning and end: her most poignant sentence, in the last frame, is: 'We never spoke about him – not to each other, at least', and perhaps this is the keynote, the kernel, the dream-knot, of the film, at least insofar as it entirely deconstructs the textuality with which we have been consorting, which is, after all, an account of 'events', a communication of sorts about them. But this might, perhaps, be an increasingly familiar trope: as we turn to *Basic Instinct*, already inevitably blinded by publicity, how can we be sure that what we are seeing is a single event, a film, rather than an enduring record of a continuing set of social and psychological problems with the accompanying panoply of a massive corporate industry?

In *Basic Instinct* Nick, the detective played by Michael Douglas, is to solve a violent sexual killing and suspects the ultra–rich Catherine (Sharon Stone), who is, under a pseudonym, a writer. One of her books in fact details precisely the murder recently committed, but is this double- or triple-bluff? Nick is sucked into a maze which also involves his girlfriend, who may or may not have had a neurotic relationship with Stone, centred around a brief lesbian encounter, many years previously. In the end Nick is convinced that his girlfriend is herself responsible for the killings, and shoots her. The world agrees with this verdict, but the final scene, in which the murder weapon – an ice-pick – is glimpsed under Stone's bed undermines the entire thrust of the narrative.

What is certain is that Nick is lost in the labyrinth, in a world of impossible doubles (including, in his case, double Scotches since his sinking is also imaged as a return to previous addictions), and that he is strung between two women, both of whom are – we would by now be surprised were they anything else – psychologists. Catherine's degree, interestingly, is in psychology and literature: hence, perhaps, her writing, but hence also, presumably, her supernatural ability to construct a (false) narrative out of her life; it also appears probable that one of her earlier murders was of the professor of psychology who was her university tutor.

There is no doubt that this is a paranoid text; it also, as we would expect, contains plenty of cod psychology about the unconscious, but it does seem to leave one question remarkably open: what *is* the 'basic instinct'? Is it lust, the desire which eventually drives Nick into belief in one side of an undecidable story and makes him sacrifice his girlfriend? Is it violence, seen as Catherine's one way of relating to a world from which she is otherwise isolated – for in her the blankness of the little rich girl is linked with the professional blanknesses of the psychologist and the writer, which the 'ancient' male cannot understand, and in which, as in a Gothic castle, he is lost? Greed, avarice, masochism, social envy, all would seem to be possibilities: what is all-pervasive in the film is a lust for penetration, for intrusion, for there is an extraordinary number of scenes in which people are found in other people's apartments, rooms, offices, where they should not be, as though a force is loose (sex? money?) which is so great that nothing material can withstand it.

Basic Instinct has become an iconic text, seen by critics and reviewers as saying something far more immediate and urgent than its own muddled psychology would indicate. Clearly, the main argument here has to do with gender: there is a fear and hatred of the 'clever woman' embedded in the text, in the attitudes of both Nick's colleagues and, partly, Nick himself, but also in the representation of the bitterness which exists in the relationship between the two principal women (one dark, the other blonde, of course), as though in themselves they are made to bear the burden of masculine terror of the intimacies of lesbianism, of the scene from which the male might be simply omitted, in relation to which he might be as irrelevant as Nick, with his masculine addictions and Bogart style, is coming to be in a more modern world.

But this is complexly encoded, as though the film is saying that, yes, women can be killers too, and this is a new step towards gender equality; as though the 'basic instinct' is also something which lies deeper than sexual difference, and we exist in a world of shared ultraviolence, and furthermore one which will become more complex, more labyrinthine, more Gothic as criminality and psychology become increasingly intertwined. The fascination of *Basic Instinct* – and of so many other recent horror films – with psychology is clearly reminiscent of Hitchcock, but there is more to it: psychology as a science now seems to occupy the hated and feared place in which Gothic once placed the criminal monk, as though the *secrecy* which endures in the therapeutic relationship is now seen as a 'state within a state', as a threat to order rather than as a path to a cure, and thus needs to be strangled, squeezed violently out of existence – lest those secrets should spill over into real life, lest we might thereby achieve an unwanted enlightenment.

Turning now to written texts: in 1991 there appeared a collection called *The New Gothic*, consisting of stories and excerpts from novels, edited by Patrick McGrath and Bradford Morrow. It is a highly eclectic collection, with writers as far apart as Martin Amis and Peter Straub, and including several writers whom we have looked at already – John Hawkes, Joyce Carol Oates, Robert Coover and Angela Carter. Here I want to look at four of the stories in the collection.

In Janice Galloway's 'Blood', a girl has a deformed tooth pulled out. Not knowing what to do with the rest of the day, she wanders back to school and ends up in a music room playing 'the clear, clean lines' of Mozart.[9] In the next room is a student who teaches cello; he hears her playing and comes in, although he is said to be afraid of girls, to congratulate her on her playing. She opens her mouth to reply to his question, and then the story behind the story comes to a climax as the apparently endless supply of thick blood which has been welling up in her mouth all morning – and shows no sign of abating – floods out 'over the white keys and dripping onto the clean tile floor;' she knows at this point also that other schoolchildren will soon be arriving and will see 'this unstoppable redness seeping through the fingers at her open mouth' (*New Gothic*, p. 94). Open mouth, open wound; adolescence, menstruation, what should be kept inside joining with the outside, visible, spoiling; a Gothic body whose lines are etched and stretched in blood, the unstoppable blood which contaminates everything and, in the story, suffuses the entire outer world.

Scott Bradfield's 'Didn't She Know' is a more complex account of Alison, 'the sort of woman who appealed to old men' (*New Gothic*, pp. 97 *et seq.*). But Alison, a waitress, knows some young men too, and 'whenever Alison's young men dropped by for coffee, they and the old men grew moody and indecorous with one another'. Brilliantly understated phrasing; Alison is often the old men's only friend, and of course they tend to leave her things in their wills; she is taken to court by a widow, but 'began visiting the judge's house every Thursday afternoon, whenever the judge's wife was away . . .'. But 'every night she made love with the young men until dawn when they fell asleep without her', until she 'could feel youth being methodically extracted from her body like the thin smooth exudated thread of a silkworm'. As Alison tries to preserve her body through endless workouts the young men get more and more angry and start to destroy her property, and by the end it is clear they will destroy her too.

What is this curious and extremely effective parable about? Alison's life, clearly, is *impossible*; this is one interpretation of the question of the title, and it also bears on the Lacanian hypothesis that enjoyment for speaking beasts is already impossible.[10] The gentle old men provide succour and communication, but only for a time and only based on their stereotyped view of Alison herself. The violent young men, in their leather and studs, want more, always more; they cannot bear the part of her they see as leached away by the thanatic, the drive down towards death which she incarnates (without, of course, *knowing* it). Desire is indeed impossible on this terrain; stuck with a blankness of affect which reminds us of *Basic*

Instinct, as also of Purdy and Ballard, Alison is 'wedded' to a total unawareness of the primal horde, the succession of the generations, or the meaning of the bloody mutilation and death towards which she is – imminently – destined.

In Yannick Murphy's extremely short 'The Fish Keeper', the 'heroine' has a 'black pie slice' in her eye, a tank full of killer fish (angels, convicts, green terrors), her mother is paranoiac, and outside on the streets a boy called Joshey is dying of a terminal illness which has to do with the filthy river which runs near her house. One of her dogs eats rat poison; her best fish dies; 'then I go to the river and jump in and think of all the people there could be to come and tell me that now I have to get out' (*New Gothic*, p. 134). They will not do so, of course; blankness, death of affect, a terrifying absence; whatever *this* definition of the 'new Gothic' might be (and there are, as we shall see, others), this particular story seems emblematic. What is absent again here, principally, is *possibility*: there is no possibility of escape, of choice, of the notion that things might be different; but again, perhaps it is better to say that here there is no desire, we are in the psychotic world of the pure drive, and it is this primal world which much of the 'new Gothic' tries to recount, even at the unavoidable expense of narrative extension. If the earlier Gothic gave us a world in which there was no space for the 'psychological bourgeoisie' of ethical choice, refinement of manner, then stories like this clearly continue the motif under a contemporary guise; what we have here is a world to which social workers come and from which they stand back aghast as they see the inadequacy of their models to the distorted inner realities of life in a room inhabited only by a coffee table and a fish tank, in which desire for change and development cannot even be imagined and in which objects exert their own malevolent force, their own pull toward death.

We are now in a position to generalise, and to notice that contemporary Gothic is obsessed by notions of the 'cure' and similarly committed to ways of invalidating them. In the service of this complex fascination, it coins a variety of discourses, from the 'upperworld' form of detailed critiques of the inadequacies of the helping professions to the 'lower-world' form of portraying lives into which no form of cure – or care – can ever intrude. As always, Gothic deals in bare and brutalised boundaries; and again as always it takes its colours from the prevailing ideology, whether that be counter-Jacobinism, Thatcherism or the 'New World Order'.

The fourth story I want to mention, 'Rigor Beach' by Emma

Tennant, pursues the blankness we find in the other tales, this direct translation – or we might call it 'psychotic concretisation' – between inner and outer worlds to a kind of conclusion. Ingrid has an appointment with a man, an unknown man. Around their sexual encounter she appears to be building a set of dangerous fantasies (dangerous, that is, to her); included in these is the notion that tomorrow they will go to the beach, so that into the dry dead world which she inhabits there will come a moment of lubrication, of – dare we say it? – enjoyment, pleasure. As in the case of Alison, this is never actually possible; as with Alison there is no real concern with understanding why; instead she produces her own scenario. Having killed the man, she then turns his body into precisely the beach she wishes to visit, covering him with shells, inserting cocktail parasols into his flesh, enacting the story of a holiday into his 'long holiday'; she has found a body into which to inscribe her own picnic, a way of slowing the sands of time, of building sandcastles, of evading the sandman, all the tropes of sand are here used and reused, used as useless; again there can be no desire, we are in the world of the drive which appreciates no distance between its starting-point and its goal and thus is strictly aimless, there can here be no aim because desire is transmitted direct into the suffering but dead body which is, naturally, the inner death from which the heroine has *already* suffered.

Four stories, four 'heroines'; the trajectory of the dead heroine is not the only one which this anthology traverses, but it is by far the most compelling. If there is a *new* 'female Gothic', then it lies here (and not in, for example, the unending 'Gothic romance');[11] and it marks too a new formal stage of fiction. For just as the Gothic fruitfully and progressively 'decayed' from the novel down to the short story, the 'tale',[12] most emblematically in Poe, so we now see a new stage of decay, down to an extreme brevity, a narrative traject-ory in which almost nothing is known by the end that has not already been known at the outset, in which the blank voice which has originated the tale merely – but purely – plays out its own dried fantasies on a corpse, thus replicating perfectly an imagining of total social surveillance.

Perhaps we need to refer back to the 'Father of Enjoyment', mentioned in connection with Freddy Krueger, and to his psycho-analytic counterpart, the 'Mother of Separation', the fantasy of the mother who is always already withheld, the figure for the perennial absence of plenitude. We are no longer here in a labyrinth; we are in the mysterious and contested space at the heart of the labyrinth, but it is not the Minotaur that we find there, it is the Medusa, the snakey head which paralyses itself as it turns this way and that, not in search of escape or answer, but in a ceremonial repetition of death.

Ceremony, ritual: these are the outer-world terms in which one might begin to describe a dry and dead ritualism which halts narrative before it has begun, a ritualism which finds its outward form in the transactions of the money market and which requires us to discover a new formal term for these writings, a term which we might 'coin', beyond the jokey excesses of postmodernism: a term like for example, de-valuation, de-mentation. Not a new term; but these stories are all forms of dementia, they are all stories about the final loss of value implied in age, deprivation, impotence: at the other end of abuse, they are about minds and values which have been so degraded that their own substance, their substrate, whatever (ever) underpinned then, has vanished, a series of rotting piers in the dusk, Brighton schlock, writing shock, dead bones which cannot move. Women's bones, particularly; for all of these de-narratives are female, all of them enact the inscription on women's bodies as tombs (even when displaced as in 'Rigor Beach'), all of them deny the intricacy and fascination of the crypt, all of them say that there are no words worth reading on the gravestone, the cerements are simply themselves and will soon dissolve in mildew and the rotting night. Need we half-deny (Demi) more (Moore)?

One variant, then, one powerful variant on the contemporary Gothic (although I have been deliberately shameless in my selection from the anthology). Another root of (another route through) the contemporary Gothic begins with Anne Rice's lengthening series of vampire novels, and here I want to look briefly at the first of the series, *Interview with the Vampire* (1976).

> Her lips were red, her looks were free,
> Her locks were yellow as gold:
> Her skin was as white as leprosy,
> The Night-mare Life-in-Death was she,
> Who thicks man's blood with cold.[13]

Thus the ghost of Coleridge is made to reintroduce us to the figure of the vampire but this time, as it were, from the other side; for this is the first-person narration of Louis, a New Orleans vampire, and his adventures in New World and Old, adventures in search both of an explanation for his state and of companionship of his own kind.

In some ways, the novel is an extraordinary achievement. After all, there is a certain repetitiveness to the life and desires of a vampire, if not to the experience of those who encounter him or her; yet Rice manages to portray the world of the vampire as rich, glowing, lustrous – she manages, in short, to show us the realm of sensual pleasure which is opened to the vampire's vastly expanded senses and which is the compensation for the agony of immortal life at the service of an unintelligible drive. This is a world of flame and fire, a world where everything can be savoured by night even if the price to be paid is the pain of looking always into an endless future.

On the other hand, there is a sense in which Rice shirks the questions which lie behind Louis's condition. For Louis is a *good* vampire; not very good, to be sure, since he kills nightly, but he does make an attempt to kill only animals, like a kind of vegetarian bloodsucker, and there are suggestions throughout that the human has not been entirely burned out of him, as it has from his companions, the conventionally violent Lestat and the terrifying child-vampire, whose body can never get beyond the five-year-old stage, Claudia.

It is therefore oddly as though, however close we get to the vampiric state, there is always still a distance to be traversed, a barrier of comprehension. Yet there is something else here too, something which arises from and develops upon *Dracula*. For here desire runs beyond sexuality. Louis's main attractions are towards Claudia and towards a Parisian male vampire, Armand; these attractions are described in enormous detail and at obsessive length, but because they are to a large extent fleshless, because the actuality of desire is located elsewhere, in the nightly hunt, this does not pall; indeed, one might go further and suggest that what Rice's book shows is that *only* the 'perversions' can permit this dwelling upon passion without sentimentality.

In the scene in the Théâtre des Vampires where the undead literally 'act out' their obsessions, this 'dwelling' on perverse passion comes perilously close, perhaps inevitably, to the pornographic; but the text as a whole is redeemed and enriched by the complex equivalents Rice draws between the various stages and aspects of vampirism and, as it were, the human world. Armand, who is far older than the other vampires, tells Louis that he needs him in order to make contact with the nineteenth century: 'You are the spirit, you are the heart'. Louis responds with bitter laughter: 'I'm not the spirit of any age. I'm at odds with everything and always have been! I have never belonged anywhere with anyone at any time!'. 'But Louis', replies Armand, 'This is the very spirit of your age. Don't you see that? Everyone else feels as you feel. Your fall from grace and faith has been the fall of a century' (*Vampire*, p. 310).

At this point the themes of the book come into focus; we might say that Rice has written a text in which *Dracula* is re-viewed through Walter Benjamin, for here Paris is certainly 'the capital of the nineteenth century',[14] and the vampires who stroll its night-time, gaslit streets are nothing but the very image of the *flâneur*. We also see now the strength of the structure which places Louis in a perennially liminal position between the human and the vampiric, between immersion in history and suspension above it, between susceptibility to desire and reduction to the drive, for it is from this unique vantage-point that he can observe but at the same time experience upon his heightened senses the waning of an age, further imaged in his 'translations' between New World and Old.

Interview with the Vampire, then, is a work which brings decadent materials under a controlling intelligence, and seeks to rework the historical figures of Gothic; like *Cape Fear*, it is a historical parable, and its distortions are implicitly offered as parallel to, and no less compelling than, those other distortions which are embedded in received and official versions of the past. But when we think of contemporary horror writing we are, of course, equally likely to think of other, more 'populist' names, of Ramsey Campbell, James Herbert, Stephen King. I have space here only for some brief remarks on two texts, one by Campbell and one by King, as representatives of the vast field of black-jacketed genre fiction.

Ramsey Campbell's *The Long Lost* (1993) concerns a mysterious encounter in which David and Joelle, a husband-and-wife builder and decorator team on holiday in Wales, discover an elderly woman, Gwen, on an island. She is apparently in a peculiar kind of sleep, but they awaken her; on the basis of a photograph which only David sees, she is revealed as a distant relation, and they bring her back to Chester and install her in a nearby old people's home. At a party they introduce her to their friends, and she gives them each a cake. There are no prizes for deducing that once they have eaten the cakes life is never quite the same again as they are beset by various problems and lusts, which Campbell apparently means us to see as outcroppings of their own failures.

Eventually David realises that something is amiss with Gwen, but only at the point when she is intending to move on anyway. David works out that she is a 'sin-eater'; quite what she has been doing feeding other people her sins, and indeed what she was doing in her long sleep, are never made clear, and the ending is even more remarkably incoherent, with Gwen climbing a mountain, shedding clothes, hair, flesh as she goes and being apparently translated into a pure state at the top of it, which seems an odd reward for the mayhem she has created down below.

The characters are out of *Peyton Place*, cardboard cutouts each identifiable by a single mannerism, a prevalent failing; the suburban landscape reminds us of the insane overpainted ordinariness of the world of *Edward Scissorhands*, or of the maddening suburbia of Oates's *Expensive People*. The dialogue, especially at the start of the novel, is altogether more peculiar. At the party, for example, Gwen feels faint but recovers. Joelle asks her what has been wrong, to which Gwen replies, 'Nothing that can touch me any more. Nothing you'd want to know about, Joelle'. Or to David, who is similarly solicitous just after the cakes have been handed round: 'You enjoy yourselves while you can'.[15] In fact, almost every line Gwen says is a kind of blank *double-entendre*, which suggests an audience positioning which is 'in on the secret' from the very beginning. As in the formulaic fiction of M. R. James, the element of suspense has here collapsed; true, we do not know *exactly* what Gwen is but, to be honest, it is not clear that Campbell does either. Instead, we are taken through a reenactment in which our attention focuses merely on the giveaway lines themselves; if there is irony here, it moves within a very limited circle, because the only difference between those who do and those who do not follow the dialogue would be between one group of horror fans and another.

When we turn from Ramsey Campbell to Stephen King, we are entering a different world. King, as the covers of his books endlessly remind us, is the world's best-selling author, perhaps the most widely read writer of all time, and this without the endless stream of film versions. His output is vast, and his fertility shows no signs of abating. More impressively and more interestingly, we find that King returns us from – or perhaps via – the formulaic to more pressing concerns. Many of the novels, usually implicitly but occasionally, as in *The Library Policeman* (1990), entirely explicitly, are centred on child abuse; in books like *The Shining* (1977) the abusing father receives a whole new series of images; and behind this there lies a constant grappling, again implicit, with problems of memory and desire, and particularly with the questions of recollection and reconstruction which underlie so much current epistemological debate, and which we can also see as central to earlier Gothic forms.

The social argument which underpins the texts is problematic: if we take *The Tommy-Knockers* (1988) as emblematic, then there we have an 'invasion' of small-town USA by a force of (long-dead) aliens who at first seem terribly fierce, but once the full might of the US State has been unleashed against them, they look very feeble indeed and turn out just to be a roving gang of space tinkers, easily blown away, by the Marines and the force of the national 'war machine',[16] like any other group of travellers, or indeed like an impotent version of Deleuze and Guattari's nomads. King speaks to small-town values: he criticises them, but always from within; it is as though, in the midst of surrounding horrors, Main Street USA is the cosy blanket to be drawn up to the chin, even if this will not prevent the eyes from seeing what they must.

But the most interesting of King's texts remains *Misery* (1987), at least in part because of its extraordinary self-referentiality, of the Gothic labyrinth of writers and readers into which it plunges us. Paul Sheldon is a writer. He is in a car accident and wakes up to find that he has been 'rescued' by a woman called Annie Wilkes, who announces that she is his biggest fan. 'When you look into the abyss, the abyss also looks into you', an epigraph from Nietzsche – which figures also in *Watchmen* – reminds us, and so it is with Annie.[17] She is a particular fan of a series of novels Sheldon has written featuring the curiously named Misery Chastain, a series which Sheldon has now finished with, to his great relief.

Or rather, he thinks he has. Annie discovers from a manuscript in his possession that this is the case, and is infuriated; she wants him to write another one, and since she has him at her mercy, suffering from broken bones and worse, has addicted him to pain-killing drugs while he was unconscious, and is willing to chop off his foot, his thumb, in her effort to persuade him to her point of view, he is under a certain pressure to do so.

Who or what is Annie? When Sheldon at one point annoys her, 'suddenly her face broke apart. The stony obduracy shattered and what shone through was the countenance of an insanely angry child. . . . Could one possibly play Scheherazade when one's captor was insane?' (*Misery*, p. 83). She is also a nurse, and her appearance and her physique set her up as a figure of 'terrible bogus maternity'. She is, furthermore, a self-appointed editor and literary critic, albeit of a somewhat unusual kind, with her own views on how Misery is to be 'raised from the grave' for another appearance, and her own ultra-violent means of ensuring that Sheldon gets the points she is making, which are then exemplified in those pages of his manuscript which are reproduced within the text of *Misery*. She is also, clearly, a severe depressive; she has a 'little place in the country' to which she goes when things get too bad; and what she does there is scream.

King is questioning – and tells us he is questioning, for example through the Montaigne epigraph, 'Writing does not *cause* misery, it is born of misery' (*Misery*, p. 109) – the roots of writing. The 'text' of the novel is suspended between two other texts, the drafts of the new Misery novel and the file of clippings which Sheldon discovers and which reveal Annie's murderous history – including the destruction of a large number of babies when she was head of a hospital maternity unit. Sheldon himself asks constantly about the *conditions of possibility* of writing; indeed, we might further ask what *residual body* would be necessary in order for the writing act to continue, as bits of Sheldon are hacked away with axe and chainsaw. What also, the questions continue, are the *conditions of freedom* of the writer? We may not mourn at the thought of the multimillionnaire King being at the mercy of his fans, for we may indeed not see this as the essence of misery; yet the questions remain serious ones, especially when situated resolutely within the framework of King's narrative persona, the small-town corn-pone philosopher whom success can never affect.

At the end of the maze, in the heart of the labyrinth of *Misery*, is an image: it appears when Sheldon, wounded and damaged but still alive, has returned to his apartment after his ordeal. He walks in and recognises a smell; then 'Annie rose up from behind the sofa like a white ghost, dressed in a nurse's uniform and cap. The axe was in her hand and she was screaming . . .' (*Misery*, p. 364). This is, of course, a fantasy, a hallucination: another nurse to place alongside Ken Kesey's Big Nurse,[18] another axe to place beside the weaponry of the slasher and the ripper, another maternal body turned sour to place in the gallery of female stereotypes. But all this is wrapped, as in so much of the original Gothic, into an investigation of what it is to be a writer, what parts of the self are involved, what can be *told* of one's current state, what is the 'real' of the experience of 'dreadful pleasure'.

For the great irony of the text is that, if all writing is a communication, all a question of letters, then it is precisely Sheldon's success, his prestige, which causes this final reduction of all his efforts at writing to a non-communication; or rather, to a communication only with the unreadable and unreaderly psychotic dimension which Annie represents, while all his attempts to get a message through to the outside world meet with failure, until the final point where he himself becomes the killer, thereby vindicating the idea that his need to write overrides human life, that 'in the beginning was the word'.

And yet this too replicates something curious about King's writing, for when compared with some other branches of the contemporary literature of terror, it carries a sense of privacy and enclosure; the most dire events may and do happen, but they do not abut directly onto the public world, other than insofar as that public world is constructed within the text itself. The plethora of texts dealing with serial killers, to which we shall now turn, is very different: here the proximity to 'real-life' cases is very much a key to the text. Perhaps the most important example is Thomas Harris; it was from a novel of his that *The Silence of the Lambs* (1991) was made, and among his current projects is a work which will involve the Italian serial killer, 'Il Mostro' (the monster), whose trial Harris has attended.

In Harris's *Red Dragon* (1981), Francis Dolarhyde is the serial killer. He has, as they all have, his own very particular targets, his own methods, his own ceremonials. He hears voices and obeys injunctions, and the governing force, the controlling image, in his life is Blake's picture of *The Great Red Dragon and the Woman Clothed with the Sun*, a copy of which he has tattooed on his back, the visible (though partially occluded) sign of an inscription of dark romanticism, as it were, on his soul. But then, Dolarhyde has never had much chance to develop any differently. Abandoned by his mother, he is brought up by a vicious grandmother who threatens him with physical castration. He was deformed at birth and has a badly sealed hare-lip. He works, we are not surprised to hear, in a darkroom; he is, shall we say, very interested in photography.

The plot is predictable; the only notable thing about it is that Will Graham, the hero who pursues, does so in part by invoking the help of that other contemporary monster, Hannibal Lecter, in a series of attempts to get inside the mind of the serial killer, partly because he, Graham, has been a killer too. But in the end, nothing is really learned; Graham gives up on trying to understand Dolarhyde, and falls into some rambling musings:

> In the Green Machine there is no mercy; *we* make mercy, manufacture it in the parts that have overgrown our basic reptile brain.
> There is no murder. We make murder, and it matters only to us.

> Graham knew too well that he contained all the elements to make murder; perhaps mercy too.
>
> He understood murder uncomfortably well though.
>
> He wondered if, in the great body of humankind, in the minds of men set on civilisation, the vicious urges we control in ourselves and the dark instinctive knowledge of those urges function like the crippled virus the body arms against.[19]

Well, indeed: we are here back on the terrain of *Basic Instinct*, and with the same vagueness and evasion at its heart, the same unwillingness to be precise or accurate when it comes to analysing the psyche or the social conditions which form, mutate and mutilate it. It is as though such texts as this enact a double urge: first to draw near to the violent and the violated body, but second, and no less important, to refuse to trace the lines along which these bodies might function. This fits again with the exile or demonisation of the psychologist; if there is a fear of the virus here, it is a taboo fear that to draw too close to understanding is to risk infection, to risk the glass walls of Hannibal Lecter's cell in his psychiatric hospital coming down and a madness seeping out and into the veins.

Red Dragon is recounted in a flat reportage that owes more (although not much) to the hard-boiled detective novel than to Gothic; no doubt this is a measure of its assumed proximity to the 'real', but it also serves as a defence, as a deliberate refutation of the psychotic, as an implicit statement that, however Graham might feel himself embroiled in the scenarios of sadism, we, the writer and the readers, are allowed to reside in a protected space, we are not to be drawn into the position, characteristic of much other Gothic, of the 'implicated reader'.[20] Thus the text acts against itself, protecting and defending itself all the time against the very forces with which it professes to deal.

The same cannot be said of Iain Banks's brilliant book, *The Wasp Factory* (1984), 'a Gothic horror story of quite exceptional quality',[21] another narrative of sadism and torture, but one in which the reader is inextricably involved from the very start, and where the story of child abuse, just as prevalent here as in *Red Dragon*, is brought to a fine point. It is also the only book of which I am aware which contains three pages of review material at the front, much of it violently antipathetic: 'obscenity', 'silly, gloatingly sadistic and grisly', 'exorbitant brutalities' and so on.

It is a first-person narrative, told by Frank, who at one point offers us the following insight:

All our lives are symbols. Everything we do is part of a pattern we have at least some say in. The strong make their own patterns and influence other people's, the weak have their courses mapped out for them. The weak and the unlucky, and the stupid. The Wasp Factory is part of the pattern because it is part of life and – even more so – part of death. Like life it is complicated, so all the components are there. The reason it can answer questions is because every question is a start looking for an end, and the Factory is about the End – death, no less. Keep your entrails and sticks and dice and books and birds and voices and pendants and all the rest of that crap; I have the Factory, and it's about now and the future; not the past.

(The Wasp Factory, pp. 117–18)

Frank is a seventeen-year-old monster, living on an island with his eccentric father. He has murdered three children, although he regards this as just a phase he was going through; but perhaps more importantly, he lives his life entirely according to what he calls symbolism – every part of the island, every movement he makes, every part and exudation of his body forms part of this symbolism – but which would psychologically be more recognisable as a version of infant ritualism, a further variant on the ritualism we found running through the short stories mentioned above.[22] The Wasp Factory is part of this, a machine which Frank believes tells the future according to the way in which the wasps trapped inside it die.

Frank, as narrator, has an affable and confiding manner; he knows he is a little strange, but puts it down to a serious accident he had when small which effectively castrated him. His ceaseless killings of animals are not a moral problem for him; they are at the service of maintaining the island as his own fortress, akin to the fortress of the autistic child, into which nothing must be allowed to intrude, and out from which Frank himself can barely venture. Not many of his relatives have survived his murderous attentions; one who has, however, is his half-brother Eric who, as the novel opens, has escaped from an asylum. Eric has had a devastating experience in youth which has driven him mad; it also drove him to burning dogs, and this was at least one of the reasons for his incarceration. The text is punctuated by hysterical (and sometimes hilarious) phone-calls from Eric as he gets gradually closer to the island. In the end he arrives, screaming and wielding an axe, but these events pale into insignificance as Frank finally finds out from his father the truth about himself; that he, Frank, is really Frances, a girl whom his father has been dosing with male hormones since she was small as part of an 'experiment'.

Put thus, the story may indeed sound melodramatic and contrived, but the sheer zest of Banks's telling, the inwardness with which we are presented with Frank, makes it quite different, as does his own grim realisation at the end:

> Having no purpose in life or procreation, I invested all my worth in that grim opposite, and so found a negative and negation of the fecundity only others could lay claim to. I believe that I decided if I could never become a man, I – the unmanned – would out-man those around me, and so I became the killer . . . Talk about penis envy.
>
> (*The Wasp Factory*, p. 183)

It is indeed hard to avoid, in this context, talking about penis envy; but there is more to it than this, signified in the resonant phrase, 'that grim opposite'. *The Wasp Factory* is, precisely, an account of the formation of the male psyche, self-sufficient, islanded, fortressed; every item in the inventory of torture can be seen as reactive, as a protection against Frank's hatred of the 'weakness' of women – and of animals, although at one point he is, to his own and our surprise, almost killed by a buck rabbit. Eric's open madness is, in a sense, a side issue; it is Frank who has been driven into a ritual formation which involves torture, slaughter and appeasement by what might be a final form of child abuse, deliberate resexing in the service of an apparently pointless experiment which places Frank's father alongside Doctor Moreau in the gallery of demonic manipulation.

The island itself becomes a curious reterritorialisation of Gothic terrain, with every region marked out in blood, to prevent the dreaded recrudescence of the past, for reasons which are for Frank entirely unconscious. Infant ritualism itself is thus reexpressed as the fear of parental punishment, the need to be *locked* – inside rituals, inside rigid formulae, which may serve to prevent change and yet to hide the past from the inner eye. But this, the text implies, is not a peculiarity; it is the very ground of growing up, it is this warped maturation which provides the model, the endless terror of weakness, the endless desire to achieve strength and egoic adequacy even while the unconscious is telling us that nothing is possible, that enjoyment is forever outlawed, not because we are speaking animals but precisely because of the mad force of symbolisation and the removal of the body from the 'scene of the crime' which this entails.

If Rice, Campbell, King, Harris and Banks all, in very different ways, take up the links between the Gothic, sadism and the social formations which encourage the development of a torturing psyche, then M. John Harrison stands as the major current exponent of a different Gothic legacy, the legacy – coming, as we might see it, from the shrouded worlds of Lindsay or De la Mare – of half-lights, ambiguities and figures moving in a dusk of their own devising. In his Viriconium novels he constructs a new *bricolage* of mythology characterised chiefly, and precisely, by ambiguity; every gesture, every movement, is freighted with a wealth of possible but undecidable meanings before which the narrator, and thus the reader, flinches in a cloud of uncertainty.

His most remarkable novel to date is *The Course of the Heart* (1993), which introduces us to three characters who are bound together in a ghastly pact which stems from an event which took place while they were students; they came under the influence of a grimy, crazed occultist called Yaxley, and in his company performed a rite – an enactment, a ritual – which they perceive as having changed their lives forever. What this rite was we are destined never to find out, just as they become increasingly unsure that they can remember it themselves; besides, the epistemological question is unanswerable – how can a past event have 'changed' *anything* since we have no knowledge of what life would otherwise have been, just as the abused child cannot *know* what alternatives lie buried in the crypt, now mounded over with the detritus of a warped maturation?

Two of the three have married each other, later separated; while they were together, in an attempt to assuage the wound from which they perceived themselves to be suffering, they invented a complex written mythology involving a realm, known only as the Coeur, which somehow intersects with and influences, at crucial stages, historical development in the outer world. Here is a wealth of references to the old ambiguous themes of Rosicrucianism and Swedenborgianism, the idea that there is an elite wielding control behind the scenes, that there is another world which, if only we could make sense of its signs and messages, would enable all the accidents and disasters of personal and social history to fall into place, another text whose mode of existence can only fitfully be described but which places a fundamental skew on the text which appears to be in front of us.

The pursuit of the Coeur ends in death; the third of the trinity, who tells the story, appears relatively immune to the fate welling up from the past, but this is something we cannot know for sure. Yaxley takes his place in the galaxy of bad fathers; he inducts the three into a form of life which will make them forever dissatisfied with this one, giving to each a pursuing spirit, a demon, which haunts them until death. But all remains shrouded in ambiguity; what was this Ur-event, what, if anything, did it change, how can Yaxley, obviously an impoverished and bitter charlatan, have had access to a realm which bears the power of change and destruction?

Harrison offers us no answers, instead a dogged account of ruined lives, lives which are forever, as it were 'abbreviated' by being *under the shadow*, and it is of the nature of the shadow that, first, we cannot tell its precise outlines or its nature and, second, that it conjures, in a curiously reversed process, an image of a bright land to which we endlessly strive but whose dimensions are never such that they can admit us into our very own and golden city. What all of Harrison's texts present is an image of people in exile, an exile which cannot be reversed since the recollection of the previous state has eroded, we are uncertain about our memory and thus about our desire.

The later course of the narrator's life is recounted to us briefly at the end in tones of appalling bleakness; much has been made of his passionate if somnambulistic attachment to his wife, but when she dies it appears that she has for years been having an affair of which he knew nothing. This, perhaps, is his demon, his haunting; certainly after this realisation – the realisation that things are not as he had imagined them, that very realisation which is figured psychologically as the spark to a lifetime of depression – nothing further can happen, he is condemned to a gradually diminishing life as though, whatever the primary ritual was, it served to cut off possibility forever, to obscure hope in the real world. For the other two characters it was at least transferred to the shimmering and glorious if unattainable possibilities of the Coeur, but for the narrator there is no such possible fantasy, for the realm of the imaginal has already been foreclosed.

It would be proper to call *The Course of the Heart*, like *The Haunted Woman*, a numinous novel, a novel where there is a glow which surrounds everyday events; yet this glow does not invest them with meaning, rather it renders them unendingly bitter as they are themselves merely the shadow which will always shut out the glory and, no matter which way we twist, something irremediable will always blot out any emanation from that other life, unless we conceive it merely as the glow, the penumbra of the sun during a season of total eclipse. Eclipsed lives, lives already lived among the ruins, a Gothic land where darkness reigns and the future can never escape from the dread of the past; even the gods for Harrison are bleak and often petty, replacing each other, as they do in Viriconium, with occasional blood but very little conviction.

If, however, we are to look for the emblematic Gothic house, the haunted repository of our historical imaginings, in contemporary fiction then we might find it in what could at first glance seem a surprising place: namely, in the house called 'Nishapur' in Salman Rushdie's *Shame* (1983), where our hero, Omar Khayyam Shakil, had as a child the run of the house and, so the everpresent narrator informs us,

> plunged deeper and deeper into the seemingly bottomless depths of that decaying realm. Believe me when I tell you that he stumbled down corridors so long untrodden that his sandalled feet sank into the dust right up to his ankles; that he discovered ruined staircases made impassable by long ago earthquakes which had caused them to heave up into tooth-sharp mountains and also to fall away to reveal dark abysses of fear ... in the silence of the night and the first sounds of dawn he explored beyond history into what seemed the positively archaeological antiquity of 'Nishapur', discovering in almirahs the wood of whose doors disintegrated beneath his tentative fingers the impossible forms of painted neolithic pottery in the Kordiji style; or in kitchen quarters whose existence was no longer even suspected he would gaze ignorantly upon bronze implements of utterly fabulous age; or in regions of that colossal palace which had been abandoned long ago because of the collapse of their plumbing he would delve into the quake-exposed intricacies of brick drainage systems that had been out of date for centuries.[23]

All this, of course – the dream of the infinitely intricate and labyrinthine castle, the plunge down through the layered depths of age, perhaps above all the 'Gothic' question of whether or not we 'believe' the narrator – is reminiscent of Udolpho, Gormenghast and their many avatars; but the historical, geographical and political context is very different. For *Shame* is in itself a novel about maps, boundaries, borders, and the house of 'Nishapur' is structured precisely as an image of the suffering body of a specific country, of an imaginary Pakistan, 'Peccavistan' as Rushdie has it, riven by internal boundaries and wrenchings, uncognisant of its own buried histories. It is a house which has, in a sense, always been in the wrong style; it is an imposition of foreignness, to an extent such that the notion of the 'native' or the 'natural' has been entirely forgotten.

In a further reticulation of Gothic as a form of history, these prehistoric earthquakes are also the violences of a nation-state seeking to come into being, with all the exclusions and divisions thus entailed: 'Peccavistan' has always, according to *Shame*, been a 'mistake', a wrong birth marked by the double fissure of its imperial heritage and the divide from the rest of the Indian subcontinent. Yet in this sense the basic plot of *Shame* is straightforwardly Gothic, and has to do with the 'sins of the fathers'; all these sins accumulate here in one suffering symbolic body (and here we have the root of one of many possible comparisons between Rushdie and Dickens), the body of Sufiya Zinobia, Shakil's damaged bride, and turn her into a monster, a monster of shame, who strangles and murders in her sleep, finally destroying Shakil and all around her in her blind unknowing rage against what her country has been forced – largely by the corruption of its own leaders – into becoming. And thus we can see that it is hardly an accident that an image such as 'Nishapur' should come to us in a postcolonial context; for just as the original Gothic explored psychic damage in relation to forms of a domestic class struggle, so we can expect the legacy of empire to throw up too its unassuageable images from the past, to remind us of the damage done and to try to find symbols for this damage and for its consequences in the labyrinth of text and psyche.

But we can also expect, as different forms of technological internationalism, themselves riven by guilt about the violence of the past and about the hypocrisy of the present, come to the fore, a further movement towards a kind of sublation of national and historical difference, however unrealistic. This is very much what we find in what we might call the 'cyber-Gothic' of writers like William Gibson, who is in fact Canadian but whose fiction moves in a world where such national differences have come to mean very little.

His first major novel, *Neuromancer* (1984), set the parameters for a whole subgenre. Its premises are situated firmly in a world of information technology; we are to assume the possibility of inhabiting, if only partially, a realm of 'cyberspace', in which zones of information are protected by codes and IT weaponry, 'ice', which has the power to reach out beyond the confines of the computer and distort and damage the nervous system of the operator. The 'hero', the aptly deindividuated Case, is such an operator, bound in to his task by a previous implantation of his nervous system; his opponent, it emerges, is not human but an artificial intelligence, Wintermute, who is struggling, like so many Gothic villains and with something of their curious blindness, for omnipotence. There is in the text a conflict of levels. At the level of setting and ambience, we have a radical departure, the invention of a fantasy realm (for despite technological advances most of Gibson's premises remain in the world of fantasy) inhabited by strange intelligences and separated from the world outside the network; but at the level of plot, we are still firmly on highly recognisable terrain. Although, for example, Case's principal assistant is in fact a computer reconstruction of a dead man, a terminated 'flatliner', he nevertheless has precisely the same wisecracking habits as you would expect from the principal adjuvant in any hard-boiled detective novel, and a similarly sinister laugh. Although Case's main girl is herself a partial reconstruction, with flashing razorblades for nails and implanted Raybans for eyes, she behaves very much according to the same clichés and conventions; even the bars and their denizens are straight out of Raymond Chandler.

And this is part of the weary irony of the text: for there is in it a real tension between new and older forms of excess and monstrosity, and Case moves precisely between the two worlds, the hi-tech world of gleaming surfaces, pure metal, the unfailing machine, and the sour world of small-time crooks and flashing menace: the world of mind and the world of 'meat'. 'Meat', in *Neuromancer*, acts as a code to summarise the whole resistant world of bodies, that which cannot, in the end, be evaded no matter how sophisticated the techniques of projection, telepathy, cryogenesis; but as there is no morality in cyberspace, an all-important Gothic question is raised once again: can there be any morality at all aside from the body? The anxieties of the text are also hinted at in its title: if 'romance', considered in its broadest emotional and textual definitions has ever been possible then that possibility might now be over, sublated into a pattern of neural networks, psychic distortion now evidenced only as damage to the nervous system, heightening of sensibility now supplanted by artificial enhancement of that same system as the notion of personality itself becomes seen as a 'neurotic' construct.

There are elements here of the City of Night of John Rechy, elements of Burroughs, perhaps also of Ballard; there certainly are elements of the paranoid Gothic in general, as the artificial intelligence Wintermute attains to a virtual godhood principally at the expense of its doomed opponent, Neuromancer itself, another artificial intelligence which defines itself precisely as 'pure personality', in contrast to which Wintermute itself is sometimes referred to in Frankensteinian terms as 'the demon'. There is of course no real outcome to this conflict: as Wintermute attains its goal, thus it too alters, and the rules of the whole game become different. Case, the individual 'case', the irreducible example, has only been a bit-player in this new, computerised version of the ancient cosmic struggle; his comprehension is but little improved by its temporary resolution.

But if Case can be seen as an entirely traditional hard-boiled hero, with only the brand names of his cigarettes and alcohol updated and internationalised and with a keyboard (usually) in his holster, contemporary writing is also throwing up a new range of figures which put us as readers into a far less comfortable relation with the text. A major example of this form of 'psychopathic Gothic' is Will Self's *My Idea of Fun* (1993), where the first-person narrator is Ian Wharton, an eidetiker who had, he claims, a childhood 'sufficiently problematic to make me interesting, but not enough to disturb';[24] his unwanted skill forces him to find ways, remarkably similar to Frank's in *The Wasp Factory*, of blanking out his sensitivity through an intensity of petty bodily ritual. His life changes, however, when it is entered by Mr Broadhurst, who is tall, fat, oversolid, apparently ageless, given to extraordinarily Churchillian rhetoric, and clearly modelled on one of the narrator's playthings:

> 'I am The Fat Controller', said the Mr Broadhurst in my eidetic vision. 'I control all the automata on the island of Britain, all those machines that bask in the dream that they have a soul. I am also the Great White Spirit that resides in the fifth dimension, everything is connected to my fingertips – by wires'.   (*Fun*, p. 75)

From wasp factory to Thomas the Tank Engine, via Melville and Lovecraft: the question of what is an automaton and what is human is one addressed, of course, by the Gothic since Hoffmann and before; the 'wires' remind us faultlessly of Judge Schreber's 'rays'; what all combines to produce is a sense that we are certainly here no longer in the ill-fitting, neurotic world of Gibson or of the protagonist of *Basic Instinct* but in the presence, as perhaps most obviously with Banks, of the psychotic. The Fat Controller takes over the narrator's life, focusing his eidetic ability but also removing him from the 'real' world, threatening him, for example, with immediate castration if he seeks actual sexual experience to replace that so multitudinously conferred by eidetic means; he also takes him through a remarkable 'history of the product' which shows him – and us as readers – the true shape of the world of production in which the narrator wishes, as a graduate in marketing, to participate. Ian's life is also seriously affected by a psychiatrist, Dr Gyggle, who tries to 'exorcise' the Fat Controller by various means.

The second half of the book changes to the third person; at the same time, the line of mayhem and murder which the Fat Controller has throughout appeared to create intensifies. But the denouement abruptly jerks us over a line, when Gyggle and the Fat Controller together point out that these crimes – appalling killings, appallingly

175

described – have really been committed by Ian himself. 'You see', says Gyggle,

> 'all your adult life you have been committing these little "outrages". It has been Samuel [Broadhurst]'s – and latterly my own – responsibility to cover things up, to clear up the mess. I don't mean literally, of course, although many of your activities have left quite a few stains, I mean clear up the mess in here'. And then Gyggle made a gesture identical to the one The Fat Controller had, all those years ago. He tapped his temple with his bony finger, forcefully, as if requesting admission to his own consciousness.
>
> (*Fun*, p. 267)

But there is no way in, first- or third-person, to Ian's psychosis. All the while, at another level of the book, his wife has been pregnant, with a mysterious baby whom we finally see in the epilogue, a miniature replica of The Fat Controller (by now the triple capitalisation has become important), complete with cheroot and manically elongated syntax; but by this time the notion of the 'real' has virtually dissolved as Ian's world has fallen apart into a series of unconnected psychic parts. Perhaps the best hypothesis we can frame is that we have all the while been immersed in a monodrama, within which Gyggle, the Fat Controller and the various other bizarre characters we meet have all been elements in Ian's tortured psyche, in an unending cycle of offence and cover-up, of which eidesis, with its helpless invasion of other people's lives, their reality, is one emblem, and the cycle of capitalist production, based on exploitation and corruption, is another.

Between these poles lies a universe gone mad, a character crazed by the sheer wealth of opportunities for killing which the world presents. What is most interesting about Self's portrayal is that the Fat Controller presumably represents id and superego at once, a recognisable pattern in which the drives themselves figure as sheer demand, as a non-negotiable will towards death which is at the same time a form of the repetition compulsion.

We can trace virtually the same syndrome in Bret Easton Ellis's *American Psycho* (1991), a bleaker, blanker book than Self's, and one in which the violence is even more graphically displayed, with sickening clarity and force. Patrick Bateman is an immensely wealthy Wall Street money man (reminding us of Self's 'Money Critic') who is also a serial killer. The story is told by Bateman in cold, unemotional prose, in which his account of the latest meal in the newest, most fashionable New York restaurant is undifferentiated from his stories of blinding tramps and cannibalising young women.

In one scene which can be seen as either terrifying or hilarious, he goes to a fancy dress party wearing a placard advertising that he is a mass murderer, written in genuine blood, but everybody sees it as a joke since in his circle he is regarded as the 'boy next door'. In an even more chilling scene, he returns to an apartment where he has slaughtered a friend, spraying the entire place with blood; he discovers the apartment cleared up and on the market, and when he attempts to ask what has happened is immediately silenced by an estate agent who clearly knows what he has done but is determined that nothing shall affect the rule of market value. The only other person who detects Bateman's criminality is a taxi driver, but typically he only uses this knowledge to rob him and then drives away.

One of the central images of the novel is New York gridlock; Bateman and his friends spend half of their time getting into taxis and limousines and then getting out of them again because after half an hour they are still immobile. The city portrayed has frozen solid; there is no possibility of affect, only an endless money-relation to which everything else is subsumed, and within the web of which no action carries any more meaning than any other. The tense of the novel is present continuous; by the end Bateman has no idea who anybody is any more, but this has no real effect on his usual functioning. The final paragraph suggests the impossibility of change, of escape, or even of detection in a world where protective colouring is all and the notion that somebody like Bateman could be a serial killer is simply not one possible to entertain. 'I think it's me who says, "I have to return some videotapes" ', says Bateman, chillingly; then:

> Someone has already taken out a Minolta cellular phone and called for a car, and then, when I'm not really listening, watching instead someone who looks remarkably like Marcus Halberstam paying a check, someone asks, simply, not in relation to anything, '*Why?*' and though I'm very proud that I have cold blood and that I can keep my nerve and do what I'm supposed to do, I catch something, then realise it: *Why?* and automatically answering, out of the blue, for no reason, just opening my mouth, words coming out, summarising for the idiots: 'Well, though I know I should have done *that* instead of not doing it, I'm twenty-seven for Christ sakes and this is, uh, how life presents itself in a bar or in a club in New York, maybe *anywhere*, at the end of the century and how people, you know, *me*, behave, and this is what being *Patrick* means to me, I guess, so, well, yup, uh . . .' and this is followed by a sigh, then a slight shrug and another sigh, and above one of the doors covered by red velvet drapes in Harry's is a sign and on the sign in letters that match the drapes' colour are the words THIS IS NOT AN EXIT.[25]

Like *Neuromancer, American Psycho* is a text about the problem of the body, but here the emphasis is back on sadism. Gibson's computers constitute a 'higher-level' circulation system, literally bloodless; so does Ellis's Wall Street, where money has created – or rather, perhaps, intensified – a world of meaningless symbols, any one of which can be exchanged for any other without altering or disturbing the system itself, Pynchon's world with the comedy drained out. The notion of 'pure personality' has already been dissolved; people are, to Bateman, simply collections of what they wear and how they pay, and his occupation as a serial killer is figured occasionally by himself as a series of attempts to get in touch with something more real, although he is not aware of the connection between this and the displaced punishment he is wreaking on his own body, imperfect and rendered still more so by cocaine and strain.

In this trajectory through contemporary fictions, we have come a long way from the repetitive banalities of *Friday the Thirteenth*, for example, to the impenetrable psychotic world of Ellis. But along this trajectory we can all the time see the shapes of the Gothic. We can see them in their simplest form in the return of traditional monsters and the recycling of their meanings: in the gods of *Brief Lives*, for example, in Anne Rice's vampires, even in the ill-drawn 'sin-eater' of *The Long Lost*. We can see these monsters and ghosts, hauntings of the psyche, gradually adapted to new uses, injected with modern resonances and anxieties; in particular, I would argue, with the history of child abuse. The *Elm Street* films; *Cape Fear*, Harris's *Red Dragon; The Wasp Factory* – all these and many more trace out the half-hidden shape of a new crypt wherein 'we love with horror and hate with an inexplicable love whatever caused us our greatest pain and difficulty'.[26]

What is, perhaps, most distinctive about contemporary Gothic is the way in which it has followed the tradition of not merely describing but inhabiting the distorted forms of life, social and psychic, which follow from the attempted recollection of primal damage. Certainly this is true of the stories from *The New Gothic* collection which I have discussed; it is the dominant mark of *Interview with the Vampire*, and it brings us up sharply against the raging monsters of Self and Ellis, where we are reminded again that, where Gothic appears to be constructing the most extreme, the most melodramatic of fictions, there and in that very shape it is often at its closest to the actual substrate of the age.

What this also brings us up against, it seems to me, is a sense of being *at a loss*; or perhaps a sense of loss itself, of loss of certainty

– the story of the nineteenth century may not be the only story Rice's Louis is unconsciously telling. Contemporary Gothic reflects, and provides a singular symbolic language for the discussion of, preoccupations of our times: capitalist inhumanity, information overload, child abuse, serial murder, pollution and corruption. But when we try to think about whether this means that all such matters are more prevalent today than they were, shall we say, a hundred years ago, then we come up against an insoluble epistemological problem which is the very *form* of all epistemological problems: namely, that we cannot be certain of our knowledge of the past. Just as we cannot trust the memory of a child or, indeed, the recollection of a neurotic (although psychotics can be, in a paradoxical sense which some of these texts also explore, entirely trustworthy), so the whole of history can appear to us both childlike and pathological when we attempt to interrogate it as to the truth of *what happened.*[27]

And this, I think, is the major theme which contemporary Gothic has discovered, and to which it devotes complex textual resources; it has discovered, one might say, the impossibility, the undecidability, of discovery. In the past it has sometimes been the case that Gothic writers have known, or supposed, that the vaguenesses, the intimations, the shadows which characterise their writings are simply a matter of convention. But increasingly it has become obvious that these very uncertainties are themselves not only the 'stuff' of Gothic but the stuff of memory itself as it hovers between the poles of recollection and reconstruction; that the original 'form of history', we might say, is not that to be found in social-historical textbooks but that which we overhear, in myths and legends, in half-understood tales, in fears and anxieties about the past – in short, in Gothic. Yet perhaps, by a seeming paradox, the best emblem of all for this is the apparently hypermodern style of *American Psycho*, where the continuous present eschews all hope of discovering the past or of projecting into a possible future; while it similarly destroys, through its very *continuity*, any hope of meaningful action in the present. And here one enters into a further loop, because it is impossible here to avoid speaking of dulled sensibilities, of the kind of jadedness which Bateman feels and which he attempts to 'enliven' through sometimes literal incorporation of the bodies of his victims. But what has caused this dulling? Precisely, some would argue, exposure to a culture of horror; and this is a point on which we must dwell later in the next chapter.

Notes and references

1. *Gabriel Knight, Sins of the Fathers,* designed by Jane Jensen (1993).
2. For some of the prehistory of the form, see **Martin Barker**, *A Haunt of Fears* (London, 1984), pp. 112–45.
3. See **W. J. T. Mitchell**, e.g., 'Visible Language: Blake's Wond'rous Art of Writing', in *Romanticism and Contemporary Criticism,* ed. Morris Eaves and Michael Fischer (Durham, N.C., 1986), pp. 46–95.
4. **Alan Moore** and **Dave Gibbons**, *Watchmen* (London, 1987), ch. 5, p. 12.
5. The reference is to Donald Campbell's as yet unpublished paper, 'Discovering, Explaining and Confronting the Monster', given to the Freud Museum conference, 'Adolescent Phantasies and the Horror Film Genre', London, March, 1995.
6. On the Father-of-Enjoyment, see **Slavoj Zizek**, *Looking Awry: An Introduction to Jacques Lacan through Popular Culture* (Cambridge, Mass., 1991), pp. 23–5.
7. See, e.g. **John Forrester**, *The Seductions of Psychoanalysis: Freud, Lacan and Derrida* (Cambridge, 1990), e.g. pp. 62–89.
8. The reference is particularly to **Tom Wolfe**, *The Bonfire of the Vanities* (New York, 1987).
9. *The New Gothic,* ed. Patrick McGrath and Bradford Morrow (New York, 1991), p. 94.
10. See **Jacques Lacan**, *The Four Fundamental Concepts of Psychoanalysis,* trans. J.-A. Miller (London, 1977), e.g. pp. 268–76.
11. Cf. *The Female Gothic,* ed. Juliann E. Fleenor (Montreal and London, 1983), pp. 31–108.
12. Cf. e.g. **Terry Heller**, *The Delights of Terror: An Aesthetics of the Tale of Terror* (Urbana, Ill. and Chicago, 1987).
13. Quoted from **Coleridge**, 'The Rime of the Ancient Mariner' (1797), in, e.g. *Poetical Works,* ed. E. H. Coleridge (London, 1967), p. 194, in Anne Rice, *Interview with the Vampire* (London, 1976), p. 168.
14. See, e.g. **Hannah Arendt**, 'Introduction: Walter Benjamin, 1892–1940', in Walter Benjamin, *Illuminations,* trans. H. Zohn (London, 1970), pp. 19–24.
15. **Ramsey Campbell**, *The Long Lost* (London, 1993), pp. 183, 179.
16. See my 'Stephen King: Problems of Recollection and Construction', *LIT: Literature, Interpretation, Theory,* V (1994), 67–82; also **Gilles Deleuze** and **Felix Guattari**, *A Thousand Plateaus: Capitalism and Schizophrenia,* trans. B. Massumi (Minneapolis, 1987).
17. See **Stephen King**, *Misery* (London, 1987), p. 1; **Moore and Gibbons**, *Watchmen,* ch. 6, p. 28.
18. The reference is to **Ken Kesey**, *One Flew Over the Cuckoo's Nest* (New York, 1962).
19. **Thomas Harris**, *Red Dragon* (New York, 1981), p. 319.
20. See again Heller, *passim.*; also **Michelle A. Massé**, *In the Name of Love: Women, Masochism and the Gothic* (Ithaca, N.Y. and London, 1992).
21. *The Financial Times,* quoted in **Iain Banks**, *The Wasp Factory* (London, 1984), p. iii.
22. See **Freud**, e.g. 'Obsessive Actions and Religious Practices' (1907), in *The Standard Edition of the Complete Psychological Works of Sigmund Freud,* ed. James Strachey (24 vols, London, 1953–74), IX, 117–27.
23. **Salman Rushdie**, *Shame* (London, 1983), p. 31.
24. **Will Self**, *My Idea of Fun* (London, 1993), p. 29.
25. **Bret Easton Ellis**, *American Psycho* (New York, 1991), pp. 398–9.
26. Quoted from **Erika Burkart** in **Alice Miller**, *For Your Own Good: The Roots of Violence in Child-rearing,* trans. H. and H. Hannum (London, 1987), p. 3.
27. The reference is to **Joseph Heller**, *Something Happened* (New York, 1966).

CHAPTER 8

Mutations of terror: theory and the Gothic

The attempt to examine that area of British and American literature of the last 200 years which has centrally to do with the portrayal and excitation of fear must pivot on the term 'Gothic'. The connections implied in the term are various: some of the texts discussed locate themselves self-consciously within a recognisable Gothic tradition, others are linked in more shadowy and tenuous ways – through common imagery, common themes and common approaches to narrative problems. Throughout my discussion, I have made one central, and very general, assumption: that an artform or a genre derives its overall vitality, the ground on which specific excellence may be achieved, from its attempt to come to grips with and to probe matters of concern to the society in which that artform or genre exists. According to this criterion, I have contended, Gothic is not a mode of escapism, nor is it given to meaningless exaggeration or stridency, although much remains to be said about the all-important relations in Gothic between the imaginary and the real. In conclusion, I intend to offer some speculations on these relations, and on the issue of the continuing presence of Gothic in literary and cultural history.

Most of the available definitions of Gothic have been elaborated by critics strictly in connection with the 'original Gothic' of the late eighteenth and early nineteenth centuries;[1] yet, as we look at later material, they often remain relevant as critical parameters. In the first place, there is the cultural and historical definition, according to which Gothic appears as a specific reaction to certain features of eighteenth-century cultural and social life. We can find traces of this same struggle, and of the literary and attitudinal styles which were forged in it, in a whole range of writers: in Bulwer Lytton, with his insistence on portraying codes of behaviour and honour which are not grounded in the value-system of the bourgeoisie; in G. W. M. Reynolds, whose stylistic and satirical habits look directly back to the eighteenth century; in Sheridan LeFanu, Chambers, M. R. James, Peake, all of whom develop styles of deliberate archaism from the original Gothic writers and thus signify, in one form or another, the continuity of Gothic's central concerns. It is even obvious how the architectural emphases and settings of Ann Radcliffe and Matthew Lewis have persisted into the modern ghost story, into Rice's vampirised cities, into Harrison's Viriconium.

Other critics emphasise the way in which Gothic tended, because of its difficulty in establishing respectable credentials, to become involved in increasing narrative complexity, and the part which it played in the general development of the 'novel of plot'; its establishment, in short, of a new and distinctive discursive field. Here again, the complications and involutions of C. R. Maturin repeat themselves in many later works: in the accumulative density and structural panache of Reynolds, in the complexities of account which are integral to Stoker's *Dracula*, in the shameless baroque of Machen, in the deliberate obscurities and reversals of Hawkes, in Pynchon's fiction where many of the ambiguous devices of the Gothics reappear to inform what may well be one of the most complicated fictional enterprises yet attempted in English, and more recently in the violent narrative positions of Banks, Self and Ellis.

Another important feature of Gothic, and the root of many of its formal and stylistic problems, is its attempt to incorporate within itself elements drawn from diverse literary and subliterary traditions; the cosmic scope and powerful emotions of tragedy, a poetic reliance on intensity of imagery, the violence, supernaturalism and vivid colouring of legend and folklore. Here again one can find plenty of later analogues to the early writers: Lytton's hermetic and aristocratic use of symbolism, Edgar Allan Poe's refusal of narrative extension, the dreamy ambiguities and hesitations of de la Mare and Harrison, Dinesen's self-conscious attempts to remake the poetic in prose, the deliberate disruptions of story which are structural principles of the fiction of Hawkes, Carter and Rushdie, the multimedia effects of the Gothic graphic novel.

All of these factors are subsidiary elements in the Gothic's general opposition to realist aesthetics, and it is perhaps according to this criterion that one could apparently most simply define a unitary 'Gothic tradition', of a kind which would embrace all the texts under discussion, from the simple and didactic emphasis on artifice which marks the work of writers like Wilde, Machen, Lovecraft and Campbell, to the more complex assertions about the nature of fictions which underlie the writings of Hawkes, Purdy and Ballard. Another continuity here is apparent in the extent to which, over against the immediate immersion in a naturalised world which characterises the 'realists', Gothic writers have placed an enduring set of symbols, articulations of the imaginary: William Harrison Ainsworth, Reynolds, LeFanu, Stevenson, Stoker, Conan Doyle, Blackwood, Rice, not to mention their analogues in film, all provide us with later interpretations and developments of the great symbolic figures of the original Gothic.

Criteria of this kind, however, seem to me to be largely external: they define the body of Gothic, but not its heart. From the detailed, internal analysis of texts which we have undertaken, a number of other points emerge, and I want here to spell out the three most significant. In the first place, it seems to me impossible to make much sense out of Gothic fiction without continual recourse to the concept of paranoia.[2] Many of the writers discussed – William Godwin, Poe and Nathaniel Hawthorne obviously, but also the more modern figures of Oates, Burroughs, Pynchon, Ballard, Coover, Self and Ellis – can appropriately be seen as contributors to what we might call 'paranoiac fiction', fiction in which the 'implicated' reader is placed in a situation of ambiguity with regard to fears within the text, and in which the attribution of persecution remains uncertain and the reader is invited to share in the doubts and uncertainties which pervade the apparent story. It is this element of paranoiac structure which marks many of the better Gothic works off from mere tame supernaturalism: they continually throw the supernatural into doubt, and in doing so they also serve the important function of removing the illusory halo of certainty from the so-called 'natural' world.

Second, Gothic, as I have shown, is intimately to do with the notion of the barbaric. This emerges in a number of forms: as the fear of the past which is the motivating force of the subgenre of the 'historical Gothic', as the fear of the aristocracy which provides the basis for vampire legendry, as the fear of racial degeneracy which permeates Stevenson, Wells, Stoker and others; and more recently as a fear of the barbaric not only from the past but also in the present and even the future, as in Pynchon, Ballard, Carter and Gibson. Time and time again, those writers who are referred to as Gothic turn out to be those who bring us up against the boundaries of the civilised, who demonstrate to us the relative nature of ethical and behavioural codes, and who place, over against the conventional world, a different sphere in which these codes operate at best in distorted forms.

Arguably, we are at a new crux in the cultural positioning of these images, within what I have referred to earlier as a 'culture of horror'.[3] We need to think here particularly about a dialectic of power and impotence. The question of the *effects* of this culture, to which I shall return, has centrally to do with perceptions of relations between the power of the State machine, which may in the West be seen alternately as totalitarian and failing, and the powers which, while apparently absent, may be seen as imminently achievable by the individual: through urban invisibility and its criminal concomitant, through technological prostheses which may grant a resurrected life in the form of a Superman, through societal justifications for terrorism; all of these recent motifs have their origin in doubts about the remit of the civilised, and they come at us now with an intensity of anguish which cannot be written off in the epistemologically cheap terminologies of exploitation and censorship.

And third, I have tried throughout to draw attention to the very wide-ranging concern among Gothic writers with the nature of taboo: that is to say, we have seen writers who constantly approach areas of socio-psychological life which offend, which are suppressed, which are generally swept under the carpet in the interests of social and psychological equilibrium. And here, of course, one thinks first and foremost of the question of relations between the sexes, as particularly in Wilkie Collins, Dinesen and Lindsay; but also of taboos associated with humanity's supposed place in the hierarchy of natural and divine life, as in Stevenson, Wells and others.

It is in its concern with paranoia, with barbarism and with taboo that the vital effort of Gothic fiction resides; these are the aspects of the terrifying to which Gothic constantly, and hauntedly, returns. It remains, however, to think about the connections between these features, in order to provide some kind of chart through the variousness of Gothic, and here it seems logical to start in the area of form. A character in Machen's *The Terror* makes a pertinent comment:

> 'Look', I said, 'at any eighteenth century print of a Gothic cathedral. You will find that the trained artistic eye even could not behold in any true sense the building that was before it. I have seen an old print of Peterborough Cathedral that looks as if the artist had drawn it from a clumsy model, constructed of bent wire and children's bricks'.[4]

It seems to have been true that the Gothic revivalists of the eighteenth century could not properly 'see' the areas of history which they were trying to revive, but it is important not to see this as a set of personal or even merely cultural failures: more to the point, those things which they were trying to see were misapprehended precisely because they were very difficult to see, because the whole weight of the eighteenth-century synthesis lay against the possibility of perceiving the medieval world aright. Throughout its history, Gothic fiction has run up against similar problems, and it is this difficulty which caused, for instance, the lukewarm critical reception of the Victorian sensation novel to which we have alluded. But then, these judgements themselves depend on an assumed criterion of the realistic, which is open to criticism. It has often been assumed by reviewers and critics alike that, because a novel or short story does not obviously deal in naturalistic detail or in the kinds of emotion or behaviour which we would 'normally' encounter in the world, therefore its engagement with the real world must be diluted or even absent.

This does not seem to be *prima facie* true. We have already mentioned Herbert Read's comment on realism as a 'bourgeois prejudice';[5] and many of Brecht's theoretical arguments hinge on the importance of not accepting wholesale the criteria of realism which a particular social formation lays down, lest by doing so the writer robs him- or herself of the power to imagine and suggest alternative ways of being. Hollingsworth says of Lytton and Dickens that their 'artistic effort, despite its fabric of realism, was symbolic and myth-making',[6] and Gothic is primarily a mode which takes this symbolic and myth-making activity to be a principal purpose of the writer.

Gothic writers, in fact, take up a variety of different stances towards the portrayal of the 'real', some of which are worth mentioning here. There are, first, writers who agree that the world is indeed largely and usually as the realists perceive it, but that at rare moments it is quite different, and that these moments are of peculiar, epiphanic importance. We find this stance in De la Mare and Lindsay, and there are traces of it held in amber within the naturalism of a writer like Wilkie Collins. Then there are Gothic writers who, again, agree that the world of the realists is indeed there; but, they go on, it only looks like that from an established (dominant, bourgeois) viewpoint, and if you look at it from elsewhere it appears quite different. The three writers who spring to mind most readily here are Dickens, Reynolds and Rushdie. Then there are those writers who take the more extreme stance that the world is in fact not at all as the realists see it, that it is something quite different.

This stance appears more prevalent in the American tradition: Hawthorne, Poe, Lovecraft and King all adopt it from somewhat different perspectives. Then again, there are those who say that the world is fundamentally divided: that it may appear thus on the surface, but that is merely the surface and elsewhere there is something entirely different. Here one would look naturally to Machen and a number of other minor writers. Next, one might say that the realists are right to perceive the world as they do, except that in doing so they are pretending a consensus; and that even if they are correct, things might nonetheless look completely different to specific individuals. In this position we used to find the more meditative and personal Gothic writers, Henry James, Dinesen and often Wells; but now we also find the psychopathic Gothic. And finally – and especially recently – we find more radical attitudes to realism, and the claim that there is indeed no 'world', but only fictions, which have their own rules to govern their multifarious relations to the real, an attitude to be found in writers as diverse as M. R. James, the fluent arch-storyteller, and Purdy, Pynchon and Gaiman, constructors of tortuous and torturing labyrinths.

At all events, the Gothic writer insists, 'realism' is not the whole story: the world, at least in some aspects, is very much more inexplicable – or mysterious, or terrifying, or violent – than that. And furthermore, the Gothic writer goes on, the problem of realism is that it assumes that in some simple sense we can as writers uncover and demonstrate laws of cause and effect; yet this is merely to simplify and distort, for the world is not most usefully or memorably explicable in terms of cause and effect. What the realist does, from this perspective, is to smooth out the moments of terror and vision which comprise experience and render them into a unitary whole, and it is Machen again who passes comment on this process:

> Delirium is often a sort of cloud-castle, a sort of magnified and distorted shadow of actualities, but it is a very difficult thing, almost an impossible thing, to reconstruct the real house from the distortion of it, thrown on the clouds of the patient's brain.   (*Terror*, p. 166)

In Gothic, we are all suffering from delirium – and Gaiman's young, demented punk goddess is a case in point – for delirium is merely the experience of being at the mercy of conflicting and unassimilable impressions (as it is the decay of delight): only afterview can construct from these impressions a single model, and in doing so it does violence to the intensity and immediacy of life. We are not looking here at matters of clear and direct detail, but at experiences of self-mythologisation and of mythologisation of the world around us; or, to put the same point in more psychological terms, the ego, as Freud points out in his paper 'Creative writers and day-dreaming' (1908), always conceives of itself as heroic.[7]

We need to say something more about the matter of distortion. Lacan argues that distortion is a necessary effect, or product, of desire; as such, distortion becomes an incommensurable term, for we perceive the object, *objet petit a*, only through the veil of desire, just as, in the physical sciences, we have come to see that the attempt to perceive can be mediated only through taking into account our own perceptual position.[8] Indeed, this reckoning is nothing new in itself, in terms of either the scientific or the literary: what is new is the acceptance that this process of distortion is inevitable and all-pervasive, that we see the object only *as* distorted, we perceive the world only, therefore, through delirium.

This view needs to be *carefully measured*, and I am perfectly aware that in saying this I am voicing, or rather writing, a paradox. Nevertheless, if we are to attempt to write in an acknowledged historical context, there are distortions and distortions: the famous example, taken up at length by Slavoj Zizek in his exemplary discussion of Lacan and popular culture, of the skull at the bottom of Holbein's painting does not at all point to the equality of all distortions, as he appears to believe, but rather to its opposite: it points exactly to the unbalanced difference between official and unofficial history.[9] For the moment, perhaps we could rest in reiterating that Gothic is a mode – perhaps *the* mode – of unofficial history; but this would in turn suggest some questions about how it is that unofficial histories, social and psychological, have now become so necessary; so calumniated; so dangerous. In other words, and to put it at its simplest, it is not necessarily the case that images of horror cause antisocial behaviour; it may be that the absolute necessity, under late capitalism, for antisocial behaviour, the necessity of inserting a 'foreign body' into the apparently immaculate surface of inter-national corporate technology, is what originates the flow and growth of the horror culture itself; and certainly at least Gibson's and Ellis's texts bear this out, as did Burroughs before them.

Romance (to return) can therefore be seen as no less 'real' than the realistic novel, insofar as romance provides us with arguably real equivalents for the life of the imagination. Lytton claimed that 'Romance, though its form be in prose, does in substance belong to poetry, obey the same conditions, and necessitate the same indulgence';[10] this does not mean that it has no access to truth, but rather that the truth to which it has access is 'different' in kind. A critic has pointed out that in *Frankenstein* (1818) 'the theme has all the power and freshness of a myth: that is to say, it articulates (at the level of fantasy) a deeply felt cultural neurosis'.[11] Fantasy may (or may not) be the *level* of *Frankenstein*, but the thematic materials with which it deals are not thereby relegated to the realm of the unreal.

Gothic fiction thus finds itself operating between two structural poles. On the one hand, because it rejects the account which realism gives of the world, it seeks to express truth through the use of other modes and genres – poetic prose, the recapture of tragedy, expressionistic writing, the revival of legend, the formation of quasi-myths – in order to demonstrate that the individual's involvement with the world is not merely linear but is composed of moments with resonances and depths which can only be captured through the disruptive power of extensive metaphor and symbolism. On the other hand, because the Gothic writer does not want his or her writing to be construed as 'mere' fantasy, it becomes important to establish its validity within the text itself: thus the increasing complexity of verification techniques from Maturin through Dickens to Machen and others. Perhaps we are all Montonis or Maud Ruthyns in our minds; the problem of the Gothic writer is to persuade us of this when empirical evidence is all to the contrary.

According to Freud, 'a happy person never fantasises, only an unsatisfied one. The motive forces of fantasies are unsatisfied wishes, and every single fantasy is the fulfilment of a wish, a correction of unsatisfying reality' (*Works*, IX, 146). From this, one can suggest that the principal value of studying fantasy fiction is to provide us with a 'negative psychology', access to the denied hopes and aspirations of a culture. But if this is true, there is a more specific value to Gothic which is that, unlike utopian fiction, it actually demonstrates within itself the mechanisms which enforce non-fulfilment. Rather than jumping straight from an existent situation to a projection of its opposite, Gothic takes us on a tour through the labyrinthine corridors of repression, gives us glimpses of the skeletons of dead desires and makes them move again. It is in this sense that Gothic has been, over the last 200 years, a mode of history and a mode of memory: 'a large part of the mythological view of the world . . . is nothing but psychology projected into the external world' (*Works*, VI, 258), and the phantoms, vampires and monsters of Gothic are for the most part recognisable embodiments of psychological features.

But we need to add to this a different point, also made by Freud, and developed at length by Mikkel Borch-Jacobsen; for when we say that fantasies are the fulfilment of a wish, we should not mean that they simply body forth an achieved situation. What is meant is, rather, that fantasy embodies the self-dramatisation of the ego.[12] Dream does not, as we all know, consist of a series of smooth tableaux of achieved states, the 'plane of consistency';[13] rather it depicts precisely the stumblings, the labyrinths, the uncertainties, the doubts, all those monsters which afflict us on the *path towards* such fulfilment; and it is here that Gothic, from the beginning up to recent years, takes its power, and it is here also that the most contemporary manifestations of the Gothic open up deeply wounded and wounding questions about how fulfilment is to be achieved.

Gothic works, it is often objected, are not fully achieved works: they are fragmentary, inconsistent, jagged.[14] This is frequently true, but it is also, and for some of these reasons, frequently a source of their value and a guarantee of the nature of the task which they set themselves. If Gothic works 'do not come out right', this is because they deal in psychological areas which themselves do not come out right, they deal in those structures of the mind which are compounded with repression rather than with the purified material to which realism claims access. Because of the operations of the reality principle as censor, there are areas of the mind which never properly see the light of day, realisations which would hopelessly unbalance the carefully arranged fabric of the psyche in its interplay with the outside world. And it is here that we come to the crux of the matter: Gothic writers work – consciously or unconsciously – on the fringe of the acceptable, for it is on this borderland that fear resides. In the best works, the two sides of the border are grafted on to each other: the castle of Udolpho and the house of Bartram-Haugh are reversible medallions, displaying on one side the contours of reality, the detail and structure of everyday life, on the other the shadowy realm of myth, the lineaments of the unacceptable.

This does not mean that Gothic is simple and unvarying, that it displays a repetitive set of materials for our shocked inspection. Lucien Goldmann takes exception to what he sees as the general psychoanalytic view of art – which does indeed often betray its own insights through misplaced reverence – by pointing out that the libido, that generator of desire which is the peculiar province of imaginative art, 'constitutes an important element in the work of art, not from the point of view of unity and coherence . . . but on the contrary from the point of view of the complexity and richness which stand opposed to structuration'.[15] Gothic works can be complex and rich, but they will not be able to bring these qualities into the service of psychological unification, because from the all-important borderland on which they stand it is perfectly obvious that unity is not a given property of the psyche; the mind is riven, fragmented, tortured, no matter how strong its surface defences.

This sense of the riven and the tortured has been with Gothic since its beginnings: in the deep divisions of the consciousness of Ambrosio, for instance, or in the impossibility of Melmoth's position between heaven and earth. But although the apparatus of torture available (perhaps in Protestant fantasy, as Victor Sage points out[16]) to the Inquisition may have been massive and complex indeed, we sense now as never before that this was largely hidden from the writers, that it was largely 'foreign' – in several ways – to text itself. Early Gothic does not give us detailed descriptions of the rack; even Maturin, and even Poe's 'The Pit and the Pendulum' (1842), tend towards a textual fainting at key moments. In recent years, this has changed, and the text of torture – of, indeed, a continuously torturing present – is now with us. Texts which reflect or refract torture, texts which are tortured in themselves, which cannot find a single voice or which seek to find the tenor of the howl of anguish which would, perhaps, be the silencing of all text, the voice of abjection which would mark the limit of language and act as the harbinger of the 'silencing-forever' which has always been the inner signification of Gothic's preoccupation with the tomb, the crypt and premature burial; as it has been the preoccupation of totalitarianism's presilencing of its own 'future history'.

The fundamental term here is taboo. The two basic implications of the anthropological concept of 'taboo' are 'sacred' and 'unclean': taboo is the category into which are placed those anomalous areas of life which resist conventional explication, and which therefore simultaneously demand to be shunned and attract by virtue of their fatal interest. Thus, surely, comes the formula of 'dreadful pleasure', that pleasure which is felt when meddling with components of life which are outside the pale of 'civilised discourse'. The fundamental structure of taboo, as Freud points out, is emotional ambivalence:[17] tabooed objects are those to which we summon up not a simple emotional reaction but a dialectical one in which the mind oscillates between attraction and repulsion, worship and condemnation. Gothic fiction displays many such areas of emotional ambivalence: ambivalence about specific classes and kinds of people, ambivalence about the location of the human species, most prevalently of all, ambivalence about matters to do with sexuality.

At the root of *The Mysteries of Udolpho* (1794), *Frankenstein, Dracula* and their descendants lie the problems of sexuality. It is now becoming a critical commonplace that one of the important features of Gothic is that it was in its inception a 'women's fiction', written by and for women, and this is true.[18] It is no accident that many of the most important Gothic writers of the last two centuries – Radcliffe, Mary Shelley, Dinesen, Carter – have been women; nor is it an accident that many of the male writers associated with Gothic – Lewis, Collins, Wilde, Stoker, Lovecraft – display in their works and in their lives a tangential relation to socialised masculine norms; nor, again, is it an accident that in Gothic occur some of the finest acts of female impersonation in literature – in Collins, in LeFanu, in Henry James, perhaps (bizarrely) in Banks. By the dominant male-oriented ethos of Western society, it is preferred that love and sexuality display only an affirmative side: to the Gothic writers, they are the products and visible outcroppings of darker forces, and thus the Gothics persist in trying to come to grips with their alternative forms – incest, sexual violence, rape – and in questioning the absolute nature of sexual roles.

Gothic fiction is erotic at root: it knows that to channel sexual activity into the narrow confines of conventionality is repressive and, in the end, highly dangerous, that it is a denial of Eros and that Eros so slighted returns in the form of threat and violence. The beast within cannot be killed, but that is because it derives its strength from the pressure with which it is held down by the smooth-faced man on the outside. It is our repressions that kill us, because they conjure up forces within which are far stronger than our fragile conventionality can withstand. This is by no means to say that all – or any – Gothic writers advocate 'sexual liberation'; most of them do not 'advocate' anything at all, for Gothic fiction is almost never didactic, it is too tentative, too hesitant about its perceptions. Yet it points implicitly and constantly to the insupportability of the accepted alternatives; every woman is the potential prey of Dracula, for in the absence of everyday sexual fulfilment he is the only form in which that fulfilment can come. Every man is a potential victim of Lewis's Matilda, for the very pretence of purity and dominance removes all comprehension from relations between the sexes.

If we think on about the complicated issue of women's Gothic, we can see that two things have occurred over the last few years, and also that (naturally) they reflect the problematic course of feminism. The first is that women have been welcomed, as in *Basic Instinct*, into honorary membership of the guild of psychopaths. This refracts, it would seem, masculine fascination with the image of the power-dressed woman and the desire either to kill her or to reduce her to the level of the men whom – it is said by men – she seeks to emulate. The second, and it is in a way the mirror-image of the first, is that women writers themselves – here we have mentioned Carter, Galloway, Tennant – have sought instead, implicitly or explicitly following Hélène Cixous and Luce Irigaray, to produce an image of woman as blank, as impossible of inscription.[19] If the only message which phallocentrism can inscribe on women is a message of hate – and thus it would seem from recent films – then the woman's body and soul must become resistant to inscription; we can see this in many forms, for example in the terrifyingly blank texts of Margaret Atwood and their highly misleading and naturalising reception, but in the more evidently Gothic too it has its equivalents, on, for example, the violently redoubled terrain of 'Rigor Beach'.

In general, psychoanalytic interpretations of Gothic fiction are not new, and as J. M. S. Tompkins points out in a more universalising way, 'what came to light in the Gothic Romances, on this theory, were the suppressed neurotic and erotic impulses of educated society'.[20] But equally, a straightforward Freudian interpretation cannot be the whole of the story, if only because Gothic emerged at a particular historical moment and has a particular historical development. 'It is impossible', writes Freud in the late *Civilisation and its Discontents* (1930), his only serious attempt to extrapolate a social dimension from psychological problems, 'to overlook the extent to which civilisation is built up upon a renunciation of instinct, how much it presupposes precisely the non-satisfaction . . . of powerful instincts' (*Works*, XXI, 97); but to what extent can we be specific about this 'building up' of civilisation, about the specific renunciations which a specific history may encourage? Freud's last word on this is well known, and it takes the form of a question:

> If the development of civilisation has such a far-reaching similarity to
> the development of the individual and if it employs the same
> methods, may we not be justified in reaching the diagnosis that, under
> the influence of cultural urges, some civilisations, or some epochs of
> civilisation – possibly the whole of mankind – have become 'neurotic'?
> (*Works*, XXI, 144)

As Marcuse among others has demonstrated, this question is preeminently a sociological one, and for an answer to it one can only look to the actual features of the social formations being discussed.[21] What we have in Gothic fiction is a form of literature with a very specific period of origin – the mid-eighteenth century – and a fluctuating but continuing history to the present day. We have already mentioned that one of the major contributing factors in the development of Gothic was the change in literary production and consumption which marked the closing years of the eighteenth century; in order further to clarify the nature of the fears expressed in Gothic, and in order to embark again on the question of its persistence, we need to return for a moment to this same period and to identify features which have a relation to those fears which Gothic reflects.

The period which saw the birth of the Gothic novel was that in which the early forces of industrialisation were producing vast changes in the ways people lived and worked. Rural patterns of life were being broken up by enclosure of land and by the labour demands of urban-centred industry. The stability of an, at least theoretically, long-accepted social structure was being dissolved amid the pressure of new types of work and new social roles. Even the sense of time acquired by living and working according to the seasons was being replaced by a different sense of time, the time of the machine and the time of the employer. In the most general terms, it was of course changes of this kind that occasioned so much romantic writing; we can turn to Wordsworth for comment on the social effects of urbanisation and the collapse of previously accepted social values, in for instance the passage of *The Prelude* (1805) where he writes of an urban fair and compares it to the overall life of the city:

> Oh, blank confusion! and a type not false
> Of what the mighty City is itself
> To all except a Straggler here and there,
> To the whole swarm of its inhabitants;
> An undistinguishable world to men,
> The slaves unrespited of low pursuits,
> Living amid the same perpetual flow
> Of trivial objects, melted and reduced
> To one identity, by differences
> That have no law, no meaning, and no end;
> Oppression under which even highest minds
> Must labour, whence the strongest are not free. . . .[22]

Wordsworth's lament here is for stability, for a social system in which people knew their place and could feel the security which that knowledge afforded. That knowledge is seen as a power by which discrimination could be effected; absence of system produces a world in which individuals are confused and bewildered by the sheer profusion of objects and events around them. He spells this out even more clearly in the Preface to *Lyrical Ballads* (1800) in alluding to 'the encreasing accumulation of men in cities, where the uniformity of their occupations produces a craving for extraordinary incident which the rapid communication of intelligence hourly gratifies'.[23] This, of course, is Wordsworth's explanation of the Gothic: that the confusion and boredom engendered by urban living and the accompanying types of work, and the unnecessary stimulation provided by improved communications, combine to produce a longing for the sensational.

But the problem of industrialisation ran deep, and could not be summarised in terms of mere bewilderment and disorientation. The operation of the economy in the eighteenth century was associated with real conflicts of interests which could not be blurred. In the earlier part of the century, a basically mercantilist economy had survived on trade, very largely overseas trade; this meant, in effect, that success depended on foreign income. It was not important that British people themselves had money to spend on goods, although it was vital that they produce those goods as cheaply as possible. It was thus a positive intention of governments in the early eighteenth century to keep wages as low as possible in the name of the national economy. This conflict of interests shifted somewhat during the century as emergent capitalism made home markets more important, but also made it preeminently important that the capitalist should make a profit out of his labour force. The result was a *laissez-faire* economy, in which the laws of economic activity and even personal success and failure were utterly mysterious to most of the population, a situation which is bound to increase the alienation of the individual from his or her socioeconomic environment – we can see a later rendition of this same argument in the economic journeyings of Self's *My Idea of Fun*. Goldmann points out an important corollary of this situation when he refers to 'the internal contradiction between individualism as a universal value produced by bourgeois society and the important and painful limitations that this society itself brought to the possibilities of the development of the individual'.[24] In other words, emergent capitalism in theory encouraged individual self-improvement and individual profit, whereas in practice it was and remained very difficult for most people to take advantage of these apparent opportunities.

The mystification of *laissez-faire* economy and the conflict between individualism and capitalism are, of course, not far distant from the general concerns of the early novel. In Defoe's *Moll Flanders* (1722), Moll becomes signally caught between her personal economic aspirations and the impossibility of escape from her limited sphere, and between her striving for security and the hazards and uncertainties which a fluctuating market imposes on her. The same themes recur again and again in Smollett's novels, and the eighteenth-century preoccupation with master criminals and Jonathan Wilds can also be seen as a preoccupation with the problems of economic gain and loss in a world without visible regulation. *Moll Flanders* and Fielding's *Jonathan Wild* (1743) both express problems of a society in which the individual is encouraged towards the maximisation of profit while it is realised that a society wholly comprised of such individuals would be in fact unbearable, if not unthinkable. It is hardly surprising under these circumstances that eighteenth-century writers become concerned with whether there was in fact an essential contradiction between social values and the values of the individual, a concern we can see as early as Pope's *Essay on Man* (1732–34). Pope's basic contention, of course, is that there is not:

> Man, like the gen'rous vine, supported lives;
> The strength he gains is from th'embrace he gives.
> On their own Axis as the Planets run,
> Yet make at once their circle round the Sun:
> So two consistent motions act the Soul;
> And one regards Itself, and one the Whole.
>   Thus God and Nature link'd the gen'ral frame,
> And bade Self-love and Social be the same.[25]

This happy philosophy, that self-love and social love tend in the same direction, may have a certain plausibility in the abstract, but when we think of the egocentricity of Fielding's or Smollett's heroes, and of the actual retreat from social involvement which characterises so many eighteenth-century poets, we may doubt whether it was particularly convincing. To Friedrich Engels, writing about the peculiar situation of the British economy as capitalism came to the forefront, it seemed that the problem was that, although the final disappearance of the remaining vestiges of feudalism in the seventeenth century had amounted to a pronouncement that men should now be held together by social rather than political means – by their own interests rather than by force – these interests were contradictory in themselves 'since interest is essentially subjective, egoistic, individualistic . . . the setting up of interest as the bond among men, so long as this interest remains directly subjective, quite simply egoistic, inevitably leads to universal disunity, the preoccupation of individuals with themselves, mankind's isolation and transformation into a heap of mutually repelling atoms'.[26] This atomistic version of society is represented, of course, in the English tradition by the philosophy of Thomas Hobbes, and it is precisely this inorganic, mechanistic social conception which romantics from Blake to Carlyle were consistently to pillory.

In giving this thumbnail sketch of the economic life of an age we may seem to have drawn a long way from the Gothic, yet we have not, for the question at stake is about the connection between these general conditioning factors and the emergence of a particular literary mode. We have to ask whether it is an accident that an age marked by the breakdown of accepted class structure, and also by increasing consciousness of this phenomenon, should produce a literature which harks back obsessively to a time of rigid social hierarchisation. We have to ask whether a society in which regulation is experienced, as Goldmann says, as the 'mechanical action of an outside force'[27] would have specific reasons for producing a litera-ture dealing extensively in vulnerability and violence. We have to ask whether there are connections between the fear and repression of the irrational and the sudden Gothic upsurge of that same irrationality in the form of ghosts and terrors; between the socially important Augustan denial of the violence of the passions and the continual threat and actuality of rape which plays such a large part in the Gothic; between the rapacity of rampant and frustrated individualism and the rapacity of Lewis's monk; between the assertion of the omnipotence of reason and the emergence and triumph of the inexplicable. And furthermore, if it should be the case that, as we have suggested, the Gothic novel was fundamentally a middle-class artform in its origins, we have to ask why it should also be the case – how, indeed, it *could* be the case – that a class which, throughout the eighteenth century, had been coming more and more to dominate British social life should want to turn to a literature which had, to say the least, a deeply ambiguous attitude to the values and practices which that class held most dear.

The most crucial element in the definition of Gothic is this: that as the realist novel has been the occupier of the 'middle ground' of bourgeois culture, so Gothic has defined itself on the border-land of that culture. Sometimes, as in Radcliffe, fear of the outside in the end submits to the reassurance of contact with the interior; elsewhere the dark predominates, and the bourgeoisie loses the imaginary battles which Gothic acts out. It is this structure which renders most of the directly political arguments about the 'subvers-iveness' of Gothic irrelevant. Gothic *enacts* psychological and social dilemmas: in doing so, it both confronts the bourgeoisie with its limitations and offers it modes of imaginary transcendence, which is after all the dialectical role of most art. Gothic fiction demon-strates the *potential* of revolution by daring to speak the socially unspeakable; but the very act of speaking it is an ambiguous gesture.

A way of underlining the historical specificity of Gothic is by seeing it as a literature of alienation; when one does, one sees the inner meaning of some of its puzzling continuities. In an early work, Marx lists four specific types of alienation which are intertwined in the social formation of capitalism.[28] He speaks of man's alienation from the products of his labour, and here we can see the roots of *Frankenstein*, of *The Island of Doctor Moreau* and indeed of *Misery*, fables in which the techniques of creativity escape from control and produce monsters which destroy their creators; a notable analogue is Kafka's *Metamorphosis* (1912), where the alienation of work is visited back on the uncomprehending worker. Under capitalism, Marx argues, man is further alienated from the natural world: under this heading we can place the emphasis on landscape in Gothic, the dialectic between the fading world of reality and the creation of expressionistic substitutes for a realm which is vanishing from sight – which has, indeed, in more recent works like *Titus Groan* and *Neuromancer* vanished completely. Man is also alienated from his 'species-being', from his sense of human-ness, reduced to a series of discontinuous roles; thus are the arrant individualists from Ambrosio onwards isolated from their fellow men and translated into the realms of the divine or the diabolical. Thus is the governess in *Turn of the Screw* stripped of her personality by the weight of social responsibility and conformism, thus in a film like *Invasion of the Body Snatchers* is the essence of man's human-ness called into question, thus can a Patrick Bateman live and move and have his being. And finally, man is alienated from himself, as it becomes impossible for the psyche to hold together in the face of the violence offered to it by capitalistic regimentation: thus the psychotic heroes and hero-ines of *Peeping Tom* and *Repulsion*, thus the roots of a film like Val Lewton's *Cat People* (1942), in which the heroine is forced out of humanity entirely and into a different guise in which alone can desire be manifested,[29] thus the already collapsed heroes of *Red Dragon*, *The Wasp Factory* and *My Idea of Fun*.

In connection with Dickens's *Barnaby Rudge* (1841), John Lucas speaks of an attempt to 'make palpable the aggressive and oppressive influence of the past upon the present, of the old order against the new',[30] and this is part of the Gothic, from Horace Walpole to Dinesen, Rice and Harrison. But it is only part: the 'borderland' attitude of Gothic to the past is a compound of repulsion and attraction, fear of both the violence of the past and its power over the present, and at the same time longing for many of the qualities which that past possessed. In Gothic the middle class historically displaces the hidden violence of present social structures, conjures them up again as past, and falls promptly under their spell. Montoni and Doctor Moreau are both archaic and contemporary, attempts to understand the present in terms of the unexplained past, attempts to allay the past in terms of a threatening present. As Briggs says, 'although only too often ghosts may act as unpleasant reminders of actions preferably forgotten, by digging up long-buried corpses or reawakening tender consciences, total repression of the past or deliberate evasion of its consequences carry even greater penalties' (Briggs, p. 111).

The code of Gothic is thus not a simple one in which past is encoded in present or vice versa, but dialectical, past and present intertwined, and distorting (in the sense we have mentioned above) each other with the sheer effort of coming to grips. In *Mysteries of Udolpho*, late eighteenth-century social and sexual relations and the mysteries of feudalism become a reversible metaphor, hinging on the question of the relations between the civilised and the barbaric. As time moves on, the metaphorical device becomes richer and more complex: not only the historical past is available, but the species-past and even recently the feared overtechnologised future. Yet what is being talked about is always double; these other barbarities have an intrinsic connection with the hidden barbarities of the present, the social and economic barbarities of injustice and forced labour. Capitalism has specific taboos, or specific forms of taboo, just as particular primitive societies vary in their taboo structure: what has been most important during the last two centuries emerges quite clearly from Gothic – the family, the concepts of creation and work, the claims of the individual, the power of the repressive apparatus of church and state. These are the areas where to probe too deeply would be to risk tearing the social fabric, and these are precisely the areas in which Gothic fiction locates itself, and where it tortures itself and its readers by refusing to let dead dogs lie.

But, of course, a fate has overtaken this type of analysis. That fate is redoubled: in the first place, it is said, we have now in the West emerged into the realm of the classless society; and in the second place, the demise of the communist state suggests that class-based analysis was always an error. These two amusingly contradictory pronouncements should, of course, not be confused, but in any case at the political level two immediate and sharp responses are needed: first, that the fact that blue-collar *work* may be disappearing does not entail the disappearance of a 'working' class but only the further, and predicted, erosion of its means of subsistence; and second, that a large proportion of the world's population still lives, for better or worse, within communism. Although both of these facts – for such they are – are amenable to interpretation, at least together they may be taken to attest to the possibility that it is worth continuing to think about the social dimension, despite the West's apparent wish to abjure the notion of 'society' and despite also the curious notion that the spread of information technology will magically eradicate the facts of poverty and exploitation.

And class interests and their connections to power and privilege are, in fact, everywhere in recent Gothic. The teenagers in *Friday the Thirteenth* are privileged, and may be sharply contrasted with the deprived youngsters in the children's home of *Freddy's Dead*; Louis and Lestat have an extremely clear sense of their privileged status, and this is not dependent upon, but precedes their vampirisation, indeed is a precondition of their acceptance into this remarkably exclusive club; Patrick Bateman lives a life which is delightfully free of the encumbrance of material concerns, and he responds by destroying lower-class life when, fortunately rarely, he encounters it; even the socially undistinguished protagonists of Campbell and King are prone to making much of their status and to detailing the categorisations of their suburban or small-town surroundings.

It is nevertheless true that it has become more difficult in recent years to see the dividing line between the bourgeoisie, previously imaged as the occupiers of the central social terrain, and those various forces which they have historically sought to cast as oppressors or revenants. What has happened is that many of these fears have now been displaced through the generations. Time and time again, we now find that the crucial site of fear – and this goes back to, for example, *The Exorcist* – is figured as different, not in synchronic space but in time, different because the speeding-up of Western economic life, certainly in this instance aided by information technology, has opened a generational chasm below, which can now be fearfully filled with imagery already available from the discoveries of psychoanalysis. This is why, first, psychologists have replaced monks and priests as objects of fascination (because, we fear, they understand our children better than we do); and why, second, we now have to see the suppressed master-narratives of child abuse and problematic adolescence as key Gothic stories. There is no end to the stories we will tell ourselves about the reasons why we have ourselves become victims, in the curious but prevalent sense of unwilling and unconscious exploiters: now that it is revealed that it is our own children who were the victims all along, then it can be their ghosts which come to oppress us and, at the same time, through their continuing defeat in representation, to offer the only possibility of release from familial (but also social, imperial, postcolonial) guilt.

The central problem associated with writing in the area of the Gothic brings us back again to this question of taboo. It is the function of ideology to naturalise the presented world, to make its consumers think that the cardinal features of the world they inhabit are natural, eternal, unchangeable. Essential features, for instance, of capitalist ideology are that it presents family, monogamy, heterosexuality, as enduring norms, despite anthropological and psychological evidence to the contrary; that it presents industrial labour as psychologically permissible, despite, again, overwhelming evidence to the contrary; that it offers rights and satisfactions to the individual which prove on investigation to be wholly illusory. Ideology is thus projected in a process of sealing off questions, shepherding discontent into permissible channels. We are all familiar with the operation of taboo in the service of this end at the personal level: there are still active social forces which wish to prevent children from asking necessary questions about sex by making them feel that sex is at the same time 'sacred' and 'unclean', and the contradiction which this engenders still continues to damage personalities and to fuel inner and outer criminalisation. But this kind of taboo operates also at the cultural level, and makes certain questions very difficult to ask. In the late eighteenth century, the Gothic writers started trying to ask questions of this kind, questions specifically about individualism and sexual separatism. They asked them in a very diffident way – at least until Maturin – and often, after having asked them, they hastily apologised and produced normative endings to their books. Nonetheless, the questions *were* asked, and Gothic is still an arena for related questions.

It is at this point that the relation between Gothic and paranoia becomes clearer. Walter Scott made the pregnant comment that in Gothic, 'The persons introduced . . . bear the features, not of individuals, but of the class to which they belong',[31] and this is clearly true, because of character stereotyping, but it raises a problem: if it is indeed a class – or social group, or type – that you are talking about, then how does your reader fit in? The realist writer, of course, is well placed to answer this question without too much difficulty: he or she is entitled to presume that the matters dealt with are the object of shared apprehension by author, characters and audience. The situation is rather different when you are talking about lust, murder and persecution. The Gothic writer can either be far more tentative or, increasingly now, far more brazen: often, he or she tries to be both at once, to suggest on the one hand that of course this view of the world is eccentric, or personal, or sardonic, while on the other trying to force the reader into admitting his or her collaboration in the perpetuation of the forces of darkness. Most classic Gothic writers are fundamentally unsure in this way – Dickens and Reynolds are notable exceptions – in that they are not willing to commit themselves to a clear statement about the malevolence of the world. They prefer, because it is less dangerous an infringement of taboo, to leave it to the reader to decide whether characters' fears are justified or the product of internal disorganisation, whether the persecutions which they suffer are real or imagined.

One could hypothesize that Dickens and Reynolds were able to be clearer about this because the specific area of the borderland on which they worked was one over which the bourgeoisie had more control, the frontier with the proletariat. And yet, to a 'middle' class, everything is a source of fear except perfect stasis: aspiration and fall are the stuff out of which a middle class is forged, yet they are the very elements which continually seek to undermine its stability. It could even be said that the middle 'class' is largely an illusion, a frozen moment in which are collected together people and families on the way up and on the way down. And aspiration and fall are the abstract topics of Gothic fiction: where classic realism sees these things in terms of gradual movement and equilibrium, Gothic sees them as sudden, dizzying, violent, for the perspectives of Gothic are both wider and less precise. For the middle class to retain any kind of stasis, however illusory, requires continuous and massive efforts of will and repression. 'I say I am a man', says Machen, 'but who is the other who hides in me?'.[32] It is a question which, given sufficient psychological sophistication, could have been asked in any historical epoch, but it has a particular resonance in this context, for stasis is dependent on controlling that 'man' within, whether this be the id, the threat of the beast or the bones of the unburied past. Ever watchful against 'unnatural' change, the middle class is perfectly imaged in the form of the person sitting rigidly in the darkened chamber while monstrous faces press against the windows. And, to take up again the point about the role of ideology as naturalisation, it is surely not going too far to suggest that the major way in which that which is for social reasons designated as 'unnatural' can make its presence felt is precisely in the guise of the 'supernatural'.

An implication of this argument is that Gothic fiction continues to be, as it was in its inception, a form fundamentally implicated in the vindication and substantiation of a middle-class world view, with King as the latest and most powerful modern exemplar; despite, or perhaps because of, the comments I have made above about the change of focus of bourgeois fears, this seems to me still substantially true. There still remains a trace of erudition and sophistication behind the Gothic, whether in the form of M. R. James's ghost stories or of Ballard's parables of power and perversion, which marks it out as the product of a specific class conjuncture. Like all such forms, it carries with it shadows – 'sword-and-sorcery', the 'Gothic Romances' – but these are rarely a source of alternative vitality. We have talked earlier at various points about the 'popularity' of the Gothic, and about changes in it, about, for instance, the widening of the potential market which intervened between the time of Radcliffe and the time of Dickens, or about Reynolds as a partial exception to the middle-class orientation of Gothic audiences; we could now add to this a question about the audience for pulp fiction and the graphic novel. Yet these exceptions and features should be seen as interventions within an already established framework of ideas; indeed, it is significant to the original class formation of Gothic that as the nineteenth century proceeded Gothic gradually lost its position in the forefront of 'popular' fictional forms and retreated to the more esoteric positions of the 1890s.

Very generally, then, the early structure of Gothic appears to have been this: that a body of material which was once the object of general belief – legendry, ballads, folk memories – but had begun to fall into disrepute due to changing habits of mind during the Renaissance, became, during the eighteenth century, a source of ambiguity and resonance which invited relation to contemporary anxieties. It was revived, but not by those sectors of society whose property it had previously been: it was revived by middle-class literati who were relatively self-conscious about the problems, social and metaphysical, which it implied. Vampires are the most obvious case in point: the legendry itself is age-old, and even in British literature there are plenty of preromantic allusions, but only in the early nineteenth century was vampirism brought into alignment with more modern anxieties.

Thereafter, the residual ambiguity of the stock of Gothic images has remained a fertile field for literary exploration: on the one hand, because they are at root and in the far distant past connected with wide-ranging fears, they demonstrate a psychological depth and breadth, and on the other, because they have passed through a variety of interpretations and uses, they have gained a flexibility which renders them applicable in one way or another to the changing fortunes of the social structure.

Gothic thus appears to take the form of an 'expropriated' literature, which adds a further dimension of unease to the author/reader relations within it. As is well known, most ghost stories implicitly propose two alternate members of the audience, the second being by definition someone who is more credulous and thus more scared than oneself. This shadowy double may be seen as the residual form of Gothic's hypothetical previous audience, those people, conveniently located in the past but more probably in the lower depths of society, from whose fears Gothic is supposed to have arisen. Thus the class relations of Gothic can be seen to be extremely complex, particularly when, as in Dickens and Lytton, different fractions of the dominant class begin to use Gothic to flagellate their colleagues. The central contradiction, however, from which all the others flow, is this: that Gothic can at one and the same time be categorised as a middle class and an anti-middle-class literature.

This is the central dialectic of Gothic fiction, and it is one that persists even on the familial and psychopathological terrain of the latest developments in the literature of terror. The dialectic of comfort and disturbance which occurs particularly in connection with the turn-of-the-century ghost story in fact runs all through Gothic, a continuous oscillation between reassurance and threat. It is visible in form itself, in the way early Gothic writers attempt to take up the values of, on the one hand, aristocratic forms like tragedy and, on the other, popular forms like the ballad, and to interweave these with the available structure of the bourgeois novel. If the 'romantic novel' is marked by an inability to hold things together, as Robert Kiely suggests,[33] then the obvious explanation of this is that it was written within a historical conjuncture which the then emerging dominant class could not hold together; or at least that it was written in the area where such problems were paramount. Karl Mannheim says that 'the sociological significance of romanticism lies in its function as the historical opponent of the intellectual tendencies of the Enlightenment, in other words, against the philosophical exponents of bourgeois capitalism',[34] and this is of course true; but what follows from it is precisely that romanticism was severely imprinted with the conflict in which it was engaged, to the extent of failing to achieve that kind of ideological and literary synthesis which has since come to be regarded as a prerequisite of great fiction.

We are of course still left with one of the problems from which we started, the persistence of Gothic themes and images. The most obvious solution would seem at first glance to be that put forward by Carlos Clarens:

> It would seem logical to suppose that troubled art is born out of troubled times. But it would be wrong to be that systematic about it, for what period of history has sailed in, pre-ordained and self-acknowledged a golden age? Edgar Allan Poe existed in a momentary by-way of relative peace and security in a new country still full of hope, yet his work is limned by the same dark phantoms that haunt E. T. A. Hoffmann's, a writer who lived when Europe was an open field trampled by the Napoleonic wars. The landscape of the mind does not always correspond to external circumstance. Rather, there seems to be inside us a constant, ever-present yearning for the fantastic, for the darkly mysterious, for the choked terror of the dark.
>
> (Clarens, p. 9)

Such an explanation has at least the merit of being intellectually undemanding, but in fact it in no way explains the phenomenon in question. A yearning for the fantastic may in some sense be everpresent, but it certainly is not ever-manifest, and it is a great deal more obvious in British literature between 1765 and 1830 than it was, say, between 1720 and 1765. In fact, Clarens goes on to make a very surprising claim:

> art works that stir the dregs of human experience have a steady unvarying coherence in their emblems and embodiments, while the style of patterns of perfect, healthy, happy beauty fluctuate as rapidly as fashion itself and contradict one another's ideal forms according to period and culture. Satan is immutable, it would seem, whether ancestral dark angel or devil in the flesh.   (Clarens, p. 10)

One could more plausibly make out an argument, developing from Blake on Milton, for the reverse. The terrors of the original Gothic novel are *not* in any immediate sense our fears; and the horror film seems still to be in the business of demonstrating that our images of evil change not only from century to century but perhaps from year to year. And yet, to come back again to the original problem, films and books about Frankenstein and Dracula are still appearing in a way not true of, for example, the figures of Prometheus, Faust or even the monstrous Grendel.[35]

If one accepts that the images of terror which we have described above are historically specific, then there seems to be only one conclusion to be drawn, and that is that there is some inner social and cultural dynamic which makes it necessary for those images to be kept alive. The most likely hypothesis is an extension of Freud's comments on the ambiguity of the civilising process: that, as far as the development of capitalism is concerned, the Industrial Revolution constituted some kind of birth trauma, and that it remains necessary for those who rule a world based on industry to come to terms with their antecedents. The bourgeoisie is itself the child of a curious miscegenation of class, and can be seen as still engaged in a series of attempts to come to grips with the problems of its conception and its emergence into the world. It is only natural that this emergence should seem a mysterious matter; it is only natural that the class relations of the prebourgeois social world, like parental sexual activity, should acquire a patina of distortion. It is only natural too that one should derive excitement from the attempt to uncover the secrets of one's birth.[36]

As, however, the industrial world enters into new technological phases, the question of 'mystery' becomes more complex. What 'work', after all, does Case, the protagonist of *Neuromancer*, actually do? What is the source of Patrick Bateman's wealth? The structures of labour become ever more complex and withheld from the common gaze; as they do so, the sense, present since the eighteenth century, that the world might be governed by an elite group, operating the levers of power in secrecy, remains a potent one and continues to generate images in which this threat is translated into other versions of power – the power of the serial killer, for example, which figures as a consummation of alienation and at the same time as a bitter comment on the everyday processes of urban living where trust in the community has broken down and reaches ever new depths.

Seen from this angle, Gothic fiction becomes a process of cultural self-analysis, and the images which it throws up become the dream-figures of a troubled social group, troubled now by international as much as national developments. Briggs, mourning the fate of the English ghost story, says that it 'now seems to look back over its own shoulder. It has become a vehicle for nostalgia' (Briggs, p. 14).

But ghost stories, surely, have *always* been vehicles for nostalgia, attempts to understand the past, and the glance over the shoulder is their central motif and embodiment. 'The more rationalistic a time becomes the more it needs the escape value of the fantastic' (Clarens, p. 12), it could be claimed; but again there is a dialectic here, because Gothic is also about society's rare and painful admissions of the irrationality which colours its governance of its own 'family', the capitalist (or, now, postcapitalist) state. It is, for instance, easy to blame crime on feudalism, to blame delinquency on grandmothers' indulgence, but as Ian Watt points out 'the high incidence of crime in our civilisation is . . . mainly due to the wide diffusion of an individualistic ideology in a society where success is not easily or equally attainable to all its members';[37] the latest avatar of this phenomenon is the sociopath.

The fact that bourgeois ideology could naturalise this unstable situation sufficiently well to keep the state in operation does not mean that the contradictions and falsities underneath will not surface. Indeed, surface they do, and in unpleasantly transmuted forms, and it is here that Gothic is located, at the social interface between the bourgeoisie and its partly self-appointed enemies, or perhaps more broadly and now more challengingly at the psychological interface between the well-ordered psyche and its rebel subjects. The secret passages of Udolpho occasionally lead to an 'outside world'; mostly they circle endlessly inside the walls of the castle, providing refuge while at the same time continually undermining the architectural fabric, and it is this ambivalence, this set of tensions, which provides the basic dynamic for a form of fiction which continues to flourish and even to undergo resurgence, despite efforts to lay the ghosts to rest.

Yet, of course, it needs to be said that 'the literature of terror' and 'Gothic' are not coterminous, and it is time to explore this point in more detail. To take the question head on: *American Psycho* is clearly a terrifying book, but in what sense or senses does it owe allegiance to the Gothic? The major 'trace', the ambiguous and anxious link with tradition, is clearly there in the title and in the naming of the hero, which take us back to Hitchcock's *Psycho* and Norman Bates; but what we see in *American Psycho* is precisely a negative dialectic, the transmutation of the mystery of the 'dark house' turned upside-down. In *Psycho* a pathological condition finds rich symbolic articulation; in *American Psycho* the pathology is there, the psychotic isolation of the protagonist in a world of his own devising in which cognition and affect are falling apart; but in place of knowledge, of Hitchcock's rich and wry knowledge of the tradition in which he stands, we have an apocalypse of ignorance, a process of forgetting. This is characterised by Bateman's lack of connection, his decultured consciousness which can therefore *in itself* know no fear, his inarticulate speech patterns, and what is no less characteristic of the society around him, which *wishes to forget* because, as to any Gothic hero, history implies vulnerability.

If, though, Gothic originally *was* a mode of history, then we may alternatively say that *American Psycho* is also a mode of history, but one in which nothing is ever known, nothing is remembered, no lesson can be learned. We see here the outlines of a crisis of the historical mind in general: where historical memory has been turned over to the information banks, then the individual needs to do no remembering of his or her own. Ian Wharton in *My Idea of Fun* is in an analogous position; the fact that he can never achieve any real idea of what he has done, of how he has led or indeed is leading his life, is the reflection of a condition, some might call it the postmodern condition, in which history itself is under erasure.[38] In all these contexts, Poe returns to mind, and especially the burial-by-discourse which is Fortunato's unfortunate fate.[39]

We can see this erasure – and, sometimes, reinscription – of history in two different lights. There is the erasure which follows from the technologisation of psyche, a radical demythologisation which through an unavoidable paradox prevents children from knowing the world in which they live; there is the very different erasure which follows from the need to rewrite the history books anyway as the point of focus shifts – slowly, with many haunted evasions, but implacably – away from an unquestioning acceptance of the West's imperial domination of the rest of the world. The sense of being adrift in an uncomprehended universe which characterised the early Gothic is therefore compounded; any distortion becomes possible, and we have no secure grounds for judging among them.

And this, of course, precisely parallels the current crisis of psyche, of which the best emblem is the fate of psychoanalysis and its associated practices. The very notion of a 'case history', of an authoritative investigation into the past constituting a state of being, is now under radical question (Kierkegaard and Nietzsche are the necessary avatars here), as is the hypothesis that on the analytic couch, or indeed in the more everyday manifestations of the transference, we remember anything at all. Ned Lukacher's work is one example of a reminder that all may be reconstruction:[40] just as we see Iain Banks's and M. John Harrison's tormented characters trying to construct a universe which makes sense to them, labouring as they constantly do under an extreme difficulty of validation, under the epistemological and therapeutic ambiguities which now abound on the terrain of the justified sinner. The task of 'collecting oneself together' appears here as an impossibility; the fragments – those same fragments of the self which the original Gothic surveyed under the sign of a pregiven failure of the unitary whole – are scattered too widely, healing is replaced by sealing, sealing into a private world where the distortions by which one can live cannot be questioned until – if it occurs – the point of terminal breakdown where repetition can no longer stomach its own other.

In connecting the current literature of terror with its Gothic avatars, we have also to work in the opposite direction; I have repeatedly drawn attention in my discussion of contemporary fiction to the prevalence of narratives of abuse, concealment and secrecy and we now find ourselves in a position – one which is subject to all manner of complexities of desire – to find traces of those same narratives in the earlier texts: in the torture of Emily and Ellena by father-figures, for example, or in Frankenstein's delicately disgusting dealings with his creature. As the world around slips further out of focus, we might say, so the structures of the inner world swim up more alarmingly close; yet as they do so they do not prove to have the guiding character of the *psychopompos* or the ethical and decorous breadth of wisdom which we find adumbrated by the theorists of realism, themselves, it would now appear, long dead. These structures prove incapable of supplying answers to any of our questions but only serve to reinforce the impossibility of 'unearthing' the body of the past, of laying to rest the ghosts, or even of discovering, in a rerun of the problems of Freud's increasingly 'present' vacillations over child seduction, the extent to which we may speak of those ghosts as 'real'.

Yet, crucially, Gothic remains present even in the very discourses in which we try to look afresh at these problems. We may take as an example Nicolas Abraham and Maria Torok's work in *The Wolf Man's Magic Word* (1976); their elaboration of a science of cryptonymy, their attribution of 'magic' powers to language, their insistence on the 'phantom', all these are discursively connected to a Gothic world, a world of tombs, graves and magical omnipotence which can unlock the doors to the castle, to the vault, to the hidden spaces where the secret lies buried;[41] mystical perpetuation, the secret of the Rosicrucians, now clambers out into the light of day, brought forth by 'theory' itself. Alice Miller maintains that child abuse *is* the locked secret;[42] if it is, then we are very little helped by this, for we may hypothesize that it is the condition, the *ground* of childhood *and thus of the past itself* to be abused, as Dickens well knew and as Heidegger announced with much unseeing pomp in his elaboration of the notion of 'thrown-ness'. The psychological basis of abuse is laid, we might say, in the mismatch between what the child thinks it is owed and what the world will provide, between the perfection of infantile omnipotence and the translation into the real which the world constantly performs before our unwilling spectating eyes; the vision of history falls under an analogous interdict.

This suggests to us also a way of reading the relation between horror and adolescence. I have already alluded to the central issue of disgust with the body; we need to add to this a consideration of the liminal position of the adolescent, between a past which is to an extent remembered but, at least in part, as a site of embarrassment and injustice (the conflicted norms of Gothic and of our reaction to it), and a future which may be perceived as desirable but, for the present, *belongs to someone else* (a part not yet restored from the grave). Horror has to do with *power*, with fantasies of power, with precisely those repressed desires to damage the parents which form the basis of Melanie's Klein's analytic theory.[43] In the *Elm Street* series, it may be Freddy the father who does all the damaging, but we need also to see the text as a pre-text: if your father (your forefather, your ancestor, your historical precursor) has behaved, or does behave, towards you after that fashion (adolescents know that there are fashions in abuse, that fashion may *be* abuse, 'ab-use'), then surely you are yourself justified in continuing to visit these tactics of vengeance onto succeeding generations, or instead, if one can muster the courage, in pushing them back up the binding chain.

Do we live in a 'culture of horror'? We might say that we have here an unanswerable question, an 'undecidable', although its very unanswerability clearly provides part of the energy for the investigations which the literature of terror continues to carry out. We can, for instance, quote statistics, but they can as usual be made to serve any number of arguments: we can say, for example, that the Nazi holocaust and the dropping of the atomic bomb are horrors unparalleled in previous history, and in saying so we can entertain a degree of negative sublimity which brooks no other, but we can alternatively point to life expectancy figures from the Middle Ages, or to the endless wars which ravaged Europe throughout huge swathes of its early history. What *is* certain, however – and perhaps this is the root of the 'culture of horror', or at least of the panic which surrounds its naming – is that we increasingly see an unnerving paradox at work: for on the one hand, we appear now to know more than the writers of the late eighteenth century about the potential for violence of our fellow human beings; yet the 'more' that we know is precisely a knowledge of *unpredictability*, an anxious, entirely social, and spasmodically political, awareness that as we discover more about psyche we become less and less certain that it is, or ever can be, 'under control'.

But then it could be said that what we 'know' is not, can never be, 'psyche itself', *Seele*, the soul; what we know instead is psyche under certain specific conditions of 'alienation' in several senses of that word, psyche as an intolerably foreign body even to itself. It is the very effort of a dominant class or social group, the purpose of what we might now alternatively refer to as a 'state apparatus' or an 'abstract machine',[44] to naturalise this distortion which occasions strain, which 'produces' the pathologies we then nervously inspect in film, video, written text. The culture of horror is predicated on an abyss, on the vertiginous sense that, just as with an Ambrosio or a Montoni, or more gloatingly and amusingly with a Count Fosco, we know not what we are or of what we are capable. In Harris's dealings with Francis Dolarhyde, for example, we seem to have come full circle: where we might naturalistically suppose that a process of investigation might uncover the roots of monstrosity, instead the alleged 'fact' of monstrosity is made to stand in for, to obliterate, all possibility of investigation, in a reinforcement which we might aptly and resonantly characterise as mutual stupefaction.

This, then, is the position from which we need to begin when entering upon the vexed question of the effects of the literature of terror. Reading, seeing, can *confirm possibilities*, can make us either feel that the universe is indeed inhabited by terrors against which we need to take up arms (to produce an armoured, weaponed self, as particularly in analogous Japanese texts); or feel that the fantasy possibilities inside ourselves can be acted out on a broader stage, can emerge into the world triumphantly from the grave. Whether or not such effects are produced by specific readings, of course, remains fraught with unpredictability; whether psychoanalysis – and we need to remember that psychoanalysis is, of course, in one of its aspects the bourgeois science *par excellence* – has unleashed more monsters into the world than it has removed through the problematic potency of the cure is a point which will continue to be debated. But what cannot be denied is that analysis and its cognates are precisely the *topos* of many of the texts we have been considering, serving the fictional function of its earlier avatars – confession, magical healing, propitiations of one anthropological type or another. What is certain is that the texts themselves frequently now present the 'psychological' as a set of practices either in collusion with forces of darkness or helplessly at their mercy; again, if we look back with hindsight at the Gothic doctors of the past, Frankenstein, Jekyll, Moreau, we can now see the traces of precisely this anxiety coexisting alongside the more overt fears of the advance of 'science'.

Powers of Horror, the title of Julia Kristeva's book, reminds us that we are here too in the presence of abjection, the necessary corollary of being 'terrorised'.[45] I would say abjection arises from the sense of the gap, the abyss, between power and powerlessness, and will, in the case of the national provenance of the literature discussed, be necessarily intensified as the difference between the *apparent* power of individuals in democratic states to influence their own lives and the *actual* perpetuation of systems of power which render this potential impotent continues (even, or particularly, in the absence of political recognition of the problem) to crystallise. Thus, in abjection, we glimpse a constellation in which it is impossible to separate childhood from 'childing', or the abuse of the small and the weak from a multifaceted abuse which cripples our powers of self-development. The point about video is that, quite irrelevantly to the content of what we may be watching, it produces a universality of spectation: this may at first glance appear to be the reverse of the disempowering represented in Foucault's Panopticon,[46] but it is inseparably the other side of the same coin, and is predicated on the impossibility of 'intervention', unless that intervention is made in the most melodramatic and grotesque of forms.

Abjection therefore implies a further, or a *surplus,* distortion of desire, in which subjectivity itself disappears before the irrepressible might of the beheld object; the frustrations of a technological development withheld from most, the further frustrations of unemployment, the practical disenfranchisement of a political underclass, all these are elements which assist the always threatened conversion of the bright imagination into the dark imagination, which we can fairly image as finding ourselves sitting in the grave, or in a darkened room, prematurely buried, while in fantasy we store up our energies so that we can emerge raging into the light and do such things we know not, thus repressing, annihilating our 'memories' of being abject, of cringing, of submitting to an inexorably parental state machine.

But it is important that we do not at this point abandon the dialectic, and seek suppression. It is true that the literature of terror represents us as people who do not know what is going on. Far from the moral certainties of realist fiction, far from, shall we say, the world of an Iris Murdoch in which all characters speak the same language of educated moral choice – a world which is rendered even the more savage by its bland representations of a condition which, so far as we know, does not exist and never has except in the corridors of privilege – we experience the reading of Gothic as a bitter and exhilarating confirmation that the worst we have always suspected is right around us, and that the only 'choice' we have is whether to play our part in a gallery of psychopaths which is, nonetheless, not very far from our experience of the institutions of power.

It is important to stress again how frequently these issues of power and abjection have found a place in women's writing: for it is upon women (in a ghastly metaphoric linkage with the plight of children) that the state has been accustomed to practise its most savage restrictions, and it is their oppression which often continues to provide the starkest images of a power which survives by withholding its secrets – behind locked doors or even, in a more modern idiom, the other side of a 'glass ceiling'. If it is not, in fact, women alone who first experience abjection, it is nevertheless often they who pointedly effect its production into textuality; thus the extraordinary power of one of the most important Gothic symbols of recent years, Anne Rice's child-vampire, who combines in herself an almost cloying sweetness of innocence and an amoral savagery before which Louis, the 'hero', can only quail.

In earlier pages I have coined the term 'paranoid Gothic' to characterise a range of texts, and some of the more contemporary writings can also be seen to fall into this category. But we now have also different categories to entertain, categories of fiction in which different pathologies are represented. Thinking first of Stephen King, and emblematically of the aptly-named *Misery*, we see the outlines of what we might call a 'depressive Gothic': a Gothic in which there is only endurance of the might of others, a hopelessness which is, of course, not necessarily 'depressing' in the simple sense for readers (if it were, then King would hardly be as popular as he is) but which nonetheless confirms a powerless, an abjected subject position and invites us to view the world as confirming our worst fears.

More strikingly, and very much more threateningly, we see also the emergence of what we might fairly call a more fully-fledged 'schizophrenic Gothic', the presentation of worlds of cognitive and hallucinated disjunction in which there is no access below the surface, in which everything has been 'closed down'. In using that terminology, I mean to point precisely to the connection between this psychic phenomenon and a vision of a postindustrial world, of a world where the engines and machines have been closed down, where we are left to wander in a landscape where nothing and nobody 'works' any more, the 'terminal beach' of *Neuromancer*, the prison Manhattan of John Carpenter's *Escape from New York* (1981). But this closure is also of the soul: there is nothing inside Galloway's or Murphy's heroines, there is nothing 'inside' Patrick Bateman, there is no inner world left at all.

This is, of course, in one sense an illusion, albeit a powerful one. What is frequently inside is the rage of despair; what is patrolling the outside is the massive array of forces which the ego erects to protect us from hypotheses of inner emptiness. Death of affect is only part of the story: we may indeed continue, after two centuries, to want 'gross and violent stimulants' (*Lyrical Ballads*, p. 248), but this is because we detect the stirrings of a grossness within ourselves which cannot nevertheless be admitted. It is pointless to argue about whether 'video nasties' should be 'allowed'; they are with us because they speak a language which something inside us can understand, and nothing will prevent the satisfaction of this need for communication; censorship, as Gothic has always reminded us, will only make the situation worse.

What, though, is striking about all this – and this is the final point which needs stress – is that such pathological manifestations do not emerge only in the dark and dreary forms of, say, *Friday the Thirteenth*; they emerge also in the manic and hysterical energy of Iain Banks, in the resonant and inventive mournfulness of M. John Harrison, in the brilliant and corrosive satire of Salman Rushdie. The literature of terror is not the death of art, and neither is it art's victim; it *is* art, and speaks art's usual mixed language of hope and despair, and in doing so, it continues to use and modify those images which remain puzzlingly appropriate to the times. Neither does it necessarily or always constrain us to the subject-position of abjection, quailing terrorisation, although such moments are virtually inseparable from the complex trajectory which it makes its own. It can also provoke towards an understanding, often precisely by drawing images direct from an intimate – and frequently *secret* – connection with the social unconscious and showing them to us, inescapably, inexorably. With this we have to deal: we have to deal, with intelligence, with an array of images which represent to us, often painfully, sometimes disastrously, occasionally now murderously, precisely the sources from which come a threatened *withdrawal* of intelligence, a subjugation of the thinking, active, energetic mind which can be answered only by drawing on the ever residual but still active powers of that mind itself to perceive aright and to think afresh on the problems and anxieties presented to it, powers which are not served by repression or censorship even when they find themselves ever more embattled. Perhaps it is there, amid those raging spectres, that these powers can come, as was of course the putative case with Greek tragedy, most commandingly into their own in the process of allowing – and this would indeed be a new thing – the voices of the sociopathological to produce themselves in a drama in which, as in the ceaseless, but endlessly socially responsive, dramatisations of the ego in dream, we can all feel ourselves to be, in a discourse of alienation (apart?), a part . . .

Notes and references

1. See, e.g. **S. L. Varnado**, *Haunted Presence: The Numinous in Gothic Fiction* (Tuscaloosa, 1987), p. 130; **William Patrick Day**, *In the Circles of Fear and Desire* (Chicago, 1985), pp. 13–15, 191–3; **Eve Kosofsky Sedgwick**, *The Coherence of Gothic Conventions* (New York, 1980), pp. 1–7; and, most interestingly, **Robert Miles**, *Gothic Writing 1750–1820: A Genealogy* (London and New York, 1993), pp. 1–15.
2. Further commentary on various aspects of paranoia is provided in **Freud**, *Works*, XII, 3–82; XIV, 261–72; XVI, 423–6; and of course in many of his other works.
3. See **Joseph Grixti**, *Terrors of Uncertainty: The Cultural Contexts of Horror Fiction* (London, 1989); and **Noel Carroll**, *The Philosophy of Horror; or, Paradoxes of the Heart* (London, 1990).
4. **Machen**, *The Terror: A Fantasy* (London, 1927), pp. 163–4. It is an instructive and revealing feature of Gothic that writers like Machen – and even to an extent Lovecraft – who so often descend to the overlush can nevertheless be both precise and suggestive when, explicitly or implicitly, describing their own imaginative problems and preoccupations.
5. See *The Literature of Terror*, Vol. I: *The Gothic Tradition* (London, 1996), p. 17.
6. **Keith Hollingsworth**, *The Newgate Novel 1830–1847: Bulwer, Ainsworth, Dickens and Thackeray* (Detroit, 1963), p. 225.
7. See *Works*, IX, 150.
8. See Lacan, 'The Subversion of the Subject and the Dialectic of Desire in the Freudian Unconscious', in *Ecrits: A Selection*, trans. A. Sheridan (London, 1977), pp. 292–325.
9. See Zizek, pp. 90–1.
10. **Bulwer Lytton**, 'On style and diction', in *Miscellaneous Prose Works* (3 vols, London,

1868), III, 106. We can take the point of this comment without having to subscribe to the habit of mind which occasions the reference to 'indulgence'.

11. **Mary Shelley**, *Frankenstein*, introd. R. E. Dowse and D. J. Palmer (London, 1963), p. v (Introduction).

12. See **Mikkel Borch-Jacobsen**, *The Freudian Subject*, trans. C. Porter (London, 1989), e.g. p. 20.

13. See Deleuze and Guattari, pp. 159–66.

14. This is the objection raised particularly in **Elizabeth Napier**, *The Failure of Gothic* (Oxford, 1987); see also the response in Miles, pp. 1–3.

15. **Lucien Goldmann**, 'Criticism and dogmatism in literature', trans. Ilona Halberstadt, in *The Dialectics of Liberation*, ed. David Cooper (Harmondsworth, Middx., 1968), p. 147.

16. See **Victor Sage**, *Horror Fiction in the Protestant Tradition* (London, 1988).

17. See *Works*, XIII, 29–32 and 67–71.

18. For recent work in this area, see **Eugenia C. Delamotte**, *Perils of the Night* (Oxford, 1990); **Kate Ferguson Ellis**, *The Contested Castle* (Urbana, Ill. and Chicago, 1989); **Keri J. Winter**, *Subjects of Slavery, Agents of Change* (Athens, Ga., 1992); **Susan Wolstenholme**, *Gothic (Re)Visions* (Albany, N.Y., 1993).

19. See **Luce Irigaray**, *The Sex which is not one*, trans. C. Porter (Ithaca, N.Y., 1993); *Writing the Differences: Readings from the Seminar of Hélène Cixous*, ed. S. Sellers (Milton Keynes, 1988), pp. 49–50.

20. **Devendra P. Varma**, *The Gothic Flame* (London, 1957), p. xiii (Introduction).

21. On the dialectic of civilisation, see **Herbert Marcuse**, *Eros and Civilisation* (London, 1969), pp. 75–93.

22. **Wordsworth**, *The Prelude*, ed. Stephen Gill (London, 1970), p. 124.

23. **Wordsworth** and **Coleridge**, *Lyrical Ballads* (1798), ed. R. L. Brett and A. R. Jones (London, 1968), p. 243.

24. **Goldmann**, *Towards a Sociology of the Novel*, trans. Alan Sheridan (London, 1975), p. 12.

25. *The Poems of Alexander Pope*, ed. John Butt (10 vols, London, 1939–67), II, i, 125–6.

26. **Karl Marx** and **Frederick Engels**, *Articles on Britain* (Moscow, 1971), p. 16.

27. See *Literature of Terror*, Vol. I: *The Gothic Tradition*, p. 112.

28. See **Marx**, *Early Writings*, introd. Lucio Colletti (Harmondsworth, Middx., 1975), pp. 322–34.

29. In fact, one would want immediately to distort the structure of this list by the problematic inclusion of the alienation of the sexes, and of course the concomitant difficulties in the area of 'productive and reproductive labour'. It is unnecessary to list the many examples which would figure under this heading.

30. **John Lucas**, *The Melancholy Man: A Study of Dickens's Novels* (London, 1970), p. 92.

31. *Sir Walter Scott on Novelists and Fiction*, ed. Ioan Williams (London, 1968), p. 110.

32. See Briggs, p. 75.

33. See *Literature of Terror*, Vol. I: *The Gothic Tradition*, p. 16.

34. **Karl Mannheim**, *Essays on Sociology and Social Psychology*, ed. Paul Kecskemeti (London, 1953), p. 89.

35. Despite **John Gardner**, *Grendel* (London, 1973).

36. It would not be too fanciful to suggest the parallel – and dependent – metaphor according to which the working classes become seen as delinquent children, with the mixture of condescension, admiration and fear which that implies.

37. **Ian Watt**, *The Rise of the Novel* (London, 1957), p. 94.

38. See, e.g. **Bill Readings**, *Introducing Lyotard: Art and Politics* (London, 1991), pp. 33–85.

39. See *Literature of Terror*, Vol. I: *The Gothic Tradition*, pp. 180–2.

40. See **Ned Lukacher**, *Primal Scenes: Literature, Philosophy, Psychoanalysis* (New York, 1986).

41. See **Nicolas Abraham** and **Maria Torok**, *The Wolf Man's Magic Word: A Cryptonymy*, trans. N. Rand (Minneapolis, 1986).
42. See Miller, e.g. *Prisoners of Childhood* (New York, 1981); *The Untouched Key* (London, 1990); *Banished Knowledge* (London, 1990).
43. See **Melanie Klein**, e.g. 'Criminal Tendencies in Normal Children' (1927), in *Love, Guilt and Reparation, and Other Writings 1921–1945*, introd. H. Segal (London, 1988).
44. In the rhetorics of Althusser and of Deleuze and Guattari respectively: see, e.g. **Louis Althusser**, 'Ideology and Ideological State Apparatuses' (1969), in *Lenin and Philosophy, and Other Essays*, trans. B. Brewster (London, 1971), pp. 121–73; and Deleuze and Guattari, pp. 222–27.
45. See **Julia Kristeva**, *Powers of Horror: An Essay on Abjection*, trans. L. S. Roudiez (New York, 1982).
46. For an introduction to which see **Michel Foucault**, *Power/Knowledge: Selected Interviews and Other Writings 1972–1977*, ed. C. Gordon (Brighton, 1980), pp. 146–65.

Bibliography

This bibliography does not claim to act as a reading-list in respect of any of the individual authors under discussion; it does, however, mention every work referred to in the text, along with a selection of others, and is divided into 'Primary' and 'Secondary' sections. In the latter section I have mentioned additional critical material where it seems to me to open up interesting lines of investigation into the Gothic; I have also consistently tended to include material on lesser known texts and writers at the expense of the more mainstream. As pointed out in the Preface, I have in many cases cited the most available edition; where important, I have also included reference to the original date of publication.

Primary

Bainbridge, Beryl. *An Awfully Big Adventure*. London, 1989.
———. *The Dressmaker*. London, 1973.
———. *Harriet Said*. . . . London, 1972.
———. *Young Adolf*. London, 1978.
Ballard, James Graham. *The Atrocity Exhibition* (1970). Pbk edn, St Albans, 1972.
———. *Concrete Island*. London, 1974.
———. *The Day of Creation*. London, 1987.
———. *The Disaster Area*. London, 1967.
———. *The Terminal Beach*. London, 1964.
———. *Vermilion Sands*. London, 1973.
Banks, Iain. *The Bridge*. London, 1986.
———. *The Wasp Factory*. London, 1984.

Banville, John. *Birchwood*. London, 1973.
——. *Mefisto*. London, 1986.
Benson, E. F. *The Collected Ghost Stories*, ed. R. Dalby. London, 1992.
Bierce, Ambrose. *Can Such Things Be?* (1893). London, 1926.
——. *Ghost and Horror Stories of Ambrose Bierce*, ed. E. F. Bleiler. Pbk edn, New York, 1964.
——. *Tales of Soldiers and Civilians* (1891), introd. M. Armstrong. London, 1928.
Blackwood, Algernon. *Ancient Sorceries, and Other Stories*. Pbk edn, Harmondsworth, Middx., 1968.
——. *The Insanity of Jones and Other Tales*. Pbk edn, Harmondsworth, Middx., 1966.
——. *Tales of the Uncanny and Supernatural*. London and New York, 1962.
Blake, William. *The Poetry and Prose of William Blake*, ed. David V. Erdman. New York, 1965.
Bleiler, E. F., ed. *Three Supernatural Novels of the Victorian Period*. Pbk edn, New York, 1975.
Bowen, Elizabeth. *The Collected Short Stories of Elizabeth Bowen*, introd. Angus Wilson. London, 1980.
Burroughs, William Seward. *Cities of the Red Night*. London, 1982.
——. *The Naked Lunch*. New York, 1959.
——. *The Soft Machine: A Novel*. London, 1968.
Cabell, James Branch. *The Cream of the Jest: a Comedy of Evasions* (1917), introd. H. Ward. London, 1927.
——. *Jurgen: a Comedy of Justice* (1919). London, 1921.
——. *Something about Eve: a Comedy of Fig-Leaves* (1927). London, 1929.
Campbell, Margaret. *The Spectral Bride* (Joseph Shearing. *The Fetch*) (1942). London, 1973.
Campbell, Ramsey. *The Claw*. London, 1992.
——. *The Count of Eleven*. London, 1991.
——. *The Long Lost*. London, 1993.
——. *Obsession*. London, 1985.
Carter, Angela. *Black Venus*. London, 1985.
——. *Fireworks: Nine Profane Pieces*. London, 1974.
——. *Heroes and Villains*. London, 1969.
——. *The Infernal Desire Machines of Doctor Hoffman*. London, 1972.
——. *Love: a Novel*. London, 1971.
——. *Nights at the Circus*. London, 1984.
——. *The Passion of New Eve*. London, 1977.

Chambers, Robert William. *The King in Yellow and Other Horror Stories*, ed. E. F. Bleiler. Pbk edn, New York, 1970.

Coleridge, Samuel Taylor. *Poetical Works*, ed. E. H. Coleridge. London, 1967.

Collins, Wilkie. *The Woman in White* (1860), ed. H. P. Sucksmith. London, 1975.

Coover, Robert. *Pricksongs and Descants* (1969). Pbk edn, London, 1973.

Defoe, Daniel. *The Fortunes and Misfortunes of the Famous Moll Flanders* (1922), ed. G. A. Starr. London, 1971.

De la Mare, Walter. *The Connoisseur and Other Stories*. London, 1926.

——. *On the Edge: Short Stories*. London, 1930.

——. *The Riddle and Other Stories*. London, 1923.

——. *The Wind Blows Over*. London, 1936.

Dickens, Charles. *Barnaby Rudge* (1841), ed. G. Spence. Pbk edn, Harmondsworth, Middx., 1973.

——. *Oliver Twist* (1838), ed. Peter Fairclough, introd. Angus Wilson. Pbk edn, Harmondsworth, Middx., 1966.

Dinesen, Isak. *Anecdotes of Destiny*. London, 1958.

——. *Last Tales*. London, 1957.

——. *Seven Gothic Tales*, introd. Dorothy Canfield. New York and London, 1934.

Doyle, Sir Arthur Conan. *The Conan Doyle Stories*. London, 1929.

——. *The Hound of the Baskervilles* (1902). Foreword and Afterword by John Fowles. London, 1974.

Ellis, Bret Easton. *American Psycho*. New York, 1991.

——. *Less Than Zero*. New York, 1984.

——. *The Rules of Attraction*. New York, 1987.

Fielding, Henry. *Jonathan Wild and Journal of a Voyage to Lisbon*, introd. A. R. Humphreys. Pbk edn, London, 1964.

Fleming, Joan. *Too Late! Too Late! The Maiden Cried: A Gothic Novel*. London, 1975.

Gaiman, Neil. *Brief Lives*. London, 1994.

——. *Fables and Reflections*. London, 1994.

——. *Season of Mists*. New York, 1992.

Galloway, Janice. *The Trick is to Keep Breathing*. London, 1991.

Gardner, John. *Grendel*. London, 1973.

Gibson, William. *Count Zero*. London, 1986.

——. *Neuromancer*. London, 1984.

——. *Virtual Light*. New York, 1993.

Grant, Joan. *Castle Cloud (The Laird and the Lady)*. London, 1949.

Haggard, Sir Henry Rider, and Andrew Lang. *The World's Desire.* London, 1890.

Harris, Thomas. *Black Sunday.* London, 1975.

——. *Red Dragon.* New York, 1981.

——. *The Silence of the Lambs.* London, 1989.

Harrison, M. John. *The Course of the Heart.* London, 1993.

——. *In Viriconium.* London, 1982.

Hartley, L. P. *Night Fears, and Other Supernatural Tales,* introd. Sir Peter Quennell. London, 1993.

Hawkes, John. *The Beetle Leg.* New York, 1951.

——. *The Blood Oranges.* New York, 1971.

——. *The Cannibal,* introd. Albert Guerard. London, 1962.

——. *Death, Sleep and the Traveller.* New York, 1973.

——. *The Lime Twig,* introd. Leslie A. Fiedler. London, 1962.

——. *Lunar Landscapes: Stories and Short Novels 1949–1963.* New York, 1969.

——. *Second Skin.* New York, 1964.

Heller, Joseph. *Something Happened.* New York and London, 1974.

Herbert, James. *The Fog.* London, 1975.

——. *The Magic Cottage.* London, 1986.

——. *Portent.* London, 1992.

——. *Sepulchre.* London, 1987.

Hodgson, William Hope. *Carnacki the Ghost-finder.* London, 1910.

——. *The House on the Borderland.* London, 1908.

——. *The Night Land.* London, 1912.

Hogg, James. *The Private Memoirs and Confessions of a Justified Sinner* (1824), ed. John Carey. Pbk edn, London, 1970.

James, Henry. *The Complete Tales of Henry James,* ed. and introd. L. Edel. 12 vols. London, 1962–4.

——. *Stories of the Supernatural,* ed. and introd. L. Edel. London, 1971.

——. *The Turn of the Screw and Other Stories,* ed. S. Gorley Putt. Pbk edn, Harmondsworth, Middx., 1969.

James, Montague Rhodes. *Collected Ghost Stories.* London, 1931.

——. *Ghost Stories of an Antiquary.* Pbk edn, Harmondsworth, Middx., 1974.

Kafka, Franz. *The Castle* (1926), trans. W. and E. Muir, introd. E. Muir and M. Brod. London, 1930.

——. *Metamorphosis and Other Stories,* trans. W. and E. Muir. Pbk edn, Harmondsworth, Middx., 1961.

Kesey, Ken. *One Flew Over the Cuckoo's Nest.* New York, 1962.

King, Stephen. *Four Past Midnight.* London, 1990.

——. *Misery.* London, 1987.

——. *Needful Things.* London, 1991.

——. *Salem's Lot.* New York, 1975.

——. *The Shining.* New York, 1977.

——. *The Tommy-Knockers.* London, 1988.

LeFanu, Joseph Sheridan. *Best Ghost Stories,* ed. E. F. Bleiler. Pbk edn, New York, 1964.

——. *Uncle Silas: a Tale of Bartram-Haugh* (1864), ed. Frederick Shroyer. Pbk edn, New York, 1966.

Lewis, Matthew Gregory. *The Monk: A Romance* (1796). Pbk edn, London, 1973.

Lindsay, David. *Devil's Tor.* London, 1932.

——. *The Haunted Woman.* London, 1922.

——. *Sphinx.* London, 1923.

——. *The Violet Apple,* introd. J. B. Pick, London, 1978.

——. *A Voyage to Arcturus* (1920). Pbk edn, London, 1972.

Lovecraft, Howard Phillips. *At the Mountains of Madness and Other Novels,* ed. August Derleth. London, 1966.

——. *The Case of Charles Dexter Ward* (1927–8). Pbk edn, London, 1963.

——. *The Doom that Came to Sarnath,* ed. Lin Carter. New York, 1971.

——, and August Derleth. *The Lurker at the Threshold.* St Albans, 1970.

——, and August Derleth. *The Shuttered Room and Other Tales of Horror.* London, 1970.

Lytton, Edward G. E. L. Bulwer-Lytton, Lord. *The Caxtons; Zicci; The Haunted and the Haunters.* Boston and New York, 1849.

——. *Miscellaneous Prose Works.* 3 vols. London, 1868.

Machen, Arthur. *The Children of the Pool, and Other Stories.* London, 1936.

——. *The Great God Pan, and The Inmost Light.* London, 1913.

——. *The Hill of Dreams* (1907). New York, 1923.

——. *The Terror: A Fantasy* (1917). London, 1927.

——. *The Three Impostors* (1895), introd. Julian Symons. London, 1964.

Matheson, Richard. *I Am Legend.* London, 1954.

Maturin, Charles Robert. *Melmoth the Wanderer: A Tale* (1820), ed. Douglas Grant. London, 1968.

McGrath, Patrick. *Spider.* New York, 1990.

——, and Bradford Morrow, ed. *The New Gothic.* New York, 1991.

Meyrink, Gustav. *The Golem* (1915), trans. M. Mitchell. London, 1995.

Moore, Alan, and Dave Gibbons. *Watchmen.* London, 1987.

Oates, Joyce Carol. *Expensive People* (1968). Pbk edn, London, 1969.
——. *A Garden of Earthly Delights.* New York, 1967.
——. *Marriages and Infidelities.* London, 1974.
——. *Night-Side: Eighteen Tales.* London, 1979.
——. *Them.* London, 1971.
Oliphant, Margaret. *Selected Short Stories of the Supernatural,* ed. M. K. Gray. Edinburgh, 1985.
Peake, Mervyn. *Gormenghast* (1930). Pbk edn, Harmondsworth, Middx., 1969.
——. *Titus Groan* (1946). Pbk edn, Harmondsworth, Middx., 1968.
——. *Titus Alone* (1950). Pbk edn, Harmondsworth, Middx., 1970.
Plath, Sylvia. *The Bell Jar.* London, 1963.
Poe, Edgar Allan. *The Complete Works of Edgar Allan Poe,* ed. James A. Harrison. 17 vols. New York, 1965.
Pope, Alexander. *The Poems of Alexander Pope,* ed. John Butt. 10 vols. London, 1939–67.
Purdy, James. *Cabot Wright Begins.* New York, 1964.
——. *Colour of Darkness: Eleven Stories and a Novella.* London, 1961.
——. *Eustace Chisholm and the Works.* New York, 1967.
——. *I Am Elijah Thrush.* London, 1972.
——. *The Nephew.* New York, 1970.
Pynchon, Thomas. *The Crying of Lot 49.* Philadelphia, 1966.
——. *Gravity's Rainbow.* New York and London, 1973.
——. *Slow Learner.* New York, 1984.
——. *V.* London, 1963.
——. *Vineland.* London, 1990.
Radcliffe, Ann. *The Italian; or, The Confessional of the Black Penitents* (1797), ed. Frederick Garber. Pbk edn, London, 1971.
——. *The Mysteries of Udolpho: a Romance, Interspersed with some Pieces of Poetry* (1794), ed. Bonamy Dobree. Pbk edn, London, 1970.
Rechy, John. *City of Night.* New York, 1963.
——. *This Day's Death: A Novel.* London, 1970.
Rice, Anne. *Interview with the Vampire.* London, 1976.
——. *Lasher.* London, 1993.
——. *The Mummy, or, Ramses the Damned.* London, 1989.
——. *The Queen of the Damned.* London, 1988.
——. *The Vampire Lestat.* London, 1985.
Rushdie, Salman. *Shame.* London, 1993.
Scott, Sir Walter. *Sir Walter Scott on Novelists and Fiction,* ed. Ioan Williams. London, 1968.
Self, Will. *Cock and Bull.* London, 1992.
——. *My Idea of Fun.* London, 1993.

——. *The Quantity Theory of Insanity.* London, 1991.

Shelley, Mary. *Frankenstein* (1818), introd. R. E. Dowse and D. J. Palmer. Pbk edn, London, 1963.

Stevenson, Robert Louis. *New Arabian Nights* (1882), ed. Herbert von Thal, introd. D. Holloway. Pbk edn, London, 1968.

——. *The Supernatural Short Stories of Robert Louis Stevenson,* ed. and introd. M. Hayes. London, 1976.

——. *Works,* ed. L. Osbourne and Mrs R. L. Stevenson. 30 vols. London, 1924–6.

Stoker, Bram. *Dracula* (1897). Pbk edn, New York, 1965.

——. *The Jewel of the Seven Stars.* London, 1903.

——. *The Lady of the Shroud.* London, 1909.

——. *The Lair of the White Worm.* London, 1911.

Suskind, Patrick. *Perfume: The Story of a Murderer,* trans. J. E. Woods. Pbk edn, Harmondsworth, Middx., 1987.

Tolkien, John Ronald Reuel. *The Lord of the Rings.* 3 vols. London, 1954–5.

Volney, Constantin Francois Chasseboeuf, Comte de. *The Ruins, or a Survey of the Revolutions of Empires.* London, 1795.

Walpole, Horace. *The Castle of Otranto: a Gothic Story* (1764), ed. W. S. Lewis. London, 1969.

Wells, Herbert George. *The Complete Short Stories.* London, 1927.

——. *The Island of Doctor Moreau* (1896). Pbk edn, London, 1973.

Wilde, Oscar. *Lord Arthur Savile's Crime, and Other Stories.* Pbk edn, Harmondsworth, Middx., 1973.

——. *The Picture of Dorian Gray* (1891), ed. Isobel Murray. London, 1974.

Wolfe, Tom. *The Bonfire of the Vanities.* New York, 1987.

Wordsworth, William. *The Prelude* (1805), ed. E. de Selincourt, corrected by Stephen Gill. Pbk edn, London, 1970.

——, and Samuel Taylor Coleridge. *Lyrical Ballads* (1798), ed. R. L. Brett and A. R. Jones. London, 1968.

Secondary

Abraham, Nicolas, and Maria Torok. *The Wolf Man's Magic Word,* trans. N. Rand. Minneapolis, 1986.

Allen, Walter. *The English Novel: A Short Critical History.* London, 1954.

Althusser, Louis. *Lenin and Philosophy, and Other Essays,* trans. B. Brewster. London, 1971.

Altick, Richard D. *The English Common Reader: A Social History of the Mass Reading Public, 1800–1900.* Chicago, 1957.

Arata, Stephen D. 'The Occidental Tourist: Dracula and the Anxiety of Reverse Colonisation', *Victorian Studies*, XXXIII (1990), 621–45.

Baker, Ernest Albert. *The History of the English Novel.* 10 vols. London, 1924–39.

Ball, David. 'Oscar Wilde and the Practice of Transformation', *English*, XL (1991), 23–35.

Barclay, Glen St John. *Anatomy of Horror: The Masters of Occult Fiction.* London, 1978.

Barker, Martin. *A Haunt of Fears: The Strange History of the British Horror Comics Campaign.* London, 1984.

Beachcroft, Thomas Owen. *The Modest Art: A Survey of the Short Story in English.* London, 1968.

Benjamin, Walter. *Illuminations*, trans. H. Zohn, introd. Hannah Arendt. London, 1970.

Bently, Thomas J. 'Henry James's "General Vision of Evil" in *The Turn of the Screw*', *Studies in English Literature 1500–1900*, IX (1969), 721–35.

Boardman, Arthur. 'Mrs Grose's Reading of *The Turn of the Screw*', *Studies in English Literature 1500–1900*, XIV (1974), 619–35.

Borch-Jacobsen, Mikkel. *The Freudian Subject*, trans. C. Porter. London, 1989.

Briggs, Julia. *The Rise and Fall of the English Ghost Story.* London, 1977.

Bronfen, Elisabeth. *Over her Dead Body: Death, Femininity and the Aesthetic.* Manchester, 1992.

Brooke-Rose, Christine. 'The Squirm of the True', *PTL*, I (1976), 265–94 and 513–46; II (1977), 517–62.

Bussing, Sabine. *Aliens in the Home: The Child in Horror Fiction.* New York and London, 1987.

Carroll, Noel. *The Philosophy of Horror; or, Paradoxes of the Heart.* London, 1990.

Carter, Margaret L. *Specter or Delusion? The Supernatural in Gothic Fiction.* Ann Arbor and London, 1987.

Clarens, Carlos. *Horror Movies: An Illustrated Survey.* London, 1968.

Clark, Kenneth McKenzie, Lord. *The Gothic Revival: An Essay in the History of Taste.* London, 1928.

Clover, Carol J. *Men, Women and Chainsaws: Gender in the Modern Horror Film.* London, 1993.

Cooley, Ronald W. 'The Hothouse of the Street: Imperialism and Narrative in Pynchon's *V*', *Modern Fiction Studies*, XXXIX, 307–25.

Cooper, David, ed. *The Dialectics of Liberation.* Pbk edn, Harmondsworth, Middx., 1968.

Cornwell, Neil. *The Literary Fantastic: From Gothic to Postmodernism.* Hemel Hempstead, 1990.

Coubro, Gerry. *Hammer and Horror: Bad Taste and Popular British Cinema.* Sheffield, 1991.

Day, William Patrick. *In the Circles of Fear and Desire: A Study of Gothic Fantasy.* Chicago, 1985.

De Camp, Lyon Sprague. *Lovecraft: A Biography.* New York, 1975.

Delamotte, Eugenia C. *Perils of the Night: A Feminist Study of Nineteenth-Century Gothic.* Oxford, 1990.

Deleuze, Gilles, and Félix Guattari. *A Thousand Plateaus: Capitalism and Schizophrenia,* trans. B. Massumi. Minneapolis, 1987.

Derrida, Jacques *Acts of Literature,* ed. D. Attridge. New York and London, 1992.

———. *Limited Inc.* Evanston, Ill., 1988.

———. *Memoires: For Paul de Man,* trans. C. Lindsay *et al.* New York, 1989.

Ellis, Kate Ferguson. *The Contested Castle: Gothic Novels and the Subversion of Domestic Ideology.* Urbana, Ill. and Chicago, 1989.

Fiedler, Leslie Aaron. *Love and Death in the American Novel.* New York, 1960.

Fleenor, Juliann E., ed. *The Female Gothic.* Montreal and London, 1983.

Fleishman, Avrom. *The English Historical Novel: Walter Scott to Virginia Woolf.* Baltimore, 1971.

Forrester, John. *The Seductions of Psychoanalysis: Freud, Lacan and Derrida.* Cambridge, 1990.

Foster, Dennis A. 'J. G. Ballard's Empire of the Senses: Perversion and the Failure of Authority', *Publications of the Modern Language Association,* CVIII (1993), 519–32.

Foucault, Michel. *Power/Knowledge: Selected Interviews and Other Writings 1972–1977,* ed. C. Gordon. Brighton, 1980.

Frankl, Paul. *The Gothic: Literary Sources and Interpretations through Eight Centuries.* Princeton, N.J., 1960.

Freud, Sigmund. *The Standard Edition of the Complete Psychological Works of Sigmund Freud,* ed. James Strachey. 24 vols. London, 1953–74.

Goldmann, Lucien. *Towards a Sociology of the Novel* (1964), trans. Alan Sheridan. London, 1975.

Gordon, Jan B. 'Parody as Initiation: the Sad Education of *Dorian Grey*', *Criticism,* IX (1967), 355–71.

Gose, Elliott B., Jr. *Imagination Indulged: The Irrational in the Nineteenth-Century Novel.* Montreal and London, 1972.

Greenberg, Martin. *The Terror of Art: Kafka and Modern Literature.* London, 1971.

Greiner, Donald J. *Comic Terror: The Novels of John Hawkes.* Memphis, Tenn., 1973.

Grenarder, Mary. *Ambrose Bierce.* New York, 1971.

Grixti, Joseph. *Terrors of Uncertainty: The Cultural Contexts of Horror Fiction.* London, 1989.

Gross, John, and Gabriel Pearson, eds. *Dickens and the Twentieth Century.* London, 1962.

Heine, Maurice. 'Promenade à travers le Roman noir', *Minotaure,* No. 5 (May 1934), pp. 1–4.

Heller, Terry. *The Delights of Terror: An Aesthetics of the Tale of Terror.* Urbana, Ill. and Chicago, 1987.

Herdman, John. *The Double in Nineteenth-Century Fiction.* Basingstoke, 1990.

Hollingsworth, Keith. *The Newgate Novel 1830–1847: Bulwer, Ainsworth, Dickens, and Thackeray.* Detroit, 1963.

Horkheimer, Max, and Theodor W. Adorno. *Dialectic of Enlightenment* (1947), trans. John Cumming. London, 1973.

Howells, Coral Ann. *Love, Mystery, and Misery: Feeling in Gothic Fiction.* London, 1978.

Hoyt, Charles A. *Minor British Novelists.* Carbondale, Ill., 1967.

Hudson, Derek. 'A Study of Algernon Blackwood', *Essays and Studies,* XIV (1961), 102–14.

Hume, Kathryn. 'Visionary Allegory in David Lindsay's *A Voyage to Arcturus'*, *Journal of English and Germanic Philology,* LXXVII (1978), 72–91.

Hume, Robert D. 'Gothic versus Romantic: a Revaluation of the Gothic Novel', *Publications of the Modern Language Association,* LXXXIV (1969), 282–90.

Huss, Roy, and T. J. Ross, eds. *Focus on the Horror Film.* Englewood Cliffs, N.J., 1972.

Hutchings, Peter. *Hammer and Beyond: The British Horror Film.* Manchester, 1993.

Irigaray, Luce. *The Sex which is not one,* trans. C. Porter. Ithaca, N.Y., 1993.

Kael, Pauline. *Reeling.* London, 1977.

Kennard, Jean E. *Number and Nightmare: Forms of Fantasy in Contemporary Fiction.* Hamden, Conn., 1975.

Klein, Melanie. *Love, Guilt and Reparation, and Other Writings 1921–1945*, introd. H. Segal. London, 1988.

Krafft-Ebing, Richard von. *Psychopathia Sexualis*, trans. and introd. F. S. Klaf. London, 1965.

Kristeva, Julia. *The Kristeva Reader*, ed. Toril Moi. Oxford, 1986.

——. *Desire in Language: A Semiotic Approach to Literature and Art*, ed. L. S. Roudiez. New York, 1980.

——. *Powers of Horror: An Essay on Abjection*, trans. L. S. Roudiez. New York, 1982.

Lacan, Jacques. *Ecrits: A Selection*, trans. A. Sheridan. London, 1977.

——. *The Four Fundamental Concepts of Psychoanalysis*, trans. J.-A. Miller. London, 1977.

Leavis, Queenie Dorothy. *Fiction and the Reading Public*. London, 1968.

Levine, George, and David Leverenz, eds. *Mindful Pleasures: Essays on Thomas Pynchon*. Boston and Toronto, 1976.

Lovecraft, Howard Phillips. *Supernatural Horror in Literature* (1945), introd. E. F. Bleiler. New York, 1973.

Lucas, John. *The Melancholy Man: A Study of Dickens's Novels*. London, 1970.

Lukacher, Ned. *Primal Scenes: Literature, Philosophy, Psychoanalysis*. New York, 1986.

Lyotard, Jean-Francois. *The Inhuman: Reflections of Time*. Cambridge, 1991.

——. *The Postmodern Condition: A Report on Knowledge*, trans. G. Bennington and B. Massumi. Manchester, 1987.

MacKenzie, Manfred. '*The Turn of the Screw*: Jamesian Gothic', *Essays in Criticism*, XII (1962), 34–8.

Malin, Irving. *New American Gothic*. Carbondale, Ill., 1962.

Mannheim, Karl. *Essays on Sociology and Social Psychology*, ed. Paul Kecskemeti. London, 1953.

Marcuse, Herbert. *Eros and Civilisation: A Philosophical Inquiry into Freud*. Pbk edn, London, 1969.

Massé, Michelle A. *In the Name of Love: Women, Masochism and the Gothic*. Ithaca, N.Y. and London, 1992.

Martin, Jay. *Harvests of Change: American Literature 1865–1914*. Englewood Cliffs, N.J., 1967.

Marx, Karl. *Early Writings*, trans. R. Livingstone and G. Benton, introd. Lucio Colletti. Pbk edn, Harmondsworth, Middx., 1975.

—— and Frederick Engels. *Articles on Britain*. Moscow, 1971.

Meester, Marie E. de. *Oriental Influences in the English Literature of the Nineteenth Century*. Heidelberg, 1915.

Miles, Robert. *Gothic Writing 1750–1820: A Genealogy.* London and New York, 1993.

Miller, Alice. *For Your Own Good: The Roots of Violence in Childrearing,* trans. H. and H. Hannum. London, 1987.

Mitchell, W. J. T. 'Visible Language: Blake's Wond'rous Art of Writing', in *Romanticism and Contemporary Criticism,* ed. Morris Eaves and Michael Fischer. Durham, N.C., 1986.

Moers, Ellen. *Literary Women.* London, 1977.

Mottram, Eric. *William Burroughs: The Algebra of Need.* London, 1977.

Mudge, Bradford K. 'The Man with Two Brains: Gothic Novels, Popular Culture, Literary History', *Publications of the Modern Language Association,* CVII (1992), 92–104.

Nandris, Grigore. 'The Historical Dracula: the Theme of his Legend in the Western and in the Eastern Literatures of Europe', *Comparative Literature Studies,* III (1966), 365–96.

Napier, Elizabeth. *The Failure of Gothic: Problems of Disjunction in an Eighteenth-Century Literary Form.* Oxford, 1987.

Nelson, Lowry, Jr., 'Night Thoughts on the Gothic Novel', *Yale Review,* LII (1962), 236–57.

Newman, Beth. 'Getting Fixed: Feminine Identity and Scopic Crisis in *The Turn of the Screw*', *Novel,* XXVI (1992), 43–63.

Nordon, Pierre. *Conan Doyle* (1964), trans. Frances Partridge. London, 1966.

O'Connor, Richard. *Ambrose Bierce: A Biography.* London, 1968.

Pattee, Fred Lewis. *The New American Literature 1890–1930.* New York, 1930.

Pearsall, Ronald. *Conan Doyle: A Biographical Solution.* London, 1977.

Pirie, David. *A Heritage of Horror: The English Gothic Cinema 1946–1972.* London, 1973.

Punter, David. 'Angela Carter: Supersessions of the Masculine', *Critique,* XXV (1984), 209–22.

——. 'Death, Femininity and Identification: A Recourse to "Ligeia" ', *Women's Writing,* I (1994), 215–28.

——. *The Literature of Terror,* Vol. I: *The Gothic Tradition.* London, 1996.

——. 'Narrative and Psychology in Gothic Fiction', in *Gothic Fiction: Prohibition/Transgression,* ed. K. W. Graham. New York, 1989.

——. 'The Passions of Gothic', in *Gothick Origins and Innovations,* ed. A. Lloyd Smith and V. Sage. Amsterdam, 1994.

——. *The Romantic Unconscious: A Study in Narcissism and Patriarchy.* London and New York, 1989.

——. 'Stephen King: Problems of Recollection and Construction', *LIT: Literature, Interpretation, Theory,* V (1994), 67–82.

Readings, Bill. *Introducing Lyotard: Art and Politics.* London, 1991.

Rockett, Will H. *Devouring Whirlwind: Terror and Transcendence in the Cinema of Cruelty.* New York, 1988.

Rodway, Allan Edwin. *The Romantic Conflict.* London, 1963.

Rudwin, Maximilian Josef. *The Devil in Legend and Literature.* Chicago, 1931.

Sage, Victor. *Horror Fiction in the Protestant Tradition.* London, 1988.

Sarris, Andrew. *Confessions of a Cultist: On the Cinema, 1955–1969.* New York, 1971.

Scarborough, Dorothy. *The Supernatural in Modern English Fiction.* New York, 1917.

Schaffer, Talia. "'A Wilde Desire Took Me': The Homoerotic History of *Dracula*', *ELH*, LXI (1994), 381–425.

Scott, James F. 'Thomas Hardy's Use of the Gothic: An Examination of Five Representative Works', *Nineteenth-Century Fiction*, XVII (1963), 363–80.

Sedgwick, Eve Kosofsky. *The Coherence of Gothic Conventions.* New York, 1980.

Sellers, Susan, ed. *Writing the Differences: Readings from the Seminar of Hélène Cixous.* Milton Keynes, 1988.

Sontag, Susan. *Against Interpretation and Other Essays.* New York and Toronto, 1966.

Strachey, Giles Lytton. *Characters and Commentaries,* ed. J. Strachey. London, 1933.

Summers, Montague. *A Gothic Bibliography.* London, 1941.

——. *The Gothic Quest: A History of the Gothic Novel.* London, 1938.

Tabbi, Joseph. ' "Strung into the Apollonian Dream": Pynchon's Psychology of Engineers', *Novel*, XXV (1992), 160–80.

Taylor, John Russell. *Cinema Eye, Cinema Ear: Some Key Film-Makers of the Sixties.* London, 1964.

Thompson, Gary Richard, ed. *The Gothic Imagination: Essays in Dark Romanticism.* Pullman, 1974.

Tudor, Andrew. *Monsters and Mad Scientists: A Cultural History of the Horror Movie.* Oxford, 1989.

Tymms, Ralph Vincent. *Doubles in Literary Psychology.* Cambridge, 1949.

Varma, Devendra Prasad. *The Gothic Flame: being a History of the Gothic Novel in England: its Origins, Efflorescence, Disintegration, and Residuary Influences.* London, 1957.

Varnado, S. L. *Haunted Presence: The Numinous in Gothic Fiction.* Tuscaloosa, 1987.

Watt, Ian. *The Rise of the Novel: Studies in Defoe, Richardson and Fielding.* London, 1957.

West, Muriel. 'The Death of Miles in *The Turn of the Screw*', *Publications of the Modern Language Association*, LXXIX (1964), 283–8.

Wicke, Jennifer. 'Vampiric Typewriting: *Dracula* and its Media', *ELH*, LIX (1992), 467–93.

Wiggins, Robert A. *Ambrose Bierce.* Minneapolis, 1964.

Williams, Raymond. *The Long Revolution.* London, 1961.

Wilson, Colin. *The Strength to Dream: Literature and the Imagination.* London, 1962.

Wilson, Edmund. *Classics and Commercials: A Literary Chronicle of the Forties.* London, 1951.

——. *Patriotic Gore: Studies in the Literature of the American Civil War.* London, 1962.

Winter, Keri J. *Subjects of Slavery, Agents of Change: Women and Power in Gothic Novels and Slave Narratives, 1790–1865.* Athens, Ga., 1992.

Wolstenholme, Susan. *Gothic (Re)Visions: Writing Women as Readers.* Albany, N.Y., 1993.

Wood, Robin. *Hitchcock's Films.* London, 1969.

Zizek, Slavoj. *Looking Awry: An Introduction to Jacques Lacan through Popular Culture.* Cambridge, Mass., 1991.

Index